YOUR TOWNS & CITIES IN W...

CUMBRIA

AT WAR 1939–45

YOUR TOWNS & CITIES IN WORLD WAR TWO

CUMBRIA

AT WAR 1939–45

RUTH MANSERGH

Pen & Sword
MILITARY

AN IMPRINT OF PEN & SWORD BOOKS LTD.
YORKSHIRE – PHILADELPHIA

First published in Great Britain in 2019 by
Pen & Sword Military
An imprint of
Pen & Sword Books Ltd
Yorkshire – Philadelphia

ISBN 978 1 47387 710 8

A CIP catalogue record for this book is
available from the British Library.

Printed and bound in England
by CPI Group (UK) Ltd, Croydon, CR0 4YY
Typeset by Aura Technology and Software Services, India

Pen & Sword Books Limited incorporates the imprints of Atlas, Archaeology,
Aviation, Discovery, Family History, Fiction, History, Maritime, Military, Military
Classics, Politics, Select, Transport, True Crime, Air World, Frontline Publishing,
Leo Cooper, Remember When, Seaforth Publishing, The Praetorian Press,
Wharncliffe Local History, Wharncliffe Transport, Wharncliffe True Crime and
White Owl.

For a complete list of Pen & Sword titles please contact

PEN & SWORD BOOKS LIMITED
47 Church Street, Barnsley, South Yorkshire, S70 2AS, England
E-mail: enquiries@pen-and-sword.co.uk
Website: www.pen-and-sword.co.uk

Or
PEN AND SWORD BOOKS
1950 Lawrence Rd, Havertown, PA 19083, USA
E-mail: Uspen-and-sword@casematepublishers.com
Website: www.penandswordbooks.com

Contents

Preface

Aside from Barrow-in-Furness, where about 25 per cent of the town's housing stock was damaged or destroyed, Cumbria was largely safe from attack from the Germans. In the first week or two after Britain was at war with Germany, boys and girls from Tyneside came to Carlisle as evacuees. Meanwhile, Silloth Airfield had twin responsibilities, Marchon moved from London to Whitehaven in 1941, and the secret Magnesite Works at Harrington was set up by the Ministry of Aircraft Production to extract magnesium from seawater.

The war was to have a lasting legacy in Cumbria, as the county became part of the front line in the Cold War. Its comparative remoteness made it the ideal place to establish Calder Hall, a nuclear power station, and Windscale, a plutonium plant used to make nuclear weapons. HMS *Resolution*, the first of Britain's Polaris nuclear submarines, was built in Barrow. She slid into the Walney Channel at noon on Thursday, 16 September 1966 almost unnoticed as CND (Campaign for Nuclear Disarmament) demonstrators paraded near the gates of the Vickers (as it was then called) shipyard, on Barrow Island.

About the Author

I am a mother of two who has worked as a journalist and as a freelance sub-editor/ proofreader. My degree was in English with Social History (Leeds University) because of my interest in the history of the north of England. I maintain a positive approach to life despite a disability that has led to setbacks.

Acknowledgements

Thanks to Ian Stuart Nicholson from Whitehaven Archives, who researches memorials for the Imperial War Museum, for his invaluable help. He has sent me details of some of the more unusual stories that you'd not find elsewhere. Thanks also to my partner Alan McClenaghan for his computer wizardry.

I have made every effort to contact family members of those written about, and copyright holders where appropriate, and will be happy to update any omissions in any future edition of this book.

Introduction

In 1974, Cumberland was combined with Westmorland and parts of Lancashire and the West Riding of Yorkshire to form the new county of Cumbria. The Lake District National Park – entirely in Cumbria – was established in 1951. On 1 August 2016, the Yorkshire Dales National Park officially grew by nearly a quarter. The boundary covers areas in Cumbria, including the market town of Kirkby Stephen and, for the first time, a small part of Lancashire.

Carlisle, where RAF Kingstown featured in one of the most audacious escapes by German prisoners-of-war during the Second World War, is the largest settlement in Cumbria (population 73,306, 2011 census). In the south of the county is the important shipbuilding town of Barrow-in-Furness (population 56,745), which was founded on the iron and steel industry. Many great warships were built at the yard before and during the Second World War, including HMS *Upholder* – the most successful British submarine of the Second World War – and HMS *Narwhal*, discovered in 2017. Today, nuclear-powered attack submarines (Astute-class) for the Royal Navy keep the town busy.

The more scenic town of Kendal (population 28,398), which once employed more than a thousand people in the shoe-making business, is the third largest settlement in Cumbria. Whitehaven (population 23,810), on the west Cumbrian coast, was once a major mining centre. It has a smaller population than the less prosperous town of Workington (25,444), which is also on the west Cumbrian coast. Penrith (15,487), in the Eden Valley, just north of the River Eamont, is the sixth largest settlement and lies less than 3 miles outside the boundaries of the Lake District.

After World War Two, the movement towards creating National Parks gained momentum. There is only a handful of major settlements within the Lake District National Park, including Keswick, known for its association with poets, and Windermere, half a mile from the largest natural lake in England. Poet Norman Nicholson (1914-1987), whose autobiography *Wednesday Early Closing* (1975) recounts growing up in Millom in south-west Cumbria, wrote in *Portrait of the Lakes* (1972):

It's easy to understand why the National Park should omit the industrial towns of the west from the area it controls, but to pretend that they do not really belong to the Lake District is merely tourist-minded, urban snobbery.

The double-headland of St Bees, 4 miles south of Whitehaven, is a fine stretch of coastal scenery. Millom (population 7,829) was built around ironworks but has struggled since the works were closed in 1968. (The town grew to a size of more than 10,000 people by the 1960s.) During the Second World War, an airfield, RAF Millom, was developed on flat coastal land at Haverigg. Post-war, this became the site of HMP (Her Majesty's Prison) Haverigg.

The biggest private employer in Cumbria is Sellafield, opened in 1956, which directly employs around 10,000 people. The largest and most widespread industry in Cumbria is tourism. Train lines include the scenic Cumbria Coast Line from Barrow to Carlisle, where there is only a single-line track between Sellafield and St Bees. The West Coast Main Line route between London and Glasgow stops

A vivid memory of those days: The iron-ore mining together with spray steelmaking – without the addition of a steelworks – transformed Millom (pictured) to a prosperous community. (wordsworthcountry.com)

Above*: Millom.* (Andy Deacon, photographer, Millom Discovery Centre)

Below*: Millom ironworks.* (With thanks to Peter Burgess)

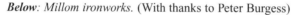

at Lancaster, Oxenholme Lake District (part of the Windermere Branch Line), Penrith North Lakes and Carlisle. Appleby and Kirkby Stephen railway stations are on the Settle-Carlisle Line, which has several notable tunnels and viaducts, such as Ribblehead in North Yorkshire.

The Ministry of Defence operates the Warcop Training Area, built for the War Office in 1942 as a tank gunnery range. Most of the armoured formations that took part in the D-Day landings trained here, according to *visitcumbria.com*. Appleby (population 3,048), a small market town that has a castle, was the capital of Westmorland until 1974.

Above*: Single track between Sellafield and St Bees.* (Ruth Livingstone, Coastalwalker.co.uk)

Below*: Map of Cumbria.* (Visitcumbria.com)

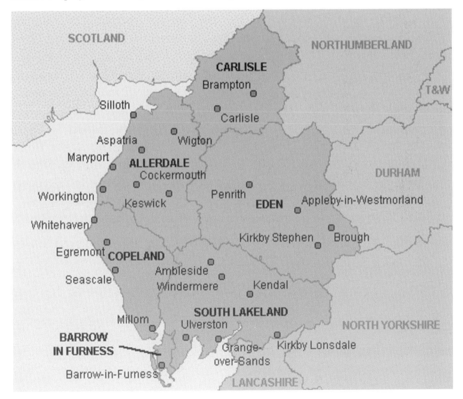

CHAPTER 1

Already War is in the Air Again

Most British families had lost relatives in what they hoped had been the 'War to End Wars', the First World War, so people preferred not to think about having to prepare for another. However, fascist governments appeared in Germany, Italy and Japan in the 1920s and 1930s and posed a serious threat to world peace.

British governments had, from 1924, quietly started preparing Air Raid Precautions (ARP) measures. In September 1935, the British prime minister, Stanley Baldwin (1867-1947), published a circular entitled *ARP*, inviting local authorities to make plans to protect their people in event of a war. Such plans included building public air raid shelters, Anderson or Morrison. And on 6 November 1935, representatives of the county councils of Lancashire, Cumberland and Westmorland and the county boroughs of Preston, Blackpool, Blackburn, Barrow and Carlisle attended a conference in the County Offices, Preston, on ARP, which was addressed by Wing-Commander Sir (Eric) John Hodsoll (1894-1971), Assistant Under Secretary of State at the Home Office in charge of the ARP Department from 1935 to 1937. County councils were recommended, should the emergency arise, to co-operate with the county boroughs as far as possible. According to a statement made to the *Lancashire Daily Post* afterwards, the proposals were being made not because the emergency was likely to arise, but as a common-sense measure.

Mention was made of arrangements for first-aid, fighting street contamination, gas scares, road-making and the maintenance of gas, electricity and water services. The speaker referred to the need for gas detectors, and the provision in houses of rooms that could be made gas-proof for a few pence (*Lancashire Evening Post*, 7 November 1935).

Barrow's unexpected visitor

Nazi officials were very much aware of the symbolic value of the *Hindenburg* Zeppelin (LZ-129), a rigid airship and passenger aircraft. The ship's first flight took place on 4 March 1936. Hitler's expansionist aims became clear on 7 March 1936, when Hitler announced that his troops had entered the Rhineland.

This action was directly against the Treaty of Versailles (28 June 1919), under which the Germans were forbidden to erect fortifications or station troops in the Rhineland or within 50km of the right bank of the Rhine. On 6 May 1936, the *Hindenburg* began the service she was built for: regular transatlantic crossings between Germany and the US.

On Friday, 22 May 1936, the *Hindenburg* flew very low over the Furness rooftops on a flight from America to Germany. The *Barrow News* on 23 May 1936 noted:

Barrow had an unexpected visitor. The (German) airship passed over Barrow at about 7.25pm flying at a moderate speed. She was very low and her registration number and name could be clearly read by people in Dalton Road and over towards Greengate Street. She was first sighted in this district from the vicinity of Bootle (west Cumbria), coming from the direction of the Isle of Man and flying steadily towards the south.

Her passage over the shopping centre of Barrow aroused the greatest interest and excitement. She appeared to be coming from the coast and steering a course that would take her across country. Every detail of her hull could be clearly made out and the deep note of her engines was the first intimation of her arrival.

Alan Wilson from Barrow, who worked for Vickers for forty-four years and retired in 1980, contacted the *News & Star* in 2009 to say he saw the *Hindenburg* (22 May 1936) while on an evening walk alongside the Walney Channel (which separates Walney Island from mainland Barrow), and the airship passed over Barrow twice in the late spring and summer of 1936:

I don't think any of us were in any doubt at that time that they were there to photograph the docks. By the mid-1930s, we knew there might be a conflict with Germany. I left the Technical School in 1934/5 and quite a few dozen of us were taken on as apprentices at Vickers. I started as an electrician and later became a draughtsman.

William Richardson (b1916) CBE DL was a shipbuilding apprentice from 1933 to 1938, and Admiralty Directorate of Aircraft Maintenance and Repair, UK and Far East from 1939 to 1946. He was chairman of Vickers from 1976 to 1983. In 1984, he lived at Hobroyd, Pennybridge, Ulverston.

The *Hindenburg* passed over Keighley, West Yorkshire, a few minutes after 8pm on 22 May 1936. As she flew over High Street, a parcel fell from the airship and was picked up by two boy scouts. The parcel contained a bunch of carnations, a small

The Hindenburg Zeppelin flying over Walney Island in 1936. (southlakes-uk.co.uk)

Raikeswood Camp was a First World War prisoner-of-war camp. (University of Leeds)

silver and jet crucifix, some postage stamps, a picture of a flying-boat and a request written upon *Hindenburg* notepaper to deposit the flowers and cross upon the grave of 'my dear brother Franz Schulte, Prisoner of War in Keighley near Leeds'. The letter, dated 22 May 1936, was signed by Johann B. Schulte. Franz Robert Schulte (d1919) had been a prisoner-of-war at the little-known Raikeswood Camp for more than 500 German officers near Skipton, North Yorkshire, whose surnames included Alex, Braun, Fiebig, Genth, Helbing, Radke, Raulfs, Scharffenberg, Schwieder, Stohr, Unbekannt, Winsloe and Zahntier. The flowers were placed in Morton Cemetery, Keighley, within an hour of leaving the airship. (Source *Keighley News 'Memory Lane'*, 1 November 2013). Of the 546 officers and 137 other ranks imprisoned at Raikeswood Camp in February 1919, 234 officers and 47 other ranks became ill. The death toll was 47 (37 officers and 10 other ranks), with 42 dying in Morton Banks Hospital and 5 in the camp. The funerals took place at Morton Cemetery, Keighley, where the men were then buried. (Source *skiptonww1camp.*

co.uk). Franz Robert Schulte was relocated to the Cannock Chase German War Cemetery, Staffordshire: Plot 14, Row 7, Grave 224 in the 1960s. (In 2014, a book of diaries, sketches and poems written by German prisoners-of-war during their time in North Yorkshire was discovered in a shoebox at Skipton library.)

Same Zeppelin

The *Hindenburg* made another trip across Furness in the early afternoon of Tuesday, 30 June 1936. The *Barrow News* of 4 July 1936 reported that she passed over the ancient village of Flookburgh, several miles west of Grange-over-Sands, at 2pm, flying very low. The residents were quickly out of doors and in the street to watch her progress. The airship passed over Barrow in a north-westerly direction at 2.15pm. She then passed over the Isle of Man on her way to America. However, due to the rise of the Nazi party in Germany, there was some concern about the possibility that the *Hindenburg* was in fact spying. And Sir Jonah Walker-Smith (1874-1964), a Conservative politician who served as MP for Barrow from 1931 to 1945, asked questions in the House of Commons whether Barrow was scheduled as a prohibited area for foreign aircraft because of the

Lakeland Miniature Village, Winder Lane, Flookburgh, opened to the public in 2001. (Jean Norgate)

nature of the industry there, and the increasing extent of the building of ships of defence and other defensible preparations.

John Nixon, an author born in Ulverston, wrote in *Wings Over Sands* (2012) about the 30 June 1936 visit:

> Could it also be that the Germans, perhaps knowing of Flookburgh's proposed airship works, were taking a sneaky look to see if any sort of aircraft industry was being resurrected at the site? With the clouds of war once more gathering on the horizon, the Zeppelin was about to pass into history, to be pushed aside by more formidable aerial weaponry, which was to give the slumbering Flookburgh site a new life and purpose once more.

Scientist, engineer and inventor Sir Barnes Neville Wallis (1887-1979), famous for developing the bouncing bomb in the Second World War, kickstarted

Barnes Wallis spent part of his early career developing airships at Vickers in Barrow. (Public Domain)

This plaque at BAE Systems in Barrow commemorates Wallis' time there as an airship designer.

his aeronautical career at the Vickers armament factory in Barrow as the First World War loomed ever closer. He went on to develop the *R80* (it made its first flight in July 1920) and *R100* airships (the *R100* had to be built elsewhere due to limitations of the Walney Island shed). In 1916, Vickers decided that it needed a larger airship construction facility than the one it operated on Walney Island. It chose a flat area called Winder Moor, south of Flookburgh, for a 900 ft-long airship shed. By late November 1916, the Flookburgh project was well under way, and construction of a housing estate, Ravenstown, to serve the airship station, started in March 1917. Despite resistance from Vickers, it was decided to abandon the project in the summer of 1917, according to

British Airship Bases of the Twentieth Century by Malcolm Fife. The government thought steel would be better put to use on warships than on airship sheds. There had also been issues concerning the foundations, for the shed was on damp ground. RAF Cark, built on the land set aside for the Flookburgh airship station, was a wartime fighter airfield that opened in 1941. Once the threat of invasion had receded, it was used for Flying Training Command and as a staff pilot training unit.

1936 Berlin

The *Hindenburg* demonstrated her propaganda value on 1 August 1936, when she flew over the opening ceremony of the 1936 Berlin Olympic Games – which remain the most controversial ever held – carrying the Olympic flag behind her. Inaugurating a new Olympic ritual, a lone runner arrived bearing a torch carried by relay from the site of the ancient games in Olympia, Greece.

The Shuttleworth family cross in Barbon. (Ian Stuart Nicholson)

The Nazis had persuaded the International Olympic Games Committee and several governments that they could stage a fair and free Olympics. Despite calls for a boycott, they were allowed to keep the 1936 Games, which were used to carry out Nazi propaganda. The five symbolic rings of the Olympic Games were everywhere in Berlin. They appeared on the white Olympic standard that fluttered beside the Swastika flag over so many houses. Berlin stressed every German victory. Only one German-Jewish athlete was permitted to play in the Games because only her father was Jewish. Reporter Philip Stockil wrote an article headlined *Berlin During the Games* published in the *Yorkshire Post* on 8 August 1936:

I have just left Berlin. My suspicions of Germany's eventual intentions were scarcely lulled by the signs which I saw of renascent military power. These were few, certainly, in Berlin – though on the evening of the Olympic opening, a large detachment of the Reichswehr, with bands playing, marched up the Kurfurstendamm. This demonstration may have been for the benefit of the foreigners dining in the street's many restaurants. If so, it was bad psychology. The marching men, with their fixed bayonets and steel helmets, must have disconcerted more than they impressed.

There were 208 participants for Great Britain: 171 men and 37 women. Lieutenant Charles Symonds Leaf (1895-1947), Royal Marines, was a gold medal winner in sailing. His son, Lieutenant Edward Derek Walter Leaf (1918-1944), Royal Naval Volunteer Reserve, whose mother's maiden name was Kay-Shuttleworth, his parents having married in 1917, was killed in action on 15 February 1944. He was buried at St Bartholomew's Church, Barbon, in the Shuttleworth family plot. Also buried there is old Etonian Major Coleridge Eustace Hills (1912-1941), grandson of the 1st Baron Shuttleworth, Sir James Kay-Shuttleworth (1804-1877), who fell while serving with the Royal Army Service Corps.

On 6 May 1937, the *Hindenburg* caught fire and was destroyed during her attempt to land at Naval Air Station Lakehurst, New Jersey. Of the ninety-seven people on board (thirty-six passengers and sixty-one crewmen), there were thirty-five fatalities (thirteen passengers and twenty-two crewmen). One worker on the ground was also killed, making a total of thirty-six dead. Many survivors jumped out of the *Hindenburg's* windows and ran away as fast as they could. The incident marked the end of the passenger airship era.

CHAPTER 2

Pre-War Build-Up

The ARP, or Civil Defence as it was later renamed, was set up in 1937. Every local council was responsible for organising ARP wardens, messengers, ambulance drivers, rescue parties and liaison with police and fire brigades. By 1938, Hodsoll's work with the ARP had shown the need for the public to be made more aware of the problems likely to affect them. It was obvious that time was, as he put it, 'running out like the tide'.

From the summer of 1938, council staff at the Town Hall and Mansion House, Penrith, were involved in the surveying of accommodation for future billeting of evacuees. On 27 September 1938, Adolf Hitler called for a military parade in Berlin to rouse patriotic sentiment. In the UK, British military mobilised for war, schoolchildren were evacuated from London, while trenches were dug in London's parks. By the end of September 1938, 38 million gas masks had been given out, house to house, to British families (*Imperial War Museum*). These had to be carried everywhere to protect against the risk of a poisonous gas attack. Even children had to carry them. As gas masks look quite scary, the government released some for children in bright colours, with a floppy nose and big ears. These were called Mickey Mouse gas masks. (At the *Millom Discovery Centre*, you can see actual gas masks that were carried. The RAF Millom display can also be seen at *Millom Discovery Centre*.) There was a baby gas mask and a gas-resistant pram. Hand rattles were issued to ARP wardens and people were told that if they heard the rattle being used, they should put on their gas masks immediately.

When the *Furness and District Year Book* was compiled late in 1938, its usual mix of pictures showing carnival queens, fetes and mayors was joined by a view of a Barrow gas mask store, according to the *North West Evening Mail* of 19 August 2016. The year book noted: *'The national re-armament programme that brought prosperity to the town in 1937 continued to exert its influence throughout 1938.'* In British history, re-armament covers the period between 1934 and 1939, when a substantial programme of re-arming the nation was undertaken. In August 1941, a gas attack drill was held in Barrow town centre using real gas, according to the town's *Dock Museum*. The routine for the drill was: 1. Remove mask from box, 2. Put mask on face, 3. Check the mask is fitting correctly, 4. Breathe normally.

An ARP gas rattle with later painted decoration for Barrow rugby league player Willie Horne (1922-2001), whose statue stands opposite Craven Park, the home of Barrow Raiders rugby league team. (1818auctioneers.co.uk)

Gas masks were never actually needed during the Second World War as gas was never used as a weapon. Had Germany launched an invasion in 1940, the British plan was to spray German troops with mustard gas from aircraft while they were still crowded together on the beaches. The idea was first proposed on 15 June 1940, just two days after Dunkirk, according to *A Higher Form of Killing: The Secret Story of Chemical and Biological Warfare* by Robert Harris and Jeremy Paxman (2001).

In November 1938, the government published the Schedule of Reserved Occupations with the goal of exempting skilled workers from being conscripted into service. These included dock-workers, farmers and miners. Overtime was compulsory at Vickers, and workmen who repeatedly refused could be dismissed and drafted into the armed forces. Women entered this male preserve. For those with children, an overnight nursery was set up at 242 Abbey Road, Barrow. (Source *The Dock Museum*, Barrow.) Abbey Road is the principal north-to-south arterial road through Barrow. Strikes were widely considered unpatriotic, but they

Barrow gas masks being fitted during the international crisis of 1938, a year before the war. (nwemail.co.uk)

did occur when workers felt that they were being pushed too much. For example, Vickers apprentices went on strike on 18 March 1941 for a 3d an hour increase. The British three-pence (3d) coin, usually simply known as a threepence or threepenny bit, was a unit of currency equalling one eightieth of a pound sterling, or three pence sterling.

The National Archives (*nationalarchives.gov.uk*) has a currency converter: 3d in 1940 was worth 49p in 2017. An article by Major Tom Harnett Harrisson (1911-1976) DSO OBE for the *Spectator* of 20 March 1942 stated: 'Many people believe that the average worker in a munitions-factory is making big money and possibly doing little work for it. Mass Observation (the social research organisation for which I am responsible) has recently made an extensive study of war industry in seven areas. Wage information was collected during this enquiry from firms employing from 20,000 down to 20 workers, and from a sample of workers personally. Of all war workers covered by the sample study, 88 per cent were receiving less than £6 per week, two thirds less than £4.' Therefore, £6 in 1940 was worth £236.08 in 2017; £4 per week in 1940 was worth £157.39 in 2017. According to *nationalarchives*, £4 in 1940 equated to two days' wages for a skilled tradesman. Harrisson, who was in the army from May 1942 until June 1944, was appointed OBE in the 1959 New Year Honours for his work as a curator. He died in a road accident in Thailand.

The first in the country

A blackout experiment was conducted by the ARP in Workington in the early hours of Saturday, 17 December 1938, and was described as 'a complete success' by ARP district organiser Captain Hill. The *Lancashire Evening Post* of 17 December 1938 reported:

> Great importance was attached to the efforts – the first in the country – to obliterate quickly the glare from extensive iron and steel works. Workington people were aware of the success of the efforts at the steel works, the glare usually to be seen for a radius of 10 to 15 miles being almost non-existent. Throughout West Cumberland, hundreds of ARP volunteers rushed to their respective posts and carried out mock duties, including firefighting rescue work and decontamination activities. On account of mist, Air Force planes were prevented from flying over the area to test the blackout. War Office officials were in the district to observe the result.

The *West Cumberland Times* of 14 January 1939 reported that Workington Town Council had discussed at length the government's evacuation scheme. A government circular detailing what was required of local authorities stressed the importance of taking a survey of their districts with a view to finding out what surplus rooms there were in private houses suitable for the reception of children. Fears as to the effect of sending large numbers of children from urban areas in the event of emergency were expressed at a meeting on Friday, 17 February 1939 of the Westmorland County Council at Kendal. Councillor William Gordon Shorrock (1879-1944), of Morland in the Eden Valley, said he felt 'there would be a great danger of pestilential disease and epidemics if billeting were carried out without careful inquiry'. He told the meeting:

> I am afraid that in some of Westmorland's isolated hamlets and villages, sanitation arrangements are primitive, while in others they are just sufficient for the needs of the present population.
>
> Undue strain would be placed on present health services, and it is more than likely they might break down, in which case the dangers to which large numbers of children would be exposed might be greater than if they were exposed to an air raid.

Sudenten German refugees, who fled in 1939 after the German annexation of Czechoslovakia, were quartered at High Cross Castle Youth Hostel, Troutbeck, Windermere. (*Leeds Mercury*, 25 February 1939.)

William Gordon Shorrock, who married Ethel Hinemoa Godby (1887-1974) in 1908. She died in Penrith. (With thanks to Richard Andrews who owns the photo)

Further appointments were sanctioned in connection with the development of the country's ARP services. These included the appointment, in February 1939, of Lady Ankaret Jackson (née Howard) of High Dyke, Cockermouth, as organiser of the ARP Women's Voluntary Services for Cockermouth urban and Cockermouth rural areas. Born in 1900 in London, she married Sir William Jackson (1902-1985), a barrister, in London in 1927, was made a barrister in 1928, lived at Rose Cottage, Strand-on-the-Green, Kew in 1929, bought Rayleigh House on the Thames Embankment in 1934, bought High Dyke with her husband in 1934, and died in April 1945 in Cockermouth Cottage Hospital from head injuries received when she was thrown from her pony while riding over Mosser Fell, above Loweswater. At the inquest, it was stated that Lady Ankaret and her 11-year-old daughter Tarn were riding ponies when sheep ran across the track. Sir William Jackson fought in the Second World War. He gained the rank of major in the RAC (Border Regiment), Territorial Army.

Lady Ankaret Jackson – granddaughter of Rosalind Frances Howard (1845-1921), Countess of Carlisle, a promoter of women's political rights and temperance movement activist – is buried at Lanercost, the family church of the earls of Carlisle. Her son, Sir (William) Thomas Jackson (1927-2004) went to Harecroft Hall Prep School, west Cumbria, between January 1936 and July 1940 and then to Mill Hill School, north London, so was probably evacuated to St Bees School before going to Cirencester Royal Agricultural College. He became 8th Baronet Jackson of the Manor House, Birkenhead. Lady Jackson's daughter was christened Ankaret Tarn Jackson (b1934) at Naworth Castle near Brampton.

She married Major Timothy Richard Riley (1928-2017), son of Lieutenant Colonel Hamlet Lewthwaite Riley (1882-1932), in 1955. She lived at Burbank House, Blencowe, Dacre, in 2003. (Burbank House was endowed as a school in

Right: The family party at Naworth Castle near Brampton. Left to right: Ankaret Jackson, Lady Caroline Howard, William Jackson, Lady Carlisle and her husband. (The Bystander, 22 February 1939)

Below: Morland is bisected by Morland Beck, which was once used to power several small mills in the village. The village church of St Lawrence dates from Anglo-Saxon times. (english-lakes.com)

Naworth Castle. Also known as, or recorded in documents as, 'Narward'. (With thanks to Philip Howard, owner of Naworth Castle)

1577 and closed c1919.) Riley gained the rank of major in the 3rd Green Jackets (Rifle Brigade). Lord Cavendish of Holker Estates paid tribute to Riley, who was clerk of the racecourse at Cartmel, in 2017. He said: 'I was close to Tim for many years. He was very much in the tradition of the retired soldiers who served racing so well after the war, and he was unbelievably loyal.' Holker Estates owns the racecourse. Riley's two daughters, Antonia and Nicola, work in racing. (Source *Racing Post*, 7 September 2017).

From 1939 to 1940, Naworth Castle was occupied by Rossall School, Fleetwood, Lancashire, which had been evacuated from its own buildings by various government departments. Among those evacuated was Peter Mutch Rhodes, much involved in sporting activities while at Rossall (1937-1944), who celebrated his Golden Wedding Anniversary in 2010. On leaving school, Rhodes, who had previously volunteered and been accepted for flying duties, joined the Fleet Air Arm and qualified as an observer. Rossall's headmaster from 1937-1957, Charles Edgar Young (1928-1977), volunteered for flying instructor duties in July 1940. He became vicar of Thornthwaite-cum-Braithwaite, Keswick, from 1957-1965. Naworth is currently owned by Philip Howard. Castle Howard, North Yorkshire, and Naworth were both owned by the Earls of Carlisle until 1911, after which the estates were split up between various members of the Howard family.

The *Scotsman* reported on 9 March 1939 that the ARP in Cumberland was said to be 'in a state of chaos'. Captain Joseph Cornelius Tobin of St James Road, Carlisle, was appointed transport officer of the ARP for Cumberland on a salary of £200 a year on 8 March 1939. (In 2017, £200 in 1940 was worth £7,869.28.) Mr A. Rowe of 63 Cumberland Street, Workington, said that in Workington and

Whitehaven there was discontent as to the class of people who were appointed to these positions. 'Some people seem to be unable to think of anybody but majors and captains,' he said. (Mr Rowe was secretary and treasurer for Cumberland and Westmorland Socialists in 1935.)

Chairman of Cumberland County Council, Charles Henry Roberts (1865-1959) of Boothby, Brampton – husband of Lady Cecilia Maude Roberts (1868-1947), who was the daughter of the 9th Earl of Carlisle – said on 8 March 1939 that Captain Tobin's appointment was urgent. Mr A. Appleby of Hesket, a civil parish in the Eden District, said that Cumberland seemed to be the last dog on the list from the ministry. There was a feeling that Cumberland was safe and that there was no need to bother.

Colonel Frecheville Hubert Ballantine Dykes DSO OBE (1869-1949) of Kepplewray, Broughton-in-Furness, and vice-chairman of the county council, replied that one could hardly say that any part of the country was a safe area. (He acquired Kepplewray, a Victorian mansion, in 1927 after the death of William Issac Barratt (1856-1924), joint managing director of the Hodbarrow company, Millom). His son, Major Thomas Lamplugh Ballantine Dykes (1912-1942), 2nd Battalion, Scots Guards, died on 13 June 1942 in Libya. He was buried at Knightsbridge War Cemetery, Acroma, Libya, and is on the Cambridge Trinity College Second World War Memorial. Lieutenant Joseph Ballantine Dykes, born in 1922, Corps of Royal Engineers, of Broughton-in-Furness received the Military Cross in 1945.

Dovenby Hall, 2 miles north-west of Cockermouth, passed from Frecheville Lawson Ballantine Dykes, MP for Cockermouth from 1832 to 1836, to Frecheville Hubert Ballantine Dykes. A private station named Dovenby Lodge between Papcastle and Dearham was provided for the family's use on the single-track Derwent branch of the Maryport and Carlisle Railway in the 1840s. There were quite a few of these stations in the county. Quite often they were a condition of the landowners allowing the railway to be built across their land. In 1930, Dovenby Hall was purchased by the Joint Committee for Carlisle, Cumberland and Westmorland, for use as a mental hospital. The line was lifted in 1935. Dovenby Hall is now the location for a high-end rally car manufacturing business.

The Women's Farm and Garden Association, established in 1899, was of interest to those who wished to adopt the government's slogan 'Be Prepared', the *Liverpool Daily Post* reported on 11 February 1939. It agreed, in March 1939, with the approval of the Ministry of Agriculture, to make arrangements to meet the needs of women who wished to take short courses on farms and gardens in their spare time and holidays at their own expense. The government re-launched the Women's Land Army (WLA) in June 1939.

Above*: Kepplewray, built on land purchased in 1899 for William Isaac Barratt.* (With thanks to Roger Baker, cumbria-industries. org.uk)

Left*: A lithograph of Dovenby Hall, sketched in 1855 and showing the estate's then owner, Mrs Dykes, in the foreground.* (Public domain)

'War, with wisdom, can be staved off,' said Wilfrid Hubert Wace Roberts (1900-1991), Liberal MP for North Cumberland 1935-1950, who later joined the Labour Party, speaking at the conference of the North-Western Union of Women's Liberal Associations at Cockermouth on 20 April 1939. He said:

> The progressive parties will have to sink their differences and we must build up not only a popular front in this country but also an international popular front to get a constructive peace, which is the universal desire.

He urged that something be done about the plight of the European refugees. 'France had taken a million while we had only received 25,000. Surely there are vast spaces throughout the Empire to be utilised,' he added. Roberts, who was commissioned in the Border Regiment at the outbreak of the Second World War, was also the owner of the *Carlisle Journal* newspaper, which ceased publication in 1969. He described

Lawson Leigh Ballantine Dykes was born at Isel Hall, Cockermouth, and gazetted to be a lieutenant in the 3rd Battalion Border Regiment on 30 April 1886. He took part in the Jameson Raid (1895-1896), South Africa, and the Matabele Campaign (1896), Zimbabwe. The plaque is at St Bridget's Church, Brigham. (Courtesy of Rev'd Canon Godfrey Butland, Team Rector, Cockermouth Area Churches)

the tradition of Cumbrian local politics in an interview with author, journalist and broadcaster Hunter Davies (b1936) for *A Walk Along the Wall* (1974):

> There's always been a branch of the Howard family which has been radical. In this area, three families have been running things for decades, the Howards, the Grahams of Netherby, and the Lowthers. I've tried to keep the anti-Tory tradition alive, fighting our traditional Tory rival families, the Lowthers and the Grahams.

The Military Training Act of 27 April 1939 responded to Hitler's threat of aggression in Europe. Single men aged 20 and 21 who were fit and able were required to take six months' military training. Men called up were to be known as militiamen to distinguish them from the regular army. It was the UK's first act of peacetime conscription and was intended to be temporary in nature. William Shepherd Morrison (1893-1961), Chancellor of the Duchy of Lancaster, speaking at a Whitehaven Divisional Unionist Rally at Holmrook, Seascale, on 3 June 1939, declared that the Military Training Act would not only provide a new permanent defence force, but would confer social benefits on the country. He said: 'Youths of all classes would have the opportunity of getting together on terms of the strictest equality. They would be housed together, fed together, clothed the same, and treated the same. They would learn to see, understand, and appreciate each other's point of view.' Morrison, a Conservative politician, was Minister of Agriculture, Fisheries and Food from October 1936 to January 1939, Minister of Food 1939-40, and Minister of Town and Country Planning 1942-August 1945. Campaigning during the general election of 1945, he attacked Socialism and pointed out that Hitler and Mussolini began as Socialists.

By the end of May 1939, 4,449 men and 2,411 women ARP volunteers had enrolled, bringing the total strength up to nearly 7,000, stated Captain A.R. Hogg, Cumberland County ARP Officer, of Lowther Street, Carlisle. The total war establishment allocated by the Home Office was 4,000. The figures for each local authority were:

Workington Borough – 532 men; 200 women
Whitehaven Borough – 430 men; 212 women
Border Rural District – 707 men; 471 women
Wigton Rural District – 817 men; 308 women
Penrith Rural District – 441 men; 247 women
Ennerdale Rural District – 359 men; 220 women
Cockermouth Urban District – 155 men; 76 women
Penrith Urban District – 184 men; 164 women
Maryport Urban District – 163 men; 103 women
Keswick Urban District – 95 men; 52 women
Alston Rural District – 50 men; 21 women
Millom Rural District – 198 men; 171 women

Lieutenant Commander Guy Howard Bolus (1902-1939) lost his life while in command of the *Thetis* submarine, built by Cammell Laird, Birkenhead, which sank on diving trials on 1 June 1939 off Llandudno. His home was at Ulverston. There were 103 men on board, twice the usual number. Seawater flooded in and the boat nosedived and was unable to resurface. The shock to the British nation was the greater for the tragedy occurring in peacetime and when the international situation was giving rise to uneasy speculation, according to *The Hunting*

Submarine by Ian Trenowden. It happened three months before the Second World War, and the *Thetis* actually grounded on Anglesey on the day war was declared.

The *West Cumberland Times* of 10 June 1939 reported that the distribution of gas masks was 'to start next week in Whitehaven'. On Friday, 7 July 1939, 4,000 gas masks for distribution in Cockermouth Urban Area arrived in the town. In August 1939, gas masks were distributed to the people of Millom area, a start was made with Seascale distribution from St Cuthbert's Church Hall, and 20,000 gas masks were distributed in Wigton Rural Area.

The Women's Voluntary Service (WVS), founded in 1938 by Stella Isaacs, Marchioness of Reading, as a British women's organisation to recruit women into the ARP services in the event of war, played a key part in the evacuation of civilians from urban areas. The *Westmorland Gazette* reported on 8 July 1939:

> A meeting was held in the National school, Sedbergh for the presentation of badges to those members of Sedbergh WVS who had passed their examinations in first aid, home nursing and anti-gas.

Miss Joan Greenwood, reporting to a meeting of the Westmorland national service committee at Kendal, said on 7 August 1939 that Westmorland had few volunteers for the WLA – not more than twenty volunteers. She appealed to farmers' wives and daughters to enrol, as people with their knowledge would not have to undergo special training. The first batch of recruits of the WLA who had been training at the Lancashire County Institute of Agriculture at Hutton, south-west of Preston, completed their training on Friday, 25 August 1939. As a memento of the occasion, they were presented with Land Army badges by the chairman of the Lancashire branch, Lady Worsley-Taylor of Town Head, Pendleton, Clitheroe. She expressed the hope that the girls would never have to be called up to serve. She hoped, however, they had enjoyed their training and had benefited by it. A further batch of recruits arrived on Monday, 28 August for a fortnight's training.

At the Threlkeld (Keswick) Flower Show on Saturday, 19 August 1939, Dr Arthur Wakefield (1876-1949), a GP from Cumbria who was educated at Sedbergh in the 1890s, told amateur gardeners that 'growing potatoes now will kill starving-out tactics in war' and 'sixteen tons of potatoes, or the equivalent, could be grown in the allotments and gardens of the Threlkeld district'. Wakefield, who joined the Royal Army Medical Corps during the First World War and reached the North Col of Mount Everest as a member of General Charles Bruce's 1922 expedition, was president of the Threlkeld and District Horticultural and Industrial Society. His selection for Everest was based on the record he set in 1905 for the Lakeland fell marathon, according to *alpinejournal.org.uk*.

Army exercises

On Great Dun Fell, Appleby, a Spitfire crashed in poor visibility on Tuesday, 18 July 1939. Pilot Kenneth Mitchell (flying solo), aged 21, of Hampshire, was undertaking a cross-country navigation exercise from RAF Catterick, North Yorkshire to RAF Kingstown, 2 miles north of Carlisle. Workers at nearby Silverband Mine, just beneath the summit of Great Dun Fell, were the first on the scene. Some of the locals managed to recover his body and brought him off the hillside on a farm trailer. Pieces of the aircraft can still be found at the crash site, according to *Peak District Air Accident Research*. At RAF Kingstown, two flights took part in local army exercises in July and August 1939, providing valuable target practice for anti-aircraft crews against towed targets.

The *Westmorland Gazette* of 29 July 1939 reported the death of Pilot Officer Joseph Murray Brockbank of Staveley, a former Windermere Grammar School pupil, who was killed in an air accident that occurred in Scarborough, East Yorkshire, on 21 July 1939. The Whitley bomber was one of a number of night bombers that left Leconfield (East Yorkshire) RAF training station on Thursday

Kenneth Mitchell's gravestone at Studland, Dorset. (With thanks to yorkshire-aircraft.co.uk)

night for flying exercises over East Yorkshire. At about 10pm, thick fog enveloped the countryside, but all machines except one returned safely. The other casualties were Pilot Officer George Buchanan Baker and Sergeant Philip Mealing. It was one of three fatal air accidents that day. The others were at Bridlington Bay and at Tilmanstone, Kent. Brockbank is on the roll of honour in St Mary's Church, Staveley, a First and Second World War roll of honour listing fifty-two names. Brockbank, who joined the RAF in October 1937, was buried in the corner of a little churchyard, Church of Saint Catherine, in Leconfield, alongside other RAF graves. He had quickly gained his wings and had often visited

The collection of wreckage as it appeared in August 2016. (peakdistrictaircrashes.co.uk)

his parents at Staveley by plane. In 1823, the Church of Saint Catherine was under the patronage of George O'Brien Wyndham (1751-1837), 3rd Earl of Egremont. Wyndham maintained around fifteen mistresses and fathered more than forty illegitimate children, though behaved no differently to most wealthy young men of his day.

Further research

Ballantine Dykes' family correspondence and estate records from 1568 to 1953 are at Cumbria Archive Centre, Carlisle. They were deposited by Captain J. Ballantine Dykes through Waugh and Musgrave solicitors of Cockermouth on 6 June 1979.

CHAPTER 3

Despite the Gathering of War Clouds

The Appleby Gypsy Horse Fair, which has existed since 1685, was held at the beginning of June 1939. Sheep-shearing was in progress in June/July. 'Happiness then Holocaust' was the headline in the *West Cumberland Times* of 12 July 1939. Three people were killed outright and burned beyond recognition and two others later died from injuries sustained when a Cumberland Motor Services coach, returning from Blackpool to Carlisle late on Sunday night, came into collision with a cotton-laden lorry and trailer. On 14 July 1939, the London, Midland and Scottish Railway (LMS) published details of forthcoming excursions. These included a grand circular tour embracing Ravenglass and Keswick each Thursday. The *Lancaster Guardian* reported on the same day: 'Kendal was in real carnival mood on Saturday, when the 10th annual Kendal Fete was held.' And £133 was collected for the Netherfield Workers' Westmorland County Hospital.

The Royal Lancashire Show at White Lund, midway between Lancaster and Morecambe, opened on Wednesday, 2 August 1939 when the war clouds were

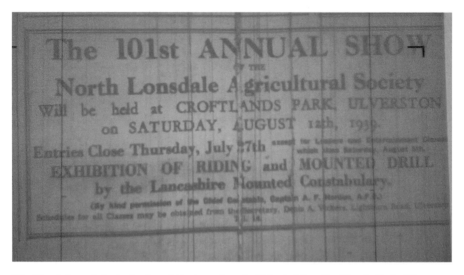

The North Lonsdale Agricultural Society show 'will be held at Croftlands Park, Ulverston on Saturday, August 12th, 1939'. (Westmorland Gazette 29 July 1939)

gathering, but there was no show until 1946 because of the war. Rain made the Cockermouth Carnival a shadow of former days on 3 August 1939. The Beetham Village Sports near Milnthorpe – held annually since 1920 – was on Saturday, 5 August 1939. Ambleside Rushbearing opened, and Grasmere Rushbearing was celebrated on 5 and 6 August 1939 (St Oswald Church, Grasmere, had its earthen floor carpeted with rushes). Although it was called rushbearing, there were no rushes involved in the ceremony in the villages of Warcop (5 miles north of Kirkby Stephen) and Musgrave (a civil parish in the Eden district) until 1939 (*Popular Leisure in the Lake Counties*, Lyn Murfin, 1990).

The Conservatives' Fete at Levens Hall, Milnthorpe, was held, reported the *Westmorland Gazette* of 5 August 1939, and 6,000 people enjoyed the varied programme. There was the best crowd for many years at Keswick Sports on 7 August 1939. Penrith Agricultural Society's show took place on 8 August 1939, though the gate receipts were considerably down owing to the international situation. Despite events such as 1,300 warplanes filling the skies over Britain on the first of several days of air defence tests on 8 August 1939, herds from three counties competed at the 62nd Cartmel Show on Wednesday, 9 August 1939. More than 4,000 spectators were present at the sheepdog trials in Rydal Park, Ambleside, on 10 August 1939, 300 more than 1938. There were more than 1,000 entries at the North Lonsdale Agricultural Society's 101st annual show held at Croftlands Park, Ulverston, on Sunday, 13 August 1939. The Silloth Show on Thursday, 17 August 1939 was believed to be the best in 112 years. On the same day, there were more than 800 entries at the 20th annual Lake District Agricultural Show at Bootle.

However, Nigel Hepper in *Life on a Lake District Smallholding* (2011) wrote:

The (Bootle) show in August 1939 was held at a difficult time before hostilities were declared. I recall being disappointed when Father and I went to the fete and found it a shadow of its former self. It took place inside a building down Main Street, as I recall it clearly in a hall, either in Captain Shaw's School or in the one attached to the Independent Chapel. There was no hound trailing either. That was the last show for the duration of the war.

Hepper (1929-2013) lived in Leeds with his parents and brothers. They went to their holiday home in Bootle, Tarn Cottage, a smallholding, on 26 October 1939 because they expected Leeds to become a prime target due to its industrial content.

In an interview for The University of Greenwich on 21 September 2010, he said:

WEST   CUMBERLAND   TIMES,   SATURDAY,

BOOTLE SHOW

Increased Entries and a Grand Quality All-Round

Clydesdales   A   Strong   Class

ST. BEES 2-YEAR-OLD v.
COCKERMOUTH FOAL

A grand quality all-round. (West Cumberland Times 19 August 1939)

We transferred from my father being a businessman in Leeds to becoming a smallholder. We'd get pigs, three pigs each – a year, to goats and lots of hens and ducks, and so on, which my mother looked after. My father looked after the pigs and the vegetables. I did what I could to help and my brother as well. We supplied eggs to the neighbours and I would go round actually selling these eggs, but we weren't allowed to sell them for more than the official price which was subsidised.

He went to Harecroft Hall as a weekly boarder during the autumn of 1939. Hepper and his family, who had a student from Leeds University staying with them at Tarn Cottage, returned to Leeds in 1942 when he went to senior school. He was a botanist at Kew from 1950 to 1990 and wrote a book (unpublished, 2000) *Happy Hepperings at Harecroft*.

The wedding of a Maryport schoolteacher in Germany took place according to German law and custom on Tuesday, 15 August 1939. John Foster of Lawson Street, Maryport, and Gertrude Margarete married before Pastor Behrmann who, in his address, said: 'Thy people shall be my people,' and expressed his wish for unity between the two countries represented by the bridal pair.

Elizabeth Pinkney 'is being married in Cumberland on 2 September to Stephen Bowen Waldron, elder son of Mr and Mrs Arthur Waldron of Ormonde House, Newbury, Berkshire. She is the second daughter of Mr and Mrs HC Pinkney of The Mount, Cockermouth,' *The Bystander* of Wednesday, 16 August 1939 reported.

The Annual Grasmere Sports, on Thursday, 17 August 1939, had its best weather for twenty-five years and its largest crowd for twenty years. A record was recognised in the adult pole-leaping contest. An American journalist was covering the story of Sir Malcolm Campbell's bid for the water speed record on Coniston, but having an insatiable thirst for copy, he had come along to Grasmere. The fell racing also interested him.

Sir Malcolm Campbell (1885-1948) first came to Coniston Water in the summer of 1939, having decided that a return to the lakes of the Swiss-Italian border region was too dangerous because of the threat of war. He was able to secure the use of the slipway normally used by the lake steamer *The Lady of the Lake*, the sister vessel of the *Gondola*. The world record bid in 1939

Nigel Hepper in 1941 wearing his Harecroft uniform. (With thanks to his son David)

was very successful, and was all over in ten days, Sir Malcolm setting a new world water speed record of 141mph on 19 August 1939 in the *Blue Bird K4*. Although well over age, he managed to get into the army during the Second World War, working mostly with motorcycles. His son Donald Malcolm Campbell (1921-1967) broke eight absolute world speed records on water and land in the 1950s and 1960s.

The annual sheep dog trials, hound trials, and hound and terrier show were held at the Hagg Field at Patterdale, at the foot of Ullswater, on Saturday, 19 August 1939. The attendance at Skelton Agricultural Show near Penrith on 19 August 1939 was believed to be a record. The following day, the Westmorland Motor Club held another one of its increasingly popular scrambles at Park Farm, Skelwith near Ambleside. Six thousand people attended the Cumberland Village Gathering organised at Dearham near Maryport. The 6th annual Flimby Fair took place on 23 August 1939. On 26 August 1939, the attendance at the Ullswater Sports, held at the foot of the lake at Pooley Bridge, was very little less than 1938's.

The Hagg Field was bought, by public subscription in 1937, from the Marshall family of Patterdale Hall (pictured) at the southern end of Lake Ullswater. (patterdalehall.org.uk)

The Lady of the Lake passenger vessel, manufactured in 1907, continued operating until the outbreak of the Second World War. She was broken up for scrap in 1950. The steam yacht *Gondola*, commissioned in 1859 for the Coniston Railway Company, was a commercial service until 1936 when she was retired. In 1972, she was given a new hull, engine, boiler and most of the superstructure. Today, at Coniston Water, the *Gondola* operates commercially as a passenger vessel by the National Trust.

The German steamer *Albert*, laden with 400 tons of timber, arrived at Whitehaven on Friday, 25 August 1939 and left hurriedly without offloading its cargo. Interviewed before leaving, Captain Kreymann declared that the German people did not want war, and he expressed the hope that if the present crisis blew over he would return to Whitehaven soon. The *Whitehaven News* reported:

> The German steamer, Albert, which arrived at Whitehaven on Friday night and entered the Queen's Dock with a cargo of timber for a local firm of timber merchants (Jacksons), left the port again on Sunday morning, taking most of the cargo with her.
>
> The destination of the vessel was not disclosed, but it was obvious that her bunkers would need replenishing, and it was suggested she was making for Dublin.
>
> Hundreds of people visited the dock on Saturday evening to see the vessel, and there was a hurried consultation with harbour officials late in the evening, when there was a suggestion that she was to leave on the tide that night.

It is understood that the necessary customs dues etc were paid by the skipper and that the authorities gave permission for the vessel to leave. Her departure about noon on Sunday was watched by a large crowd, but there was no suggestion of a demonstration of any sort during the time the Albert was in the dock.

About 250 excursionists returned to their north Lancashire and south Cumberland homes by two trains after a day at Southport Flower Show on Saturday, 26 August 1939. The first train, which stopped at various stations, drew up at Kirkby-in-Furness. Some passengers alighted from the train, which then drew further along the platform and stopped again. It began to move again, but had not got past the platform when it was struck behind by the second train, which was not due to stop before it reached Millom. The guard's van and last coach of the first train were badly smashed and other coaches damaged, and the engine of the second train was also damaged. A door was burst open and two women were thrown right out of the train by the impact. The guard, from Workington, lost his arm. St Bees Women's Institute trippers were involved.

The *West Cumberland Times* of 26 August 1939 had the whole of page five dedicated to Maryport Carnival with the headline 'Joys of a Thoroughly Organised Carnival – Maryport Shows Cumberland the Way to go Gay Despite Anxious Times'. Revellers staged their 'Royal landing' on the North Quay and held their 2-mile procession around the town. Carnival queen and princess were presented with bouquets from the Revellers' Committee. Maryport (population 11,262 in 2011) was ranked with Merthyr Tydvil, Wales, and Cleator Moor from 1924 to 1938 as one of the three places in Britain with the highest unemployment. There was a minor boom during the Second World War, when coal from north-east England was diverted to Maryport.

On page eight is a verbatim speech to Workington Rotary by Dr Rudolf Speier of Katwoice, Poland, guest of the Reverend J.C. Wilson of Broughton Moor. Dr Speier told Workington Rotarians that his country would fight to the last man:

We all don't know what will happen within the next few days. Perhaps we are meeting immediately before the most terrible mankind catastrophe. Ask the people of all nations, of all professions, if they want war. I am convinced all abhor it, not excepting the population of Germany and Poland. But I am sure should the Poles be forced to go to war they will fight to the very last man, because they would prefer to die for their country than to live as slaves.

JOYS OF A THOROUGHLY ORGANISED CARNIVAL

Maryport Shows Cumberland The Way To Go Gay Despite Anxious Times

Miss Ethel Cowan,
Crosby Vilia,
The New Carnival Queen

Miss Isobel Millar,
The Retiring
Carnival Queen

Marguerite Rook,
The New Carnival Princess

Margaret Skelton,
Retiring Carnival Princess

The queens walked from the Town Hall to the Memorial Gardens at Netherhall Corner, where retiring carnival queen Miss Isobel Millar laid a wreath on the war memorial. (West Cumberland Times, 26 August 1939)

Ennerdale Show took place on Wednesday, 30 August 1939. For the first time in the history of the show, a lady – Mrs M. Hutton of Keswick – won the supreme cattle championship. The annual show of the Burton, Milnthorpe and Carnforth Agricultural Society – the Burton Show – took place on the following day at Dalton Park, Burton-in-Kendal. There were 636 entries. A new feature was a section for home industries such as dressmaking. And arrangements had been made by the LMS Railway for extensive cheap travel facilities to be available for soccer enthusiasts during the forthcoming football season.

CHAPTER 4

Industrial Revival

In October 1935, the Whitehaven collieries all ceased production, causing much hardship. However, once again, coal and iron were needed to make military equipment and weapons. Haig Colliery and William Pit in Whitehaven were reopened in March 1937 by a new concern, the Cumberland Coal Company. The following poem, *Cleator Moor*, published in Norman Nicholson's collection *Five Rivers* (1944) about Egremont, Whitehaven and Cleator Moor, reflects the way workers became – without being consulted – part of the arms business. The last three verses show that the poem is not just descriptive, it is also critical, and critical of war:

Cleator Moor by Norman Nicholson

From one shaft at Cleator Moor
They mined for coal and iron ore.
This harvest below ground could show
Black and red currants on one tree.

In furnaces they burnt the coal,
The ore was smelted into steel,
And railway lines from end to end
Corseted the bulging land.

Pylons sprouted on the fells,
Stakes were driven in like nails,
And the ploughed fields of Devonshire
Were sliced with the steel of Cleator Moor.

The land waxed fat and greedy too,
It would not share the fruits it grew,
And coal and ore, as sloe and plum,
Lay black and red for jamming time.

The pylons rusted on the fells,
The gutters leaked beside the walls,
And women searched the ebb-tide tracks
For knobs of coal or broken sticks.

But now the pits are wick with men,
Digging like dogs dig for a bone:
For food and life we dig the earth –
In Cleator Moor they dig for death.

Every wagon of cold steel
Is fire to drive a turbine wheel;
Every knuckle of soft ore
A bullet in a soldier's ear.

The miner at the rockface stands,
With his segged and bleeding hands
Heaps on his head the fiery coal,
And feels the iron in his soul.

The accident rate went up (*Cumbria Archive Service*). On 2 March 1937, Richard Hocking (1880-1937) of Cleator Moor was killed when buried under a fall at Sir John Walsh iron ore mine, Bigrigg (closed June 1939). There was a 'pit boy' strike by young miners at Harrington No. 10 Colliery, Lowca (opened 1910, closed 1968) in January 1939. The *Lancashire Evening Post* reported on 14 January 1939:

Lowca Colliery was idle today owing to a lightning strike of pit boys. About 500 men and boys were affected. Two boys have been seriously hurt this week in one of the workings, and the boys allege that this place is too dangerous. It is expected that a settlement will be reached before Monday.

On 17 October 1939, hewer John William Clark (1902-1939) of Grasmere Avenue, Workington, was killed by a fall of stone at Harrington No. 10 Colliery.
    In July 1939, John H. Clarke (1900-1939) of Great Broughton was found dead in a gas-filled section of Risehow Colliery, Flimby (opened 1918, closed 1966). For the first time since the First World War, D.J. Mason, Coroner for West Cumberland, conducted an inquest into a mining fatality without the

assistance of a jury at Cleator Moor on Monday, 18 September 1939. He explained that, under a Home Office order, coroners had been asked, except where there were exceptional circumstances, to dispense with juries for the duration of the war.

Injured by a fall of stone in Walkmill Colliery, Moresby (closed 1961) on 1 November 1939, James Garner (1889-1939) of Moresby Parks, Whitehaven, died six hours later. A colliery deputy, John Peel of Flimby, a great-great-grandson of John Peel, the huntsman, was killed at St Helen's Colliery, Workington, on Saturday, 3 May 1941 (*Lancashire Evening Post*, 5 May 1941). In accordance with custom, war or no war, the pit was closed the following day. On 30 September 1941, miner James Edward Blair (1909-1941) died at his home in Queen Street, Cleator Moor, following an accident while working in Crowgarth iron ore mine, Cleator Moor, a few hours previously. It had only been three months since his father, Thomas Blair, was killed in an accident at Moresby Colliery.

On 3 June 1941, there was an explosion at the William Pit. Twelve lives were lost: Engine-hand William Ernest Harker of Bransty was a member of the William Pit Home Guard (the Home Guard was set up in 1940); Jonathan Curwen of Kells was in the ARP; Robert McGrievy, who lived on the Greenbank housing estate, was a member of the Coal Company ARP and attached to 'D First Aid Post'; and Pit Deputy Charles Martin of Bransty was a sergeant in the colliery platoon of the Home Guard. Servicemen home on leave were among scores of volunteers who rushed to the pit head to offer their help. Richard Todd (1908-1942) of North Road, Egremont, was struck on the head by a piece of soft ore in Florence iron ore mine, Egremont, on 31 March 1942 and died.

Hungarian Jew Nicholas 'Miki' Sekers (1910-1972) and his cousin Tomi de Gara, who both fled Budapest in 1937, set up West Cumberland Silk Mills, Richmond Hill, Hensingham, Whitehaven, in 1938. During the Second World War, West Cumberland Silk Mills was required to make parachute silk. When supplies of silk ran low and the new experimental product, nylon, was introduced as a replacement, Miki Sekers began experimenting with the new synthetic fabric, seeing its potential for dressmaking. (The Sekers Fabrics factory in Hensingham was demolished in 2010.)

On 5 May 1939, the *Hull Daily Mail* reported the reopening of Queen's Dock, Whitehaven, on the completion of £30,000 improvements. 'Vessels will take coal cargoes in the next few days,' it said. A seam of barytes (minerals) was struck on Caldbeck Fells by the Caldbeck Mines at its new mine near John Peel's birthplace, the *West Cumberland Times* of 19 August 1939 reported. It said:

The mine is now producing about 100 tons of high-grade washed barytes weekly with a single shift, and big developments are contemplated in the future. Barytes is used extensively in the manufacture of explosives. As most of the supplies used in Britain are imported from Germany and Greece, this new enterprise is of great national importance and would be invaluable in the event of war.

Three tons of khaki (cotton) arrived during the week at Redmayne Tailors, Wigton, who were doing their bit in making army uniforms for the War Office. 'This is the second time in the history of the firm that they have been asked to assist in clothing the Army,' the *West Cumberland Times* of 26 August 1939 reported. (The factory in Station Road, Wigton closed in the early 1980s and was demolished in 1987. But the company continues today as a tailors in High Street, Wigton.)

The Millom and Askam Hematite Iron Company was formed in 1890. After the First World War, there was a sharp downturn in the iron market, and economic constraints dictated that the company had to close one site down. By 1938, the Askam works had simply vanished. (Hodbarrow mine and Millom Ironworks closed in 1968.) The *Liverpool Daily Post* reported on 8 December 1939:

A new, highly-modernised blast furnace started production at Millom Ironworks yesterday, after having been lighted by Sir Andrew Lewis, the chairman of the Millom company. There are now two furnaces in use at the Millom works, each capable of making about 3,000 tons of iron per week.

A report on the same day in the *Hull Daily Mail* said that Gerald Grant (1897-1939), 25, the South Cumberland rugby union player, had died from injuries received while at work at Millom Ironworks on 6 December 1939. He was struck by a heavy jib that fell from a crane. Millom furnace worker Charles Edward Armstrong, aged 29, of Garthlands, Kirksanton, was also killed. Evidence showed that he had fallen into a ladle (*Liverpool Daily Post*, 16 February 1940). The bodies of four men entombed by a fall of haematite ore at Hodbarrow Mines were recovered by rescue teams on Thursday, 3 December 1942. The victims, Albert Gillbanks (1887-1942), William Martin (1910-1942), George Patrick (1912-1942) and George Rigg (1901-1942), were all from Haverigg near Millom.

The Second World War found Tom Fletcher Mayson (1893-1958) VC, who was born at the John Bull pub, Silecroft, serving in the local Home Guard and working at Millom Ironworks as part of the railway gang in the shunting

Above: The laying of a memorial stone and service for Tom Fletcher Mayson VC at Silecroft War Memorial in July 2017. (Taken by the Author)

Below: The 'E' company of Workington Home Guard on parade outside High Duty Alloys, 1944. (Public domain)

yard. The former farm labourer was given the Victoria Cross for his heroic actions during an attack on the German lines at Wieltje in Belgium, 1917. Members of the community gathered on 30 July 2017 at Silecroft Village Hall to remember him.

High Duty Alloys' factory in Distington, later known as Pechiney Aviatube and then as Alcan Pechiney, opened in 1940 and closed in 2007. Work was frenetic at High Duty Alloys during the war years. The foundry, forge and extrusion presses produced parts for virtually all British aircraft engines and the workforce reached a peak of almost 3,000 men and women working around the clock, seven days a week, according to *Cumbria Archive Service*. In January 1944, an Anti-Aircraft unit was set-up within the works. This was formed from men who had joined the Workington Home Guard.

Records relating to the site including order books are held by Cumbria Archive and Local Studies Centre, Whitehaven.

Haweswater Dam completed

The farming villages of Mesand and Mardale Green, west of the village of Shap, included a school built in 1883, Holy Trinity Church, Measand Hall, Dun Bull Inn, and the Parsonage. They vanished when Mardale Valley was flooded in 1935 to create Haweswater reservoir to serve Manchester, and most of the villages' buildings were blown up by Royal Engineers, who used them for demolition practice.

At the last service in Holy Trinity Church on 18 August 1935, the Bishop of Carlisle spoke to the 72 people who could fit inside. Outside, more than 1,000 stood in the fields and listened as the service was relayed over loudspeakers. The church was dismantled and the stone used in constructing the dam. All the bodies in the churchyard were exhumed and re-buried at St Michael's Church Shap, built in 1140.

Despite the war, Haweswater Dam – which raised the water level – was completed in 1940. According to *Tatham History Society*, the first 9 mile section of the 72 mile aqueduct from Haweswater to Heaton Park reservoir in Manchester was completed in 1941. Construction of the rest of the Haweswater aqueduct started in 1948. 'Twenty-five million gallons of water a day are now pouring through a pipe line from Haweswater to Manchester. But it will be many years before the project is finished,' reported the *Lancashire Evening Post* of 16 May 1955.

It was said that a new church was to be built above the new water level of the lake. This never came to pass. Manchester Corporation also promised that a new Dun Bull Inn would be built. Nothing came of it. Today, when the water in the reservoir is low, the remains of Mardale Green can be seen, including stone walls and the village bridge.

Above: *Mardale re-burial ground at Shap cemetery, which is up the hill from the church. There are no wartime commemorations here.* (John Lowis.)

Below: *Flake Howe Farm, with the lake of High Water behind in the distance.* (mardale. green.talktalk.net)

During the war, John Edmondson Coulston (1907-1998) of Pooley Bridge by Ullswater, whose grandfather once farmed at Flake Howe Farm, Mardale, served as a special constable and used to patrol Ullswater for planes (*Cumberland & Westmorland Herald*, 28 March 1998). He held a special affection for Mardale and, during hot summers when the reservoir water level fell, he would act as a guide – using his memories to point people in the direction of the former local landmarks.

Among the poems of blacksmith Thomas William Greenhow (1888-1971) of Crosby Garrett, a village near Kirkby Stephen that once had a railway station (closed 1952) on the Settle and Carlisle line, is a lament to the 'drowned village' of Mardale and the trauma of hearing of the Second World War. His descendants have compiled a book of his poems and prose, *Vulcan: The Blacksmith Poet* by T.W. Greenhow and David Ramshaw (2015).

In the drought summers of 1976 and 1984, the water level in Haweswater dropped so much that the ruins of the village reappeared. The more recent hot spell (2018) exposed Mardale Green's remains again.

Crosby Garrett Viaduct on the Settle and Carlisle Railway, 1984. Also closed in 1952 on the Settle and Carlisle railway line were Ormside and Cotehill stations. (David Ingham)

Crosby Garrett. (Jean Norgate)

CHAPTER 5

K Shoes' 250,000 Pairs of Service Boots

For more than 160 years, shoes and boots were manufactured at Kendal's K Shoe factory at Netherfield. Total sales for 1897 reached 173,555 pairs of footwear. For 1913, production reached 230,526 pairs. During the Great War, a large part of the factory's output was reserved for the War Office and to make 'K Service Boots' for officers. Major contracts were also carried out for the French Army and for the Russian Army.

By 1920, the available local workforce could no longer meet production demands and the first outlying factory was built in Lancaster (Netherlune, closed 1990). This was followed over the years by a second factory at Kendal (Low Mills, 1951), and factories at Askam (1953-1996), Distington (1965), Workington (Lilyhall, 1967-1980), Shap (1971), and Millom (1973-1991), and Millom 2 (1979). In 1923, production reached 200,641 pairs. By 1939, production had risen to 890,205 pairs. During the Second World War, the factory concentrated on government contract work, not only for serviceman's boots and shoes but also kitbags, tents, gaiters and all sorts of items for use by the forces. And more than 100 men of Netherfield went to join their Territorial battalions.

Norman Lancaster (1916-1994), who was then a clicker (the person who cuts the uppers for boots or shoes from a skin of leather or piece of man-made material), was transferred to work for the Ministry of Aircraft production on a newly completed floor at Netherfield, accessible initially only by ladder.

Their first task was to make a Plessey engine cover. This was followed by a contract for 100 covers for Anson aircraft, using fabric supplied from Morton Sundour of Carlisle. The joiners made a pattern out of plywood and the cutting of the material was done on a bench 30ft long by 5ft wide. There were 80 to 90 machinists stitching this material, which was extremely heavy to handle. Then came a contract for huge tents, designed to allow aircraft to be inspected and serviced under cover, and then, the most awkward contract of all, a huge tarpaulin heavily roped at the corners. The material was very tarry and dirty to handle. The ladies concerned with this work had to change their overalls in a lift, as there was no other changing room, and it was part of Norman's duty to stop the lift between floors to ensure their privacy.

Nobody knew what this huge tarpaulin was finally used for, as they saw it folded up and carried away on a large RAF transporter.

(K Shoes – The First 150 Years, *Spencer Crookenden*)

Later contracts included top-secret flying boots, with hidden compartments in the heel and elsewhere, where escape materials could be hidden in case RAF aircrew had to come down in enemy territory. Some replicas of Luftwaffe officers' flying boots were also made with German materials, stamping and sizes, and with a page of the *Berliner Zeitung* put in between the inner and outer sole. Some of these flying boots were fitted with a zip, so that the leg-part could be detached if necessary, and the boots transformed into walking shoes.

The total range of contracts carried out between 1939 and 1945 included more than 250,000 pairs of service boots, 29,000 kitbags, 4,500 pairs of gaiters, 145,000 pairs of RAF flying boots, officers' shoes for both the US Army and the British Army, covers for aircraft, dinghies, wood soles and, finally, demobilisation shoes.

Twenty-four members of Netherfield were killed on active service in the Second World War. Lance Corporal Elwin Sedgwick Ferguson (1918-1944), 4th Battalion, Border Regiment, of Mint Street, Kendal, was killed in action in Burma on 4 July 1944 and was buried at Imphal War Cemetery, India. Sergeant

Taukkyan War Cemetery, Burma was opened in 1951. (RegentsPark, under CC BY-SA 3.0)

Ronald Whyte (1923-1945), 5th Queen's Own Cameron Highlanders, died in hospital in Mansfield, Nottinghamshire, on 23 April 1945 from wounds sustained in Germany. He was buried at St Oswald's, Burneside, Kendal. Lance Corporal Ernest Winskill, 2nd Battalion, South Lancashire Regiment, was killed in Burma on 18 April 1945, and was buried at Taukkyan War Cemetery, Burma. Gunner Samuel Wolstenholme (1920-1945), Royal Artillery, died on 16 March 1945 while a prisoner-of-war in Sarawak, a Malaysian state on Borneo. He was buried at Labuan War Cemetery, Malaysia.

Second lieutenant joined K Shoes

Second Lieutenant Spencer Crookenden CBE MC DL (1919-2006) joined the Royal Engineers and, in April 1941, constructed landing strips and laid minefields in the Western Desert. In September 1941, he contracted a serious case of dysentery, and was for some time on the War Office's 'Dangerously Ill' list. In 1942, he rejoined the fighting with the 50th Division on the southern section of the Alamein defensive line, where the German advance had been halted but fighting was still heavy. One of the Royal Engineers' dangerous tasks was to patrol the no man's land between the lines and report back on the position of enemy minefields. In 1943, while commanding a night-time attack across a minefield and over an anti-tank ditch near Mareth in southern Tunisia, he was awarded an MC and was promoted to major.

After the Battle of Mareth Line (16-31 March 1943), he was put in charge of the 42nd Field Company Royal Engineers, which helped expel the Axis troops from North Africa. He wrote to his brother Lieutenant General Sir Napier Crookenden (1915-2002) in May 1943: 'It is not every day that one sees the complete staff of 21 Panzer Division driving in without escort in its own cars to give itself up or of watching vast groups of Germans and Italians driving down the road asking the way to the nearest POW camp.' Sir Napier survived the war as an airborne commander. Their brother Henry Crookenden joined the 2nd Battalion Queen's Westminster Rifles, later becoming the 12th Battalion King's Royal Rifle Corps. In a night attack in September 1944, he was badly wounded and, after much suffering, had both legs amputated.

After the war, Spencer Crookenden went to Cambridge to read History. In 1947, he joined K Shoes in Kendal, he became chairman in 1975, and he lived at Reston Hall, Staveley. He died on 5 December 2006 at Edenbridge, Kent, his final home (he moved there in 2004). A thanksgiving service for him was held at Holy Trinity Church, Kendal on Saturday, 17 March 2007.

CHAPTER 6

This Country is at War with Germany

The government had asked Carlisle Corporation to make accommodation for 12,000 refugees (*Lancashire Evening Post*, 24 August 1939). On 30 August 1939, Whitehaven's underground ARP headquarters at the town hall were ready for an emergency. On 1 September 1939, Carlisle received 4,000 children from Newcastle upon Tyne. Evacuees arrived at Lancaster for the Lunesdale and Lancaster rural areas from Salford, and two trains, each carrying 750 children and their leaders, pulled into Egremont station (normal passenger traffic ended along the line in 1935). Workington's first batch of evacuees arrived from Newcastle after 12 noon to be welcomed by townspeople.

On the same day, 800 schoolboys from the Royal Grammar School, Newcastle, founded in 1545, arrived in Penrith by train, clutching their rucksacks, kitbags and gas masks. They were billeted with local families or in large houses. The school used Penrith Wordsworth Street Methodist Church as its base, and shared buildings and facilities with local children. In the afternoons, the senior pupils used the classrooms at Queen Elizabeth Grammar School, Penrith, which moved to its present grounds on Ullswater Road in 1915. Morning lessons were held in hired rooms in other parts of the town. (The last ever reunion for students of Newcastle Royal Grammar School who were evacuated to Penrith took place in the George Hotel, Penrith in September 2004.)

'Penrith seems to have been fortunate in its evacuated guests. 850 blue-blazered boys now throng the streets, well disciplined, respectful and anxious to lend a hand,' wrote Tom Sarginson, *Cumberland & Westmorland Herald* editor, in September 1939. John Hurst, a former editor of the *Cumberland & Westmorland Herald*, in *Come Back to Eden: Lakeland's Northern Neighbour*, wrote that Penrith not only provided homes for the boys, but the arrival of some 400 others – teachers, officials and parents – meant that every scrap of empty property was snapped up. The main cause for concern, arising from the influx, was the strain on the water supply, then dependent solely on Hayeswater, Mr Hurst wrote. (Hayeswater was dammed in 1908 to provide a reservoir serving Penrith, but it was restored to a mountain tarn in summer 2014.) The Dean Road Girls' School, South Shields, was also evacuated to Penrith.

'Blind people numbering 350 will assemble in readiness to journey by bus and train to Egremont, Carlisle, Keswick and Cockermouth,' the *Newcastle Evening*

Hayeswater, formerly a reservoir. (Courtesy of Bob Tinley)

Chronicle of 1 September reported. And, working at high speed, the town hall staff of Newcastle and Gateshead were completing last-minute plans for the evacuation, on 2 September 1939, of expectant mothers and children below school age, cripples and blind people.

Evacuation lists for Newcastle schools relocated to Cockermouth can be found at *Whitehaven Archives* (SUDC 1/1202). Under an arrangement between Salford City Council and Ulverston Town Council, more than 1,000 children arrived in Ulverston on 2 and 3 September. Those who were of secondary school age and had been admitted to grammar schools in Salford were entitled to go to Ulverston Grammar School. In addition to these evacuees, Ulverston Grammar School played host to 114 'private evacuees'. These were pupils from at-risk parts of Britain whose parents arranged for them to stay, many with relatives, in the Ulverston area.

Not a glimmer of light was permitted, for Hitler's bombers may be flying overhead

Blackout regulations were imposed on 1 September 1939 – the day that the German army crossed the Polish frontier. These required that all windows and doors should be covered at night with suitable material such as heavy curtains, cardboard or paint, to prevent the escape of any glimmer of light that might aid enemy aircraft. Morton Sundour Fabrics' weaving factory in Denton Hill, Carlisle, invented a type of material to cover windows in factories so they could keep working throughout the night. (The Denton Hill Works closed in late 1980.) Its chairman was Sir James Morton (1867-1943) of Dalston Hall near Carlisle, knighted in 1936 for his services to the dye and colour industries. His son Alistair James Fagan Morton's (1910-1963) delicate health prevented him from taking an active role in the Second World War. Instead he was a photographer for the National Buildings Record, created in 1941 to photograph and document the historic fabric of England before it was lost.

External lights such as street lights were switched off, or dimmed and shielded to deflect light downward. Essential lights such as traffic lights and vehicle headlights were fitted with slotted covers to deflect their beams towards to the ground. On the same day, rain and international news cut attendance at Gosforth Show by half. The Lowick Agricultural Show, which should have been held at Lowick Bridge on Saturday, 2 September, was postponed. The Cockermouth Annual Show was also cancelled.

The Lowick Show has been celebrated by communities along and around the Crake Valley for more than 150 years. (lowickshow.com)

Annie Ferguson from Whitehaven, who spoke to the BBC in 2005, worked as a screen lass all through the war. This involved picking metal and stone out from the coal. She said:

> If I'm not mistaken, it was Sunday, 3 September when we heard there was going to be a war. We hadn't had what we call a 'wireless' very long. Everybody was new-fangled with the wireless then. We all listened to Mr Chamberlain on the radio on the Sunday morning saying we were at war.

At 11.15am on 3 September, British prime minister Neville Chamberlain announced on BBC Radio that the deadline of the British ultimatum for the withdrawal of German troops from Poland expired at 11am and that 'consequently this country is at war with Germany'. Winston Churchill (1874-1965) was appointed First Lord of the Admiralty on 3 September, the same position he had held during the first part of the First World War.

The National Service (Armed Forces) Act 1939 was enacted by Parliament on 3 September. It enforced full conscription on all males between 18 and 41 who were residents in the UK. Exemptions included people working in reserved occupations such as farming and engineering. Soon after war was declared, ARP became Civil Defence General Services. Volunteers were involved in such duties as wardens, rescue, first-aid, welfare, fire watchers and messengers.

William 'Billy' John Peel Pennington (1921-1990) was born at 8 Green Cottages, The Mill, at Torver (the mill was converted into cottages in 1911-1912 and the farmhouse let to tenants), and worked at Vickers as a mechanic. When war broke out, he applied to join the RAF and he was accepted until they found out that he worked at Vickers. He was told that, as his job was a reserved occupation, he was excluded from joining the forces. He was sent from Vickers to Scapa Flow harbour, Orkney, Scotland, where he repaired the boats of the British Fleet. Here, HMS *Royal Oak* was sunk (see page 66), The Churchill Barriers were built (1940s) and, in 1941, the hunt for the German battleship *Bismarck* began. His sister Joan Pennington (1916-1995), also born at The Mill, had met and married Fred Rostrom and settled in Preston. She returned to be with her mother Jean Pennington at The Mill during wartime and her first daughter, Anne, was born in 1944.

The first British shots of the war

HMS *Ajax*, a Leander-class light cruiser that served with the Royal Navy (RN) during the Second World War, was built at Vickers in Barrow and completed in April 1935. When war was declared, she took up her appropriate station and patrolled off the River Plate on the south-eastern coastline of South America. There she stopped, shelled and sank the German merchant ship *Olinda* – bound from Montevideo in Uruguay to Germany with a cargo of wool, hides, cotton and scrap iron – at 4.30pm on 3 September 1939 with scuttling charges after the crew was placed aboard British tanker *San Geraldo*. Twenty-four hours later, on the afternoon of 4 September, the German steamship SS *Carl Fritzen* was intercepted by HMS *Ajax*. As with *Olinda*, *Ajax* was forced to scuttle *Carl Fritzen*. Captain Charles Henry Lawrence Woodhouse (1893-1978), appointed to command *Ajax* in 1937, was in a hurry to get on with the war. The Battle of the River Plate, which took place on 13 December 1939, was the first major naval battle of the Second World War and included *Ajax*. (*San Gerardo* was hit by a U-boat on 31 March 1942; fifty-seven died.) HMS *Cumberland*, built in Barrow and launched on 16 March 1926, arrived at the River Plate at 10pm on 14 December 1939, after steaming for thirty-four hours. *Cumberland*, *Ajax* and *Archilles* patrolled the River Plate estuary, resulting in the German raider *Admiral Graf Spee* being scuttled by her crew on 17 December 1939.

HMS Cumberland in 1945. (Public domain)

CHAPTER 7

Take Special Care

The Threlkeld Sheep Dog Trials had been abandoned, the Cumberland Agricultural Society's Show abandoned, the Shap Show and Sports for Saturday, 6 September cancelled, the Brough Show for 14 September cancelled, the Ousby and Culgaith Agricultural Society Show for 23 September cancelled, and the Nenthead Hound Trail, Alston Moor, cancelled. However, the Lunesdale Agricultural Show, established in 1839, was held in the usual field in Kirkby Lonsdale on 15 September 1939 (*Lancaster Guardian*, 22 September 1939). Held at Egremont on Saturday, 16 September 1939, the first hound trailing event since the outbreak of war attracted a big crowd. At the autumn show of Lakeland sheep at Millom on Monday, 18 September 1939, there were large winners.

Colonel Sir Henry Clayton Darlington (1877-1959), who served in the First World War in Egypt, and Lady Darlington of Melling Hall near Kirkby Lonsdale, offered part of their residence to the Lunesdale Rural District Council as an emergency hospital for sick children among the evacuees in the areas of the Lunesdale and Lancaster Rural District Councils, the Carnforth Urban District Council, and the Lancaster City Council (*Lancaster Guardian*, 8 September 1939). Until 1952, Melling railway station was served by the nine-and-a-half mile Furness and Midland Joint Railway (the line is still in use today as part of the Leeds to Morecambe Line, although there are no stops). Melling Hall was built in 1792 by the ship-owning Gillison family. It was a hotel until 2000. Today, Melling Manor is the East Wing of the former Melling Hall.

More than 500 mothers and their children under school age arrived in Kendal in two batches on Saturday, 9 September 1939 (*Westmorland Gazette*, 16 September 1939). Meanwhile, in the early hours of the same day, soldier John George Norris (1907-1939) of Dobbinson Road, Carlisle, was knocked down and killed by a Lytham St Annes (Lancashire) Corporation bus in the blackout. Acting Coroner Mr A.L. Ashton, who returned a verdict of accidental death, had had a number of blackout inquests. On Saturday, 16 September 1939, retired postman John Greenwood Ratson (1879-1939) of Castle Rise, Kendal, was knocked over by a car at Helsfell, Windermere Road, Kendal, during the blackout.

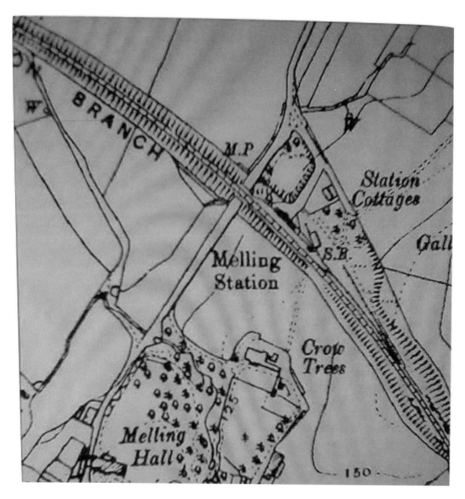

The location of Melling Hall, near the Furness and Midland Railway, 1891 OS map.

The first case under the lighting regulations in North Lonsdale was heard by Ulverston magistrates on 28 September 1939. A pharmacy in Broughton-in-Furness was fined 10s (in 2017, this was worth £19.67) for failing to obscure a light inside the premises at 10.30pm on 9 September. The defendant said her desire had been to comply with regulations. Robert Largue (1872-1939) of Holden Road, Salterbeck, Workington, was knocked down by a car on Friday, 6 October 1939 and fatally injured. Colonel D.J. Mason, Coroner for West Cumberland, said at the inquest of Largue on 11 October 1939: 'This is the second blackout accident I have had in a week, and I hope it will be a second warning that people, if they want to protect themselves, must stick to the pavement.' If blackout conditions continued, motorists would have to consider if they were justified in taking their cars out at night, he said.

John Trevelyan, Director of Education to Westmorland County Education Committee, appealed to South Shields Education Authority to stop, if possible, the drift back to Tyneside of child evacuees, the *Newcastle Journal* reported on 20 October 1939. He said:

> It seems such a pity that the mothers should take the children home when, apart from the question of the children's safety, their health has so obviously improved in the country air. I am certain that the children are happy. Apart from the unfortunate effects on the children themselves, there are the unfortunate effects on our Westmorland folk, as they have already got very fond of the children.

Trevelyan was the first director of British Families Education Service, an organisation set up by the government in 1946 to run schools for the children of British military and government personnel serving in West Germany.

The *Westmorland Gazette* of 11 November 1939 reported, in connection with the evacuation of Newcastle and South Shields Elementary School Children into the Westmorland county area, that 1,300 evacuees had returned home. The girls of Heaton Secondary School, Newcastle, were by 23 December 1939 receiving their education at the Allen Technical Institute, Station Road/Beezon Road, Kendal.

> The *Newcastle Evening Chronicle* of 28 November 1939 reported: A concert was given in the Memorial Hall, Preston Patrick, Westmorland, by children of Endmoor School (near Kendal). Among the infant performers were 17 evacuees from Elswick Road School, Newcastle. The spirit of the infants revealed how happily they had settled down to their temporary surroundings. Items in the programme included songs, dances, singing games, and a performance of a short sketch 'The Turnip Seed'.

Children of Northumberland Road School, Newcastle, were evacuated to the village of Ings near Windermere, and children of Westgate Hill School, Newcastle, were evacuated to Kirkby Stephen. The *Newcastle Evening Chronicle* of 29 November 1939 reported: 'About 38 per cent of the Westgate Hill children have returned home, but it is hoped that the drift back is now over. The children have plenty to occupy their time. In the evening, there is a young people's club, at which Newcastle children meet for games, sing-songs and other

Issued by the Ministry of Health between 1939 and 1945. (Public domain)

activities.' On 18 December 1939, nearly 800 parents went from Newcastle to Cumbria to visit their evacuated children.

The Phoney War was an eight-month period at the start of the Second World War during which there were no major military land operations on the Western Front. During the quiet months of the Phoney War, parents began to question whether it was really necessary to keep their children in the countryside. War rations made it difficult to get fuel, and rail fares had soared, so it was too expensive for most people to visit their families, according to *True Stories of The Blitz: Usborne True Stories* by Henry Brook (2012). A parent's letter in the *Newcastle Evening Chronicle* of 6 November 1939 is headed 'To See Children':

Sir – The Government advises us to leave our children in safe areas. That is quite right, but we would like to see them sometimes.

My children are at Millom and the train fare for one adult is £1 3s 1d return. What chance have working class parents of visiting their children? Could the railways not issue cheap tickets once a month or six weeks, more especially for the Christmas holidays, and so give us encouragement to let the children stay?

By January 1940, almost half of the evacuees returned home, according to *iwm.org.uk*. The government produced posters such as the one above, urging parents to leave evacuees where they were while the threat of bombing remained likely. Additional rounds of official evacuation occurred nationwide in the summer and autumn of 1940, following the German invasion of France in

May-June and the beginning of the London Blitz in September. Evacuation was voluntary and many children remained in the cities. From 7 September 1940, London was systematically bombed by the Luftwaffe for fifty-six out of the following fifty-seven days and nights. Most notable was a large daylight attack against London on Sunday, 15 September 1940, Battle of Britain Day. The RAF shot down sixty-one planes. The RAF lost thirty-one planes (*bbc.co.uk*).

'Extinguish your fires', November 1939

In bygone days, the curfew bell (established by William the Conqueror in 1069) rang out at 8pm with its message: 'Extinguish your lights and fires, or cover them up, and retire to rest.' The purpose of the old curfew was to prevent fire danger in the wooden houses of the towns.

After 1650, there seems to have been a minor architectural revolution. Timber-framed houses were no longer built and, in their place, load-bearing masonry was universally adopted for building purposes (*Life and Tradition in the Lake District*, William Rollinson, 1974). The fireplace was not only necessary for the warmth and comfort of the family but also essential for the preparation of food.

From 29 November 1939 in Penrith, the bell (that for years tolled the hour of eight) rang out at blackout time, 8pm, carrying a message very similar to the original. Today, curfew bells ring at Richmond, North Yorkshire, and Dumfries (Greyfriars Church).

CHAPTER 8

Immense Sacrifices Demanded from All

The petrol rationing scheme, which came into effect on 16 September 1939, compelled the Ribble Motor Services, with a territory stretching from Carlisle to southern Lancashire, to cut down their services by around 50 per cent. At the Penrith depot, six drivers and twelve conductors were affected. Local services suspended included Penrith-Howtown, Kirkby Stephen-Shap, and Kendal-Kirkby Stephen. 'Further amendments are being made on several routes to meet the requirements of country children who attend Penrith schools and who, owing to the 'double shift' arrangement with the evacuees, will be at school only in the mornings,' the *Penrith Observer* of 26 September 1939 reported. There was an immediate reduction in the number of private cars on the road. (Ribble Motor Services ceased operation in 1989).

Using the information gathered on National Registration Day, on Friday, 29 September 1939, when every householder had to fill in a form giving details of the people who lived in their house, identity (ID) cards and ration books were issued. The ID card was important in helping the government plan rationing, knowing how many could serve in the armed forces and how many could be employed in industries vital to the war effort, such as the shipyard in Barrow. Ration books and ID cards of deceased persons had to be surrendered to the registrar at the time of registration of a death. In June 1940, Norman Walter Goodchild (1901-1970), the chief constable of Barrow from October 1939 to 1944 and chief constable of Wolverhampton from 1944 to 1966, reminded people to carry their ID cards at all times. (With the 1941 census not taken, the 1939 National Register taken on 29 September 1939 will have been used as a census substitute.)

On the night of 13/14 October 1939, the battleship HMS *Royal Oak*, which had fought in the Battle of Jutland in 1916, was sunk at anchor at Scapa Flow by torpedoes fired by *U-47*. More than 1,200 men and boys were serving on *Royal Oak* on the night; 834 lost their lives, including: Leading Sick Berth Attendant Robert Leslie Collins (1916-1939), son of Herbert Summers Collins and Mary Collins of Carlisle; Signalman Alan Raymond Hodgson (1919-1939), born in Cark-in-Cartmel and son of Geoffrey Stanley Hodgson and Isobel Hodgson of Kendal; Engine Room Artificer Gordon Mellenby Sandham (1916-1939) of

World War Two Loans Box

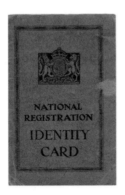

National Registration Identity Card

ID (Identity) cards had to be carried at all times. It was important this document was not lost as it had to be **presented on demand**. In June 1940 the Chief Constable of Barrow reminded people to carry their I.D. Cards at all times.

Why were ID cards introduced at the start of the war in 1939 in Britain?

It was an immediate **census*** and told the **government** how many people there were in Britain their **ages** and **gender**. It was really **important** in helping the government plan **rationing**, knowing how many could serve in the **armed forces** and how many could be **employed** in **industries vital** to the **war effort** (like the **shipyard** in Barrow).

*A census is finding out and recording information on everyone in an area.

The Dock Museum, North Road, Barrow-in-Furness, LA14 2PW

dockmuseum@barrowbc.gov.uk; 01229 876400

ID card. (Dock Museum, Barrow)

Brigham (remembered on the family gravestone at St Bridget's Church, Brigham); Leading Seaman John Robert Simpson (1918-1939), son of Robert and Elsie Simpson of Barrow; and Ordinary Telegraphist Gilbert Todd (1920-1939) of

Muncaster (named on the Muncaster War Memorial). In the immediate aftermath of the sinking, *Royal Oak's* survivors were billeted in the towns and villages of Orkney. Survivor Arthur Smith, of Middlesex, died on 10 December 2016. *Royal Oak* and many of her crew sleep in the waters of Scapa Flow in a protected war grave. (Sick berth is a rank that existed from 1833 to 1965, when the rank became medical attendant, Imperial War Museum researchers decided in October 2017.)

Official rationing began on 8 January 1940 with bacon, butter and sugar, but there was a shortage of animal feedstuffs. In March 1940, the Penrith Agricultural Society, which had the premier show in Cumberland for shorthorn cattle, decided not to hold an agricultural show and to invest instead the society's balance in war loan to support the war effort. Meat rationing came into force officially in Britain on 11 March 1940. To help householders cope with limited amounts, there were demonstrations on food economy, some of them at Electricity House, Penrith.

Lieutenant Edward Smith VC DCM (1898-1940), who worked at Oughterside Colliery until 1917, was a VC hero of the First World War. As the Second World War loomed, he re-enlisted with the Lancashire Fusiliers and was among the first

Above left: *Gilbert Todd, first Muncaster casualty of the Second World War.* (Whitehaven News)

Above right: *Every year, the RN Northern Diving Group raise a battle ensign on the upturned hull of the wreck.* (hmsroyaloak.co.uk)

of the British Expeditionary Force (BEF) to sail for France. Having achieved the rank of lieutenant, he was killed in action in France on 12 January 1940, possibly due to friendly fire. His parents, of North Quay, Maryport, were notified by the War Office on Saturday, 13 January 1940 that he had died from wounds in France.

On 21 January 1940, *U-22* sank British destroyer HMS *Exmouth*. Her crew of 135 were all lost, including Chief Petty Officer Stanley Fleming Graves (1902-1940) of Endmoor, just south of Oxenholme in the parish of Preston Patrick. (The wreck of *Exmouth* was discovered in the Moray Firth in July 2001.) Graves is remembered on the Preston Patrick memorial, a large stone cross at St Patrick's Church. British destroyer HMS *Cossack*, built by Vickers Armstrong of Newcastle upon Tyne and Vickers of Barrow, forcibly removed 303 British prisoners-of-war from German oil tanker and supply vessel *Altmark* in neutral Norwegian territorial waters on 16 February 1940, sparking the Altmark Incident. (*Cossack* was sunk on 27 October 1941 by *U-563*.)

The Royal Army Service Corps (RASC) was the unit responsible for keeping the British Army supplied with provisions (the exceptions were weaponry and ammunition). Private Alfred Ernest Davey, a coppersmith with the RASC, died in France from carbon monoxide poisoning on 4 April 1940. It was surmised that he had been in an accident. He was the son of the late Ernest Davey, who played for Barrow Rugby League Club, and was buried at Bois Carre British Cemetery, Thelus, France.

The Minister for Agriculture, Colonel Sir Reginald Dorman-Smith (1899-1977), announced in the House of Commons on Thursday, 18 April 1940 that, having regard to army needs, the government was unable to grant further releases on agricultural grounds after the present number of applications had been exhausted. Wilfred Roberts (Liberal, Cumberland North) asked: 'Does that mean that it is no use any farmer, in any circumstances, making application to have men released from the Army?' Sir Reginald replied: 'Yes.'

Conscription in Britain was extended to age 36 on 9 May 1940. And the Phoney War ended with the German attack on France and the Low Countries on 10 May 1940 that lasted six weeks. On the following afternoon, the Air Ministry announced that 'Altogether, some 20 of our aircraft are missing.'

Home Guard

Churchill became prime minister on 10 May 1940, Sedbergh old boy Brendan Bracken (1901-1958) helping him into Downing Street. Bracken, a minister in the British Conservative cabinet, served as Minister of Information from 1941 to 1945.

Churchill visited Barrow on Saturday, 11 May 1940, the day after he was made prime minister, to watch the aircraft carrier HMS *Indomitable* – (see page 252) one of Britain's newest and biggest aircraft carriers – being launched.

Churchill's elevation to the premiership restored Anthony Eden (1897-1977) to the Foreign Office. In a broadcast to the nation on 14 May 1940, Eden appealed 'to all men between 17 and 65 who had handled any weapon of offence or defence, and were willing to enrol in a citizen army to be called Local Defence Volunteers'. Local Defence Volunteers was considered too much of a title and it became the Home Guard. Home Guard battalions were formed on a district basis. Within each battalion, companies were also formed on an area basis, covering specific parts of towns or districts. Uniforms – of sorts – were issued in July 1940. The first daylight raids began in Britain at the beginning of July 1940.

Home Guard battalion areas in Cumberland and Westmorland:

1st Battalion HQ: Longtown
2nd Battalion HQ: Carlisle
3rd Battalion HQ: Carlisle
4th Battalion HQ: Cockermouth
5th Battalion HQ: Workington
6th Battalion HQ: Whitehaven
7th Battalion HQ: Millom
8th Battalion HQ: Penrith
9th Battalion HQ: Keswick
10th Battalion HQ: Kirkby Stephen
11th Battalion HQ: Kendal
12th Battalion HQ: Warwick-on-Eden

In the four days following Eden's call, more than 1,000 Workington men had applied to join the Home Guard. Drilling took place in the Drill Hall on Edkin Street, now under St John's Precinct, and the men took up arms consisting of dummy rifles (for the steelworks division), assorted firearms collected by the police, and molotov cocktails. The Workington battalion, 5th Battalion, was then organised into six companies: Workington Iron and Steel Works; the town company; railway and other transport employees; Clifton to the east of the town; High Duty Alloys at Distington; Coast-battery detachment; Headquarter Company, Signals and Intelligence; and a GPO Battalion.

There is a painting in the Imperial War Museum's Second World War collection entitled *The Grasmere Home Guard* by Professor Gilbert Spencer (1892-1979), dated 1943. Professor Spencer had served with the Royal Army

The Kendal Home Guard protected Windermere because of the risk of German flying-boats landing there. There was also an important aircraft factory based near Ambleside that used the lake to test their planes. (Kendal Archive Centre)

Medical Corps (RAMC) in the First World War. Research for the BBC TV programme *Hidden Paintings* (2011) identified the painting as possibly a scene from Rydal Water, a small body of water located near the hamlet of Rydal, between Grasmere and Ambleside. At the Armitt Library and Museum in Ambleside is a painting of the Ambleside Home Guard by Royal College of Art (RCA) student Frederick Brill (1920-1984), painted in 1943. Brill was a sergeant in the Ambleside Home Guard.

The Armitt Museum also holds works by Kurt Schwitters (1887-1948), a German artist who moved to Barnes, London, in August 1942 and then to Gale Crescent, Ambleside, in June 1945. He died in Kendal on 8 January 1948 and was buried at St Mary's Church, Ambleside.

While on duty on Wednesday, 3 July 1940 with the Home Guard, in which he was an officer, Captain Cyril Wardlaw Distin MC of Newrough, Little Salkeld, Penrith, suddenly collapsed and died, aged 50. Distin, who was wounded in the First World War, was a poultry farmer in 1929 and the managing director of Cumberland and Westmorland Poultry Farmers Ltd. He is commemorated on the Second World War parish war memorial inside Addingham/Glassonby Parish Church. His son James Wardlaw Distin (1920-1943), Royal Corps of Signals, is

Above: *The Armitt Museum and Library, Ambleside, open to the public.* (The Armitt Museum and Library)

Below: *Ambleside Home Guard by Frederick Brill (1920-1984).* (Courtesy of The Armitt Trust)

commemorated on the same memorial. He was reported missing in North Africa (*Yorkshire Post and Leeds Intelligencer*, 7 June 1943).

The rationing of tea, in July 1940, along with margarine, cooking fats and cheese, came as a surprise in a broadcast that Lord Woolton, Minister of Food, made after shops had closed to avoid housewives laying in stocks overnight: 'From today (9 July), as soon as the shops open, tea can be bought only on the surrender to a housewife's usual grocer of one of the 'spare' coupons in the current ration book.' A woman reporter for the *Lancashire Daily Post* wrote on 9 July 1940 that: 'It is the men of Britain who are going to suffer by tea rationing.' She added: 'The greatest problem which the rationing has brought is that of communal tea drinking at workshops and offices. The afternoon cup of tea has become an institution in many buildings. Incidentally, if we are at the moment a nation of tea drinkers, the next generation may alter things, for several women told me that their children had never known the taste of this beverage.' A Whitehaven grocer was fined 20s (£37.38 in 2017) at Whitehaven on 11 November 1940 for disposing of sugar in excess of coupons issued by him and fined £3 (£118.04 in 2017) for disposing of tea not accordance with the number of coupons issued to him.

The Second World War memorial inside Addigham/Glassonby Parish Church lists three casualties. (Ian Stuart Nicholson)

On 1 September 1940, Barrow had its first compulsory blackout. On 12-13 September 1940, 300 incendiaries were dropped on Salthouse, an area of Barrow. Vickers was the main target for bombing alongside Barrow's steelworks. A 5-year-old boy became Barrow's first civilian victim. Cambridge Street School was hit, but not burned down. (It was in April and May 1941 that Barrow was bombed in earnest.)

Leading Aircraftman Henry Albert Briggs died on 31 August 1940 as a result of a car crash 4 miles from Silloth and was buried at Silloth (Causewayhead) Cemetery. Chief Officer Kathleen Ackerley (1894-1940), WRNS, of Liverpool, Leading Aircraftman John Stanton Adair (1907-1940), and Aircraftman Lawrence Christie Scott were also killed. Aircraftman Alastair Charles Macintyre was seriously injured, and Mary Anthony WRNS of Liverpool injured. The car in which were the two members of the WRNS was travelling towards Silloth. It is understood that a second car containing RAF men was emerging from a side road when the vehicles collided.

The Ministry of Food's Dig for Victory campaign, announced on BBC radio on 10 September 1940, encouraged self-sufficiency. Hepper wrote:

> Throughout 1940, we increased vegetable production to such an extent that we had a surplus in the following year. As we were more than self-sufficient, Father took vegetables to the shell-filling factory canteen near Bootle Station and to Mr Harrison's grocer's shop in Bootle village. On one occasion, we even took a load of potatoes to Millom market. He did not seek to make a profit from them; he was simply helping to 'feed the nation' in a very small way... During our residence at Tarn Cottage, the Cumberland War Agricultural Committee (War Ag) controlled almost every aspect of farming and smallholding. [Farmers received instructions from the committee]

ARP Warden Thomas C. Graham of Distington (1897-1940), originally from Wigton, died on 10 October 1940 as a result of injuries sustained while on ARP duty on the night of 8/9 September 1940. Before the Second World War, he worked as a carpenter for the Distington motor trade firm of Myers & Bowman. While on the lookout for unobscured lights, he was struck by a car near the Black Cock Inn, Distington. His name is on the Distington war memorial.

On 17 October 1940, a Vickers Wellington bomber flown by 25-year-old Pilot Officer J.E.S. Morton from New Zealand – returning from operations over Kiel, Germany – ran out of fuel in bad weather. The crew was forced to abandon the aircraft near Penrith and parachuted to safety. The Wellington itself continued until it crashed on to Brown Rigg hill near Plumpton. The aircraft burned after crashing as it still carried a load of bombs and mines. Finds of armaments at the site were made in 1973. Later, a German bomber returning from a raid, probably on Liverpool, dropped its last six bombs, which landed on Stainmore and Musgrave.

The *Cumberland & Westmorland Herald* of 23 November 1940 has an article about Czechoslovakian refugees at Patterdale Hall Forestry Hostel giving a concert of their native song and dance to more than 300 people on 16 November 1940. There were Polish people in Penrith during the war. A lot of them worked on the farms.

Unescorted British liner *Western Prince*, owned by Furness Withy (a British transport business from 1891 to 1980), was torpedoed by *U-96* in the Atlantic on 14 December 1940. Fifteen passengers died and 154 passengers survived; 98 crew members and 55 passengers were picked up by the *Baron Kinnaird* (sunk by *U-621* on 10 March 1943; there were no survivors) and one crew member by HMS *Active*.

Arthur Norman Gardy, a marine engineer of South Gosforth, Newcastle, was a passenger on the vessel travelling from New York to Liverpool. He told the *Newcastle Journal* of 20 December 1940: 'A torpedo struck the ship at six o'clock on a bright moonlit night. The boats were cleared in about six minutes and the vessel started going down.

'An electrician belonging to the ship, who was in the same boat as I was, was asked to return to the Western Prince and release a lifeboat, the electric apparatus of which was not working properly.

'He then accomplished the task and then leapt into the water. But, owing to the heavy seas, it was not possible for him to be picked up by any of the boats. Shortly afterwards, the submarine, which had fired the torpedo, surfaced. The *Western Prince* sank in 15 or 20 seconds.'

On board *Western Prince* were two west Cumbrians: Angus Beattie of Cockermouth, a representative of Messrs Sandberg of London; and Pat Martin of Workington, who held a position with the consolidated Edison Company of New York. The *West Cumberland Times* reported on 4 January 1941: 'Mr Martin will be remembered as a footballer of renown, playing for Maryport. Mr Beattie is at present staying with Mr and Mrs J.R. Mason at Wigton.'

Clarence Decatur Howe (1886-1960), Canadian Minister of Munitions and Supply, was on board. He survived the sinking and eight hours in a lifeboat. During the Second World War, his involvement in the war effort was so extensive that he was nicknamed the 'Minister of Everything'.

CHAPTER 9

Ashville's Big Move to Windermere

Upon the declaration of war, Ashville College, Harrogate, North Yorkshire, was thrown open to boys whose parents preferred them to be in the safety of the Harrogate area. Their time in those early days was fully occupied in work and in the digging of a trench system from Elmfield House to the bottom of the running track. Then came the news that Ashville College was required: the buildings became occupied by the Women's Auxiliary Air Force (WAAF) for training. After considering a number of options, headmaster Joe Lancaster chose the Hydro hotel, Windermere, where the boys remained until 1946.

Ashville started its Lakeland life on 2 October 1939. Already the Hydro was overflowing, so twenty Ashville boys slept at nearby Mrs Balmer's guest house, about ten at Oak Bank, while the remainder were cared for by Miss Thornburrow at Biscay House. The kindness of Windermere Cricket Club enabled Ashville to have a good deal of fun with bat and ball. Bowness Boys Club gave a kindly welcome to members of the upper school.

A 13/14-year-old boy kept a diary from January to July 1940. On Friday, 31 May 1940, the bells had to be stopped as they were mistaken for gas warnings. S. Duncan Packett, at Windermere from September 1939 to 1941, said he played cricket against the staff at the prisoner-of-war camp near Hawkshead. It was a beautiful summer in 1940:

> Sometimes we felt energetic and rose as early as 5am to go down to the lake. There was a super boathouse and the door had been fixed so that we could change and have a swim.

In 1941, the school had more than 200 boys, and only 3 masters remained. Some masters were in the army and some were with munitions. By February 1942, the school had only half its normal complement of maids. The decrease of staff was countered by the willingness of the boys to give a hand.

Summer term 1943 had 201 boarders and 4 day-boys. Forms IVa and IVb gave up free time to go turnip thinning on Matson Ground Farm, Windermere. Their reward – a pint carton of tuberculin tested (TT milk) – was much in evidence during school tea. In 1945, after more than six years in exile, Ashville was about

Above: *The whole school assembled outside the Hydro for the first term at Windermere.* (With thanks to Andi Barker, Ashville)

Below: *Boys arriving at the Hydro.* (With thanks to Andi Barker, Ashville)

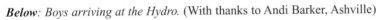

Group of Ashvillians outside the Hydro hotel in October 2014 for a weekend celebration. (With thanks to Andi Barker, Ashville)

to return home. What made Ashville's wartime prospect so pleasing was its surroundings – the lake and hills, fells and valleys.

On 18-19 October 2014, almost 100 old Ashvillians, including 19 who attended the school during its Windermere days, gathered at the Hydro hotel for a weekend celebration. Saturday evening's black tie dinner was finished off by a rousing three cheers led by Ian Wilson, one of the Windermere boys.

Mill Hill School

Mill Hill School, north London, an independent school, came to St Bees School, also an independent school (closed 2015). Lieutenant Colonel J.D. Mitchell,

Thomas Kingston Derry (1905-2001), historian and writer on international affairs and headmaster of Mill Hill, and Lieutenant-Colonel J.D. Mitchell, secretary to Mill Hill, at speed on Cold Fell. (Illustrated Sporting and Dramatic News, 10 November 1939)

Mill Hill first fifteen as guests of Egremont School. (Illustrated Sporting and Dramatic News, 10 November 1939)

secretary to Mill Hill, commanded the St Bees Home Guard. Mill Hill returned to its London home for the autumn 1945 term.

St Aubyn's School, London

During the late summer of 1938, it was decided it would be useful for St Aubyn's Prep School, Woodford Green, Essex, to have a country retreat, to which the school could retire in event of hostilities. In August 1939, headmaster Colonel William Harold Colley (1888-1971), whose son Harold (1927-2011) served in Palestine during the Second World War, took up residence at Whitehall, a medieval tower house in Mealsgate, 16 miles from Carlisle. It became, from 20 September 1939, St Aubyn's Boarding School for six years and one term. 'A few of our local boys took advantage of its presence and enrolled,' according to *Binsey Link* magazine (October 2017) serving the Bassenthwaite area. The earliest reliable record is that the Manor of Whitehall was restored by Sir Henry Percy (1604-1659), second son of the 9th Earl of Northumberland and brother of

Countess of Carlisle Lucy Hay (1599-1660), and that it then became the property of the Salkeld family. It was later bought by lace merchant George Moore (1806-1876), who served an apprenticeship at a draper's in Wigton before going to London, where he became wealthy. He built a west wing. The last person to be resident at Whitehall was William Parkin-Moore (1865-1937). It was bought by the county council, and most of the mansion house was demolished in the 1950s. According to *mealsgate.org.uk*, Whitehall was also used during the war as a rest home for airmen stationed at nearby airfields.

Royal College of Art

The Royal College of Art (RCA), Kensington, was closed in the autumn of 1939 and subsequently relocated to Ambleside, under the guidance of painter Gilbert Spencer (1892-1979), younger brother of the painter Sir Stanley Spencer (1891-1959). Enrolment fell from 334 in 1937-38, to 142 in 1941-42, and to 92 in 1943-44. The men set up home in The Queen's Hotel, and the women in The Salutation, where some rooms were also used as a studio space. Studies were also created in the market hall, which became a school for mural painting. A converted barn behind The Salutation became a sculpture school. The initial reaction from locals was not positive. The students looked very different and were wearing fashions the locals did not recognise. But reactions changed. One reason was that many of the students and lecturers joined the Home Guard. Gordon Ransom, a lecturer evacuated to Ambleside with the RCA, painted Ambleside's rushbearing mural on the west wall of St Mary's Parish Church in 1944. It was a thank you to the people of Ambleside and local children were used as models.

Underley Hall

Lady Henry Cavendish-Bentinck (1869-1939) inherited Underley Hall, a private manor house near Kirkby Lonsdale built between 1825 and 1828, in 1893. In 1916, Lady Henry, whose husband Lord Henry (1863-1931) went to war in 1914, opened the Hall as a convalescent home for soldiers. In September 1939, she offered the Hall to the County Council for any war purpose. She died in November 1939. It had already become a reception centre for children evacuated from the Newcastle and Middlesbrough areas. The staff consisted chiefly of VAD helpers and a few fully trained nurses, and there were about sixty or seventy beds in all, according to *Underley Hall, A History of House and Occupants* by John D Battle, 1969.

When the evacuees were sent home in 1940, a boys' preparatory school, Hordle House in Hampshire (founded in 1926), rented Underley for the remainder of the war. Peter Dodd wrote *Life at Hordle House, 1938 to 1942*, published in 2016. He said:

The main bedrooms (Underley Hall) on the first floor were vast and were turned into dormitories for about twelve boys. I think we were fed pretty well. We were put to work collecting firewood from the woods in the estate, which was sawn up and stacked at the back of the building – the fireplaces were enormous and gobbled up logs. Christmas 1940 was spent in Kirkby Lonsdale – my parents came up and we all stayed in a local pub. The richer parents stayed in the Royal Hotel. My father, who had been drafted into the Ministry of War Transport, was not very well paid on civil service rates and I think struggled to pay my school fees. I was allowed home in the 1941 Easter holidays – just in time for a renewal of the London Blitz, so spent most of the nights in our air raid shelter which was really very comfortable. Thereafter I came home for the holidays and a School Special train was laid on which ran from Redhill to Carlisle via Reading, Didcot and Crewe. We got off at Carnforth and were picked up by a bus from the school. I timed the journey once and it took 13 hours. Each school had a carriage to itself.

From 1976 to 2012, Underley Hall was an independent residential special school for boys with behavioural difficulties. Walhampton Prep School in the New Forest, Hampshire, is the result of the 1997 merger between Hordle House and Walhampton Prep School.

Moved to Keswick

Roedean School, Brighton, an independent school for girls, was used by HMS *Vernon*, a torpedo and electrical training establishment, during the war. The school was moved to the Keswick Hotel, which provided a safe haven for 350 girls between the ages of 11 and 16, and returned in January 1946. St Katherine's College, Liverpool, was evacuated to the Tower Hotel, Portinscale, Keswick. The Keswick Steam Laundry had to take in washing from the schools and colleges that were evacuated to Keswick, as well as soldiers' washing.

Further research

During the Second World War, the Lingholm estate, Keswick – centred on a grand Victorian mansion – was used for a short time as a boarding school for children evacuated from the North East. The estate received a letter in 2015 from a lady named Dawn Evans that gives a glimpse of those days. An extract from the letter can be found on *thelingholmestate.co.uk*. Dawn Evans, who was evacuated early in the war when her father was a bank manager in Newcastle-on-Tyne where the bombs were falling so fast, said the best part was hearing the stories by Beatrix Potter (1866-1943). Potter was an English writer, illustrator, natural scientist and conservationist best known for her children's books featuring animals, such as those in *The Tale of Peter Rabbit*. Potter and William Heelis enjoyed a happy marriage of thirty years, continuing their farming and preservation efforts throughout the Second World War. She died of pneumonia and heart disease on 22 December 1943 at her home in the village of Near Sawrey, 2 miles from Hawkshead, leaving almost all of her property to the National Trust.

Prunella Scales CBE (b1932), the actress best known for her role as Basil Faulty's wife Sybil in the BBC comedy *Fawlty Towers*, was evacuated to Windermere with her school in the Second World War. According to *Wikipedia*, this was Moira House Girls' School, Eastbourne.

The Liverpool Orphanage moved to an orphanage in Cumbria in 1944, Wanlass Howe, a large house at Waterhead near Ambleside. Grenda Walton has written a book about memories of events at the orphanage from 1944 to 1952, entitled *The House on the Hill – Lake District Revisited: Liverpool Orphanage 1944-1952* (*AuthorHouse*, 2011). According to *childrenshomes.org.uk*, the boys at the Liverpool Orphanage were despatched to the property Hawse End near Keswick. Wanlass Howe is now called the Ambleside Hotel. The Liverpool Orphanage closed in the early 1970s.

Nicholaswinton.com lists children transported from Czechoslovakia to Britain in the nine months leading up to World War Two with whom contact has yet to be made. Nicholas Winton's online list, last updated in 2013, includes: Jiri Bekefi (b1925) to Maryport; Dalibor Brochard (b1924) to Carlisle; Sidonie Guns (b1928) to Barrow; Helene Mueller (b1925) to Carlisle; and Otto Pick (b1925) to Appleby Grammar School.

Brochard (1924-1945), in the care of Mrs Nicholson in the small village of Southwaite, was at Carlisle Grammar School. In 1941, he enlisted as a volunteer with the Czechoslovak Auxiliary Corps. On 1 September 1944, he received the Czech Military Cross. He was killed in an aircraft crash (*Liberator C MkVII EW626*) on 14 March 1945, and was buried at the RAF military cemetery in Lajes on Terceira Island, in the middle of the North Atlantic Ocean (*fcafa.com, cswikipedia.org*). He is commemorated on the Carlisle Grammar School memorial.

Edmond Castle, north of the village of Hayton, Carlisle, was used to house Czech refugees from around June 1940 onwards.

CHAPTER 10

Companies Evacuated to Cumbria

The *Lancashire Evening Post* reported on 21 April 1939 that the new silk factory at Hensingham was obtaining orders from Paris, London, and other big centres, adding that the tannery at Millom was employing thirty-five males and fifteen females and may soon be extended. The newspaper reported:

> A factory at Maryport has been let to a Berlin manufacturer of knitted woollen wear and production will start within a few weeks. Two more factories at Maryport will be occupied immediately on completion, and the machinery of another concern, which will manufacture buttons, is stored at Maryport.
>
> Negotiations are proceeding at Workington for the building of a specialised factory for an English firm which now employs 2,500 workers. If the scheme is sanctioned, the first unit of this factory will be 81,000 square feet and production will have to start next autumn. More industries are also contemplated for Workington.
>
> Alterations are proceeding at Cleator Mill so that a firm making crepe and gummed paper may obtain early occupation.
>
> Negotiations have also started for the erection of a large factory in the Cleator Moor-Whitehaven area which will employ many male and female workers.Following visits to the War Office of Development Council officials, some contracts for rearmament work have recently been obtained for West Cumberland.

The £40,000 Millom tannery (now disused) was built close to Haverigg village in 1938 (£40,000 in 1940 was worth £1,573,856 in 2017).

Paper Trade Journal, 1939, reported: The Cumberland Paper Company, London, manufacturer of paper towels and napkins, paper board specialities, etc. has recently acquired a large section of the former Cleator Mill at Cumberland, and will occupy at once for general expansion in paper-converting mill.

The Bata Shoe Co, founded in 1894 in the Czech Republic, had a factory in East Tilbury, Essex. In 1940, it started a shoe factory at Grasslot, Maryport, to help with the demand for rubber footwear. This plant, like the East Tilbury plant, was purposely sited in an area of heavy unemployment. Bata said that probably the most outstanding feature of its factory at Maryport had been the excellent attendance of all workers right through the bad months of winter. The factory was closed down during the war in accordance with the instructions of the government. 'This plan was to do with the concentration of industry and happened at a time when preparations were being made to open a new rubber factory which Bata had built adjacent to the original building,' according to *batamemories.org.uk.* The factory reopened in 1946, once wartime tenants had vacated the property, and operated until 1980.

Harrington Magnesite Works

Prior to 1936, Britain had been dependent on imported magnesite from Austria and Greece. A secret project saw the Steetley Company (formed in 1885) begin to construct the Harrington Magnesite Works, on the site of the former

The Harrington pill-box (coastal observation) was manned by the 5th Battalion Workington Home Guard. (RW Barnes.)

Harrington ironworks immediately below the pill-box (pictured). Work started on 3 July 1940 and it was officially opened on 27 October 1941. Magnesia was produced from seawater, by reacting it with calcined dolomite. The magnesia paste produced was turned into magnesium oxide powder before being sent away by rail to Workington and then to the Magnesium Elektron Company, Manchester, for use in vital aircraft components, flares and incendiary bombs.

'Magnesite' was a secret project at the time, and the new railhead was referred to throughout the railway system as 'Harrington Ironworks' in a bid to fool the enemy. The output of this establishment was 40,000 tons per annum. White dust covered the houses and gardens of the surrounding area. Harrington Magnesite Works closed in 1953, following a brief revival during the Korean war. The site was gradually dismantled and developed into Harrington marina. The adjacent communities formed by Christian Street, Nook Street, Stanley Street, Stanley Square, Henry Street, Curwen Street and William Street were also demolished.

Edgards

H. Edgard and Son, civil and military tailors and riding habit manufacturers in Chelsea, came to Whitehaven in 1940 with a nucleus of keyworkers and found a temporary home at Catherine Mill, Catherine Street, where they began to train local labour in the manufacture of military, naval and air force uniforms:

> Thousands of military uniforms were produced for His Majesty's Forces by the girls of Edgards' Whitehaven factory – and sometimes those saucy single sewing machinists would pop a secret note into the breast pocket of a jacket, hoping for a reply from some dashing young serviceman who might find it.
>
> In its heyday, it employed around 500 women, and a handful of men who were more than happy to be outnumbered. A machinist wasn't a true member of the sewing sisterhood until she had suffered the agony of a sewing machine needle through a finger or thumb.
>
> (*News and Star*, 19 December 2008)

In 1947, Edgards took over the (vacated) Romney Pram Factory in Cart Road, off Preston Street, where in 1966 they had a staff of about 450, mainly women. (*Whitehaven: a Short History*, Daniel Hay). Catherine Mill was converted into flats quite a few years ago.

Marchon

In December 1939, Frank Schon and Fred Marzillier started Marchon Products in London. Schon was born in Austria and had lived in Czechoslovakia. His family was Jewish, so he came as a refugee to London. Marzillier had been educated in Germany, but came to London in 1934. Both premises that they occupied in London were bombed. Just before the end of 1940, Schon visited Whitehaven and, together with Otto Secher, set up an office in part of a small derelict house in Hensingham, Whitehaven. The garage of the house became the company's first manufacturing premises. Two months later, three condemned cottages nearby were converted into stores and the manufacture of firelighters was begun. At the same time, Marchon began to market, on a very modest scale, chemicals that could be regarded as raw materials in the detergent field. In 1943, the factory was moved to a disused site at Kells. By 1944, the number of employees had crept up to thirty-nine. In the next two years, the pace quickened and the number was quadrupled. With the end of the Second World War, scientists and technicians who

The AJR commemorative plaque for Lord Schon, unveiled outside his family home at Corkickle.
(2ndww.blogspot.com.)

had been employed at local ordnance factories became available for employment and, by 1951 the staff had grown to 586. (Marchon, once employing 4,500 staff, closed in 2005.) Marchon was a major user of the Queen's Dock until 1992.

On 29 September 2016, the Association of Jewish Refugees (AJR) unveiled a commemorative plaque at Corkickle, Whitehaven. It was the latest in an ongoing project by the AJR, founded in July 1941, to honour prominent Jewish émigrés who fled Nazi-occupied Europe and who went on to make a significant contribution to their adopted homeland.

Models and castings of the Mulberry harbour

Bassett-Lowke was a toy company in Northampton, founded by engineer Wenman Joseph Bassett-Lowke (1877-1953) in 1898/1899. It specialised in model railways, boats and ships, and construction sets. W.J. Bassett-Lowke and his friend R. Proctor-Mitchell, representing Narrow Gauge Railways Ltd,

A close-up of a model Pierhead Pontoon, which was one of the important units of the famous "Mulberry" pre-fabricated harbour. Scale ¼-inch to the foot. 1/48th actual size.

D-Day Mulberry harbour model, Bassett-Lowke. (Brighton Toy Museum)

acquired the Ravenglass and Eskdale Steam Railway (Ratty) in 1915 as a base for testing their little locomotives. (R. Proctor-Mitchell wrote *Visit Eskdale: By the World's Smallest Public Railway*, published in the 1920s.) During the Second World War, Bassett-Lowke built models of the Mulberry harbour. Mulberry harbours were temporary portable harbours developed by the British to facilitate the rapid offloading of cargo onto beaches during the Allied invasion of Normandy in June 1944.

During the German occupation of the Channel Islands, quarrymen were evacuated from Alderney to Shap Granite Works (opened in 1865). It was here that castings of sections of the Mulberry harbour were made. Prototypes of each of the designs were built and tested at Rigg Bay, on the Solway Firth in south-west Scotland. The *Guardian* reported in September 2012:

> Until four years ago, there was what looked like a small oil rig in the bay. This was a legacy of the Mulberry temporary harbour project. Across the bay is a path up to the remains of Cruggleton Castle.

The Ratty (Ravenglass and Eskdale Railway) did not carry passengers during the Second World War because the railways could take as much ballast as they could carry from the quarry on the line, so freight carryings were very high (Source: Ravenglass Railway Museum, 2017). The stone navigation tower at Ravenglass harbour was demolished in the Second World War to avoid it being used by enemy invaders.

Special wartime steel-making at Workington

During the Second World War, an electric steel furnace that produced steel for aircraft engine ball bearings was moved to Chapel Bank, Workington, from Norway to prevent it falling into Axis powers – the coalition headed by Germany, Italy and Japan.

Construction at Workington started in February 1941 and the first electric steel was made in June 1942. There were seven electric furnaces built at Workington, one at the Moss Bay steelworks, adjacent to the Bessemer plant, and six at the Chapel Bank steelworks. Only five of the six at Chapel Bank were used. All were managed by the United Steel Company on behalf of the Ministry of Supply (a department of the government formed in 1939 to co-ordinate the supply of equipment to all three British armed forces, headed by the Minister of Supply). The electric load of these furnaces was such that a new supply line was constructed to feed electricity to them from the recently built power station at Willowholme, Carlisle.

Chapel Bank had a further wartime role. It was one of the control points for Workington's air raid sirens. It was operated from a small room to the right-hand side of the main entrance foyer where the master clock and time-signalling equipment was kept. On the wall was mounted a small black motor starter with the legends 'Red Alert' and 'Raiders Passed' clearly visible adjacent to the red and green buttons. This box operated the huge motor-driven siren that was mounted on the roof at the front of the machine-shop end.

Windermere's *Sunderland* factory

Short Brothers, founded in 1908, was Britain's leading aircraft manufacturer. In 1915, its Seaplane Works was established on the River Medway in Rochester, Kent. The *Sunderland* flying-boat was developed in 1937. During the Second World War, the *Sunderland* was used in the North Atlantic Campaign by Coastal Command to protect the convoys of ships and hunt U-boats. In 1940, German bombers were targeting Rochester, so the Ministry of Aircraft Production moved some of the production of the *Sunderland* to a more secure location. As the aircraft needed a large expanse of water from which to take off, and because of its relative isolation, it was decided to locate a factory on the shores of Windermere at White Cross Bay.

The Windermere factory began production in 1941 and at its peak employed 1,571 people. They were trained by a core of skilled workers brought from the factory in Rochester and other aircraft factories around the country. The factory consisted of the detail shop and the huge hangar at the lakeside where the fuselages were built in steel frame jigs. The hangar was large enough to construct three *Sunderland* flying-boats at a time. Thirty-five aircraft were built at Windermere, and it is thought that a further twenty-five were refurbished.

When Shorts moved a section of its skilled workforce to the Windermere factory, it was placed in local billets. Elterwater Independent Hostel, Ambleside – formerly Elterwater YHA – was used as accommodation for Shorts' workers in the Second World War, according to an interview in the October 2017 *Cumbria* magazine. In 1941, building work began on a piece of land at Troutbeck Bridge in order to provide 200 married quarters and separate hostels for the 300 unmarried workers. By the end of 1942, there was a complete community with a primary school, two shops, a canteen, assembly hall, club house, laundry, sick bay, policeman and a football team. The settlement, made up of people from industrial towns across the country, was known as Calgarth.

Above: Hangar being built in 1941. (Allan King/LDHP)

Below: Elterwater Hostel. (Pete Savin, Independent Hostel Guide)

Jeff Gill, born in 1925 in Kendal, left K Shoes in 1942 to work at the Shorts factory. He started work in the detail shop and moved shortly afterwards to the hangar to work as a dolly boy on the riveting. He left in 1944 to join the forces.

Right and below: Wing Commander Derek Martin as a 20-year-old captain of aircraft on 210 Squadron. (Pembroke Dock Heritage Centre, sunderlandtrust.com)

Born in 1917 in Kent, Les Hills worked for Shorts in Rochester. He was in the factory when it was bombed in 1940. When the factory was built at Windermere, he applied to be relocated. He worked in the jig and tools department until the factory closed in 1945. He lived in a billet in Ambleside until he was allocated a house at 17 Park Hill Road on Calgarth Estate, a wartime housing scheme built for aircraft factory workers employed at White Cross Bay, in 1942. He moved to Droomer Estate in Windermere in 1958.

Wing Commander Derek Dudley Martin (1920-2014) OBE MID BSc, born in Cheam, Surrey, was, in 1940/1941, the captain of a *Sunderland* flying-boat with No. 210 Squadron. In 1942, when in charge of a training unit for Sunderland aircrews, Martin travelled by train to Windermere to collect the first plane built at White Cross Bay, *DP176,* and fly it back to his base at RAF Pembroke Dock, south-west Wales. Martin was not a member of 210 Squadron when he collected *DP176.* By then, he was Commanding Officer of the Ferry Training Unit at Pembroke Dock. The Ferry Training Unit trained up the aircrews which took their *Sunderlands* to west Africa and other overseas locations.

Martin was a member of the Guinea Pig Club, a social club and mutual support network for British and Allied aircrew injured during the Second World War that had 649 members by the end of the war. In March 1941, Martin, returning after a twelve-hour search for a U-boat in the Atlantic, began his descent towards Oban on Scotland's west coast in total darkness. The *Sunderland* hit the water and broke up. Four of the crew were killed and the remaining seven injured. Martin's scalp was torn off and one eye was hanging from its socket. After three weeks in a local hospital, he was transferred to the Queen Victoria Hospital in East Grinstead, West Sussex, and underwent several operations. Martin was very proud to have been the only Coastal Command airman to become a 'Guinea Pig', John Evans at Sunderland Trust informed me in 2018.

The Guinea Pig Club's memorial, carved from green Cumbrian slate and over 2 metres tall, is located at the National Memorial Arboretum in Staffordshire, and was unveiled in 2016.

Royal Ordnance Factory

Royal Ordnance Factory (ROF) Drigg, constructed in early 1940 between the railway line and the sea, specialised in high-explosive TNT. ROF Sellafield, constructed in 1942, specialised in propellant. These isolated and remote coastal sites were chosen because of the hazardous nature of the process and to minimise the risk of enemy air attack.

When complete, the two ROFs employed 3,000 workers, with much of the production workforce recruited initially from the local construction workforce. There was an accident at an ROF in the north-west on Wednesday, 4 March 1942, as a result of which a girl operative suffered severe injuries from which she later died (*Lancashire Evening Post*, 6 March 1942). From mid-1942, women played an increasingly large role. There was an explosion on 5 June 1943 at ROF Drigg. William Bernard Darby (1916-1943), from a large family living at Cleator Moor, managed to get out of the building but went back into the burning building to try and save Ada Bawden (1917-1943), his fiancée, who was born in Pica, Workington. They both lost their lives. A small number were injured. A summary of the inquest appeared in the *Whitehaven News* on 17 June 1943. They are not officially listed by the Commonwealth War Graves Commission (CWGC) as war casualties. Darby, whose brother Stoker Bruno Darby (1922-1943) was lost when HMS *Beverley* was sunk on 11 April 1943, was buried at St Mary Roman Catholic Churchyard, Cleator. Ada Bawden was buried at Distington Parish Church.

Wellbank Hostel (built 1941-42), Eskmeals, housed 500 workers engaged in the construction of ROF Hycemoor, Bootle, initially a shell-filling factory. Unskilled labour for the construction of the ROFs was recruited locally, mainly from Whitehaven and Cleator Moor. Wellbank Hostel was transferred to the Admiralty in November 1943, and work began to adapt the site as a transit camp where new Fleet Air Arm Pilots were to assemble on their return to the UK after completing their preliminary flying training in the Service Flying Training Schools in Canada. RN Hostel Wellbank was commissioned on 17 November 1943 as HMS *Macaw*. According to *royalnavyrsearcharchive.org.uk*, the western edges of the camp were damaged by an explosion at 10.17pm on 22 March 1945, when a rail freight wagon, part of a south-bound munitions train, caught fire. The wagon, one of seven being hauled, contained fifty-two depth-charges and was spotted as being on fire by the signal box at Bootle Station. The train crew stopped the train about 770 yards past Bootle Station to investigate, roughly in line with Wellbank Hostel. Despite efforts to isolate the wagon and seek help, the charges exploded – killing the engine driver and injuring the fireman and guard. The blast caused light damage to HMS *Macaw* 400 yards away. Wellbank has been derelict for many years, and a housing and hotel plan has been approved.

During the Second World War, Holmrook Hall was requisitioned and locals told it was a recuperation hospital for those who had suffered shipwrecks. In fact, strategically located between ROF Drigg and ROF Sellafield, it was the RN bomb and munitions training school between 1943 and 1946, under the title HMS *Volcano*. Among the graduates were Noel Cashford MBE (1922-2011) and Lionel 'Buster' Crabb OBE. Cashford also trained at HMS *Firework* at Barrow. In 1944, he worked on mine clearance in the West Country. In May 1945, he was part of Force 135, which liberated Jersey from German occupation. On the island, he dealt with hundreds of tons of German ammunition, much of it booby-trapped. Crabb (1909-presumed dead 1956) was a RN frogman and MI6 diver who vanished during a reconnaissance mission around a Soviet cruiser berthed at Portsmouth Dockyard in 1956.

High Mill, Egremont, which stood empty for many years after Wyndham Mining Company closed it down, was bought by a Mr Heyworth in the mid-1930s with the intention of making it into a piggery. The project never came to fruition. During the Second World War, it was used by the military, and many soldiers were billeted within the confines of the mill. (High Mill was demolished in 1989.)

Further research

Who Do You Think You Are? is a BBC series in which celebrities trace their ancestry. The first half of the programme shown on Monday, 13 August 2018 told the story of Robert Rinder's maternal grandfather Maurice, who was one of the Jewish orphans airlifted from the concentration camps to Calgarth. Maurice lost every member of his family to the gas chambers at Treblinka. Robert Rinder (b1978), also known as Judge Rinder, is an English criminal law barrister and TV personality.

Gleaston Water Mill near Ulverston is open for the Heritage Open Days programme. There is a 'teaser' on their entry about the mill housing British evacuee children.

CHAPTER 11

RAF Silloth's Double Role

Silloth Airfield, located 1 mile north-east of Silloth, opened in June 1939 as a maintenance control station (22MU). It was soon assigned to the Coastal Command Group Pool with the 22MU remaining as a station within the aerodrome. *Ansons*, *Beauforts*, *Bothas* and *Hudsons* were assigned as aircraft. 215 Bomber Squadron with *Ansons* and *Wellingtons* operated from the field.

Commemorative stone, just inside the modern main entrance to Silloth Airfield, in memory of Silloth Airfield and all who worked there from 1939 to 1960. It was unveiled on 27 November 2011 by Kenneth Bannerman, director general of the Airfields of Britain Conservation Trust. (Ian Stuart Nicholson)

A display at Silloth Library on 9 October 2017. (Ian Stuart Nicholson)

Construction of RAF Kirkbride, 1 mile south of Kirkbride village, began in 1937. Delivery of a large variety of aircraft was gaining pace during June 1940 at RAF Kirkbride. The landing ground was almost complete, the hangars were now all available and additional areas of land available for dispersal were being inspected. A misjudged approach by a *Bristol Beaufort* on 30 July resulted in the aircraft crash-landing short of the runway. *L4473* was a total write-off, but the crew walked away unharmed.

Work began on the new RAF airfield at Crosby-on-Eden, Carlisle, in the summer of 1940. And work began at the airfield at Longtown, 8 miles north of Carlisle, in the middle of 1940 (three runways were laid). The country was fighting for survival in the Battle of Britain and many pilots and aircraft that served in the conflict would end up flying from Crosby. A site at Scaleby, 2 miles north-west of Crosby, was a night ('Q') decoy for Crosby Aerodrome. Records indicate that it was operational in August 1942. Built in the style of a bungalow, it was manned by two airmen.

When the Royal Aircraft Establishment (RAE) used Silloth Airfield to experiment with flares dropped by a *Handley Page Hampden*, a British bomber of the RAF, in 1940, the airfield was bombed. On 15 July 1940, just before 1am, a yellow air raid warning signalled. Around 150 bombs, with parachutes attached, were dropped by an enemy aircraft to the south of the airfield. Only the wing of a *Wellington* was slightly damaged by splinters. Another raid was carried out in the early hours of 25 September 1940. Damage was caused to a farm.

Silloth's last brush with the enemy came on the morning of 24 October 1940, according to *Cumbria Airfields in the Second World War* by Martyn Chorlton. An enemy aircraft dropped a bomb near to what was known as the 'cemetery' site on the southern side of the airfield. The device, which was attached to a parachute, left a large crater in a nearby field.

Polish airmen found their way to Silloth Airfield. One of these was Eugeniusz John Antolak (1909-1997), who had flown with the Polish Air Force in 1930 and the French Air Force in 1939 as a fighter pilot. After France fell to the Germans, he fled to England in the hull of a coal ship when the French air fleet was rendered unserviceable. Once in England, he enrolled as an Allied aide for the RAF. He was attached to the RAF 309 flight squadron, and then he was sent to Silloth as a test pilot. While in Silloth, he met his future wife Patricia M. Hodges, who had been born in Silloth, and he settled in the town. He was awarded the Gazette Victory Award in May 1995 as part of the VE Day anniversary celebrations. He died in Silloth Nursing Home, Silloth, in May 1997.

Patrick and Doris Barker, whose son Tim Barker set up the Soldiers in Silloth toy soldier museum at Marine Terrace, Silloth, were both born in Silloth, married in Christ Church in 1939 and both served on Silloth Airfield during the Second World War. When it was clear that Britain might be going to war, Patrick Barker

Brave Pole who vowed to fight his enemies

**Eugeniusz John Anto-
lak, Polish World War
Two hero, of Silloth,
aged 88**

BORN in Warsaw in January, 1909, Silloth man Eugeniusz Antolak ended up travelling all over Europe, joining the fight against Germany during World War Two.

For his endeavours he was awarded the Gazette Victory Award in May 1995 as part of the VE Day anniversary celebrations.

Eugeniusz flew for the Polish Air Force, which he joined in 1930. After Hitler triggered off the war by invading Poland he had to travel to Greece before catching a ship to France, where he joined the French Air Force in 1939 as a fighter pilot.

After France fell to the Germans, Eugeniusz fled to England in the hull of a coal ship when the French air fleet was rendered unserviceable.

When asked why he fled to England he said: "It was necessary to fight the enemy."

● **EUGENIUSZ ANTOLAK:**
World War Two hero

Once in England, he enrolled as an allied aide for the Royal Air Force. He was attached to the RAF 309 flight squadron and then he was sent to Silloth MU as a

test pilot.

It was here that Eugeniusz met his future wife, Patricia.

During his time as a fighter pilot, later with Flight Squadron 302, the Pole took part in many operations over Germany, including Dortmund and Bremen.

After his time with the squadrons, and after the Channel Islands were liberated, he was asked to escort King George and Queen Elizabeth on their visit there.

He was demobbed in 1948 after 18 years of service

In 1975 he felt honoured after receiving tickets for the Service of Thanksgiving for Victory, which took place in Westminster Abbey.

Eugeniusz used his skills with the Air Training Cadet Force after he was demobbed, working voluntarily for twelve years.

Eugeniusz leaves his wife of 54 years, two children, four grandchildren and one great grandchild.

He died in Silloth Nursing Home on Tuesday. The funeral service was taking place today at Carlisle Crematorium.

Brave Pole Eugeniusz Antolak. (Cumberland News 23 May 1997)

volunteered his radio skills for the RAF volunteer reserve and was sent to France with the BEF in 1939. He was one of many slightly older volunteers sent out at the beginning of the war who were already experienced radio operators while younger recruits were still being trained. He was evacuated from St Nazaire after the defeat of Dunkirk and eventually posted to Silloth Airfield. Among his duties at Silloth, Barker worked as an operator on the Silloth Trainer – the forerunner of flight simulators. Doris, along with many local women, helped on the airfield driving a canteen wagon for the WVS.

Air accidents

During the evening of 21 December 1941, the crew of *Hudson AM624* were undertaking a night-time local flying training exercise around RAF Silloth where they were based. The aircraft was later seen flying in the area of St Bees. At around 9.35pm, it flew into the ground on Dent Fell, Cleator. The wreckage caught fire and all four on board were killed. Observer Sergeant Earl Douglas Parrish RCAF (b1918) of Medicine Hat, Alberta, Canada, was buried at Silloth Cemetery on 24 December 1941. (RCAF: Royal Canadian Air Force)

The crew of *Lockheed Hudson Mk 1 N7325/B-9* of No. 1 (Coastal) Operational Training Unit left RAF Silloth late on 5 September 1942 for a night navigation exercise. The planned route was from Silloth to South Rock light off Northern Ireland, turning south to the Kisk Bank lightship off Dublin, then eastwards to Skerries lighthouse off Anglesey before returning direct to Silloth. While returning to Silloth in cloud, the crew strayed off track. It flew into the southern side of Cross Fell on Willie Bank above Crowdundle Beck, Penrith. On 7 September 1942, the crash site was located and reported to the RAF via the police in Penrith. The following were killed: Pilot Officer Paul Arthur Bourke (1914-1942), who married Josephine Moore in Wigton in 1942; Sergeant John Bumpstead (1914-1942) of Darnall, Sheffield; Sergeant Robert Band (1913-1942); Sergeant Leslie Thomas Griffin (1911-1942); and Sergeant Richard William Hewitt (1927-1942). Band was buried at Woking Crematorium, Surrey.

Hudson Mk V AM680 took off from RAF Silloth on 10 November 1942 for a night navigation exercise. The aircraft was eventually located by the local police late in the afternoon of 11 November 1942. It had flown into the western side of Beda Head, to the south of Ullswater, and burst into flames. Pilot Flight Sergeant John Frederick Saunders (1915-1942) of London, Flying Officer Derrick Issac Jones (1920-1942) of Carmarthen, Wales, Sergeant Stanley Alfred Veasey (1913-1942) of London, and Sergeant Harold Dickinson (1916-1942) of Leeds were all killed. Saunders was buried at Enfield Crematorium, London, Jones at Carmarthen Cemetery, Veasey at Camberwell New Cemetery, and Dickinson at Silloth Cemetery.

During the war, Lawrence William Hamilton Coe (1912-1944), remembered at Runnymede Memorial, Surrey, a memorial dedicated to men and women from air forces, was posted to the RAF Volunteer Reserve. On 21 November 1942, he was promoted to flight sergeant. During the evening of 16 September 1945, he piloted a Wellington bomber, flying out of RAF Silloth. The aircraft crashed into the Irish Sea, 5 miles west of St Bees Head. Two bodies were picked up by SS *Green Isle* and taken to Whitehaven Infirmary, but two were never found – including the

Frederick Charles Jordan. (Silloth Tourism Action Group)

body of Coe. Flight Officer Oswald John Lander (1918-1944) of Bodmin, Cornwall, was buried at Silloth Cemetery, and Flight Officer George Edward Lumley at Darlington West Cemetery, Durham.

Flight Officer Frederick Charles Jordan (d1996), after completing his active tour of Gibraltar in 1943, was posted to Hooton Park and then to Silloth for instructional duties, arriving in Silloth in August 1944. At 9.05pm on 16 September, he took off from Silloth with five other crew-members in a *Wellington Mk X HF179* to practise Leigh Light homings. Leigh Lights were powerful searchlights fitted to aircraft to illuminate targets such as submarines or lifeboats. They were fitted in a 'dustbin' turret under the fuselage and could be raised or lowered. Approximately two hours after take-off, the plane flew into the sea, 5 miles west of St Bees Head, killing four of the crew. Survivors Jordan, who sustained two broken ankles, a broken arm and cracked ribs, and one other man were picked up by the SS *Green Isle* and taken to Whitehaven Infirmary. The RAF 1180 Accident Report Form relating to the crash states the following: 'Aircraft flew into sea during Leigh Light Exercises. Pilot homing on a ship burning full navigational lights was seen to fly into sea. Leigh Light not burning at time.' The subsequent inquiry found that it was error of judgement when carrying out a training dummy attack. 'Too low, hit the sea. Instructions given not to fly below 300 feet,' the inquiry said. (This story was told by Brian Jordan, Frederick Jordan's son.)

Recovered by medical personnel from RAF Silloth

On 8 February 1942, the crew of *Wellington Mk IC T2714* were on a cross-country navigation training flight from RAF Wellesbourne Mountford near Stratford-upon-Avon when their aircraft crashed near the summit of Burn Tod in the Uldale

Fells to the north of Skiddaw, Keswick. All but the rear gunner, Sergeant John Gascoyne Rutherford (1917-1943) of Bevendean, Sussex, were killed in the crash. Rutherford made his way off the hill to the hamlet of Longlands – no more than a collection of six houses – near Bassenthwaite to summon help. Following this, the bodies of the victims were recovered by medical personnel from RAF Silloth while the wreck was dismantled and recovered by 83MU, formed at RAF Woolsington, Newcastle. The three Canadian members of the crew were buried at Silloth Cemetery. Rutherford was later killed on 31 March 1943 while on board *Whitley BD412* of No. 10 Operational Training Unit, which was on detachment to RAF St Eval, Cornwall, to carry out anti-submarine patrols of the south-west approaches. The aircraft disappeared on one such patrol with the loss of all the crew. He is remembered on the Runnymede Memorial, which commemorates more than 20,000 airmen and women who were lost in the Second World War during operations from bases in the UK and north and western Europe who have no known grave.

Runnymede Memorial near Egham, Surrey, unveiled on 17 October 1953 by Queen Elizabeth II. (CWGC)

Betty Burleigh. (Silloth Tourism Action Group)

WAAF at RAF Silloth

Betty Burleigh joined the WAAF in 1942 and was stationed at the Silloth Airfield RAF Camp from 12 April 1945 to 19 October 1945 as a corporal in charge of the WAAF personnel, who were billeted at the time in The Solway Hotel. She worked in the RAF HQ office on the airfield, mainly controlling the movement of vehicles entering and leaving the airfield. Betty was demobbed in late 1945. She later worked as a civilian Radio Telephonist in The Silloth Airfield Control Tower, from 1955 to 1960.

Silloth Causewayhead Cemetery, Silloth Airfield

In the 4-acre cemetery, just a few hundred yards from the end of the runway, are the graves of fifty-six airmen who lost their lives training for war. Most of the airmen buried here were serving with the RAF at Silloth. Within the airmen section, there was one German buried, Blome Herwart, who was interred on 14 July 1942. He was exhumed on 26 August 1962 under licence for re-internment at Cannock Chase Military Burial Ground.

Aircrew of all nations lie side by side in the cemetery to the south of the airfield. (CWGC)

Further research

Each RAF Silloth air crash had to have an inquest. They are all listed in the West Cumbria Coroner's Inquests calendars, which are at Whitehaven Records Office (YTCR3/4 & 5). It would be possible to put together a list of all those killed in crashes from there. There are eight names on one page relating to two crashes a week apart.

CHAPTER 12

The One That Got Away, 1940

More than 170,000 British prisoners-of-war were taken by German and Italian forces during the Second World War. Most were captured in a string of defeats in France, North Africa and the Balkans between 1940 and 1942. They were held in a network of prisoner-of-war camps stretching from Nazi-occupied Poland to Italy. According to historian Niall Campbell Ferguson (b1964), 3.5 per cent of British prisoners-of-war held by Germans died, and 0.03 per cent of German prisoners-of-war held by the British died.

British prisoners in Germany included Private Fred Johnson, who came from Millom to Burnley, reported missing in May 1940. Joining up on the outbreak of war, he went to France with the Auxiliary Military Pioneer Corps (AMPC) in October 1939.

It was announced on 19 August 1940 that the Hon David Charles Feilding (1913-1966), who married Elizabeth Fletcher of Arlecdon in 1938, was a prisoner-of-war. 'Many Westmorland soldiers, previously reported missing, have now been officially listed as prisoners-of-war,' reported the *Lancashire Evening Post* of 23 August 1940. The third Border Regiment officer to be notified as a prisoner-of-war was Second Lieutenant Christopher Gerald Deighton (1915-1968), well-known throughout South Westmorland, of Foxhill in the village of Holme, the report said. (He was recommended for the award of Military Cross in 1940).

Second Engineer Norman Eric Frank Mant (1916-1986) of South Road, Kendal, was listed as a prisoner-of-war in August 1940. He was on the liner *Orama* (see page 262) when she was sunk by German warships. Sapper I. Hewer and Corporal John Hewer of the Royal Engineers, both well-known footballers from Parton, about one mile north of Whitehaven, were prisoners-of-war in Germany, the *Lancashire Evening Post* of 4 September 1940 reported. It also reported that Corporal Walter Grant, missing for three months, had sent a message to his wife who lived at High Bridge, Braithwaite, that he was a prisoner-of-war. He said: 'I am well; don't worry; good food.'

Private James Peters

Private James Peters (1913-2004), Border Regiment, born in Whalley, Lancashire, lived in Haverigg in 1936, as he was a cricket professional for Haverigg Cricket

Club. He lived in Penrith in 1939 and was a professional for the Penrith Cricket Club in the 1939 season, described by the *Penrith Observer* of 4 April 1939 as 'a sound batsman'. He was badly wounded in his right hip on 11 June 1940 at Fecamp, Normandy. At Fecamp, he was with Oliver Robin Bagot (see page 120) from Levens Hall and Captain John Elliot Brade Whitmore (1910-1992), Border Regiment, from Cockermouth.

Fecamp was the last significant engagement that the 4th Battalion (apart from D Company) of the Border Regiment had with the German Army in 1940.

They were attempting to evade capture and trying to make their way to safety. On 17 June 1940, Peters was captured by German forces whilst attempting to hide out on farmland at Etretat, Normandy. He was a prisoner-of-war at Stalag XX-A (also called 357 in the early part of the war) in Torun, Poland, in September 1940. In Germany, Stalag was a term used for prisoner-of-war camps. An Oflag was a prisoner-of-war camp for officers only. Bagot and Whitmore were both held prisoner-of-war at Oflag VII-B in Eichstatt, Bavaria. (On 22 May 1940, all 1,336 Polish prisoners-of-war were transferred to Oflag VII-A Murnau, Bavaria, and were replaced with British, French and Belgian officers taken prisoner during the battle of France and Belgium.)

In October 1940, Peters escaped on his own and was on the run for three days. On capture, he was badly beaten by SS (Schutzstaffel), a major paramilitary organisation under Hitler and the Nazi Party. In December 1940, he was at Bromberg, Poland, a sub-camp of Stalag XX-A. He served on farms near the Marienwerder region of East Prussia from August 1941, and, from November 1941 he was at Stalag XX-A in Torun. In March 1942, he was transferred to BAB 20 (Bau und Arbeits Battalion 20) in Reigersfield, Heydebreck, Upper Silesia, which was part of the Blechhammer Concentration/Labour Camp, Poland, a massive industrial complex. He worked at the IG Farben Chemical Industries plant at Heydebreck.

On 17 July 1944, he escaped from the factory with Herbert Collier Holt (1921-1947), Manchester Regiment, from Atherton, Lancashire. He was recaptured near Oppeln, Poland on 20 July 1944 and taken to Stalag 344 at Lamsdorf, Upper Silesia.

Conditions were a lot better at Stalag 344 than at BAB 20. The prisoners-of-war had several sports that were allowed to be played, cricket being one of them. They played test matches in the camp, which were played in a compound on a matting pitch, and they played in their usual clothing. These test matches were played between England, South Africa, Australia and New Zealand. Peters played with the England team in a series of their test matches then represented The Rest of the World versus Australia and New Zealand. It was when he was here that an Australian suggested he contact him after the war and he would get him a contract to play with Queensland.

On 22 January 1945, he set off from BAB 20 on a death march of more than 500 miles with a column of 1,000 prisoners-of-war, with little and sometimes no food. The death march was a forced march of prisoners-of-war or other captives or deportees in which individuals are left to die along the way. On 23 April 1945, the prisoners were liberated by the Americans at the village of Winklam, Bavaria.

James Peters' son Robert Peters kept his father's writings. He emailed me the following, an extract from Tuesday, 1 May 1945:

Air alarm in Ostende. We left for England at 6pm on a boat called Ben My Chree, which is Manx for Girl of My Heart. It was pretty rough. I fed the fish all the way. We arrived at Tilbury (Essex) at 1.30pm. Back in England. When they weighed me, I was seven stone. I had made it back. Hundreds of chaps have perished. Lost a lot of good mates, who had made it through the camps, but missed making it through that last journey. It was only the Red Cross, and never giving up hope that had kept me alive. If anyone is to ever tell me go 'Go to hell', I will be able to look them straight in the eye and say, 'I have already been'.

Peters returned to Queen Street, Whalley, on 12 May 1945, having lost 5½ stone of his pre-war body weight. He was admitted to St Mary's Military Hospital at Whalley, which was on the site of Calderstones Hospital.

'When he met his mother, she did not recognise him. As she was profoundly deaf, she could not hear his voice. It took him several years to regain his pre-war fitness,' Robert Peters said in August 2018.

After the war, he did not contact the Australian who had offered him the cricket contract, as after he was put on to what was referred to as the Z Reserve. Following the Second World War, a new Z Reserve of soldiers and officers who had served between 3 September 1939 and 31 December 1948 were available for recall if under 45 years of age. He also did not wish to go to Australia, and the harder surfaces in Australia may have affected his hip wound.

He returned to being a cricket professional with Great Harwood, Lancashire, in 1946 and 1947. He also played as a professional with Atherton Cricket Club from 1948 to 1956. Further information about his achievements at cricket can be found on *cricketarchive.co.uk/lancashireplayers*.

(With thanks to his son Robert Peters, who lives in Blackburn, Lancashire.)

John Miller (d1942) of Wigton, who served as a gunner with the Royal Artillery, 51st Anti-Tank Regiment, was a prisoner-of-war. On 9 May 1942, aged 24, he was shot by a German guard for smoking a cigarette when with a working party from BAB 20. He was buried in the local area, probably Cosel.

Following the war, he was re-buried at the War Graves Commission Cemetery at Rakowicki, Krakow, in the southern part of Poland.

Private James Walker Serginson (1914-1972) from Cockermouth was a prisoner-of-war at Stalag XX-A, according to *The Wartime Memories Project* (*wartimememoriesproject.com*). John William Osliff (1916-1986) from Barrow, Coldstream, was a prisoner-of-war at BAB 20. He lost two toes in an accident while working at the chemical factory at Heydebreck. (With thanks to Robert Peters.)

The British Army identity disc of James Peters. (With kind permission of his son, Robert Peters)

Keswick's Cumberland Pencil Company (closed 2008) produced a special spy pencil sent in care packages to British prisoners-of-war held in foreign prisons. They each had a small compass concealed inside the fittings for the rubber on the end of the pencil and a map rolled up in the partially hollow centre of the pencil. The graphite used in pencils was originally mined in Seathwaite Wad Mines, Borrowdale.

Meanwhile, in Britain, there were hundreds of prisoner-of-war camps and each one was assigned a number. Below is a list of prisoner-of-war camps of interest, listed as per the camp's number.

1. Grizedale Hall, Hawkshead
13. Shap Wells Hotel, Shap, Penrith
18. Featherstone, Haltwhistle
76. Merrythought Camp, Calthwaite, Penrith
103. Moota Camp, Cockermouth
104. Bela River, Milnthorpe

1. Grizedale Hall

Grizedale Hall, a mansion that had been built anew in 1905 for Harold Brocklebank (1853-1936), but had latterly been owned by the Forestry Commission until being requisitioned in 1939, is associated with *The One That Got Away*, the story of German pilot Franz Xaver Baron von Werra (1914-1941).

The original site of Grizedale Hall (above) was used for The One That Got Away, *in 1957, before being finally pulled down.* (Battle of Britain London Monument)

Von Werra was shot down over Kent on 5 September 1940, successfully crash-landing his Messerschmitt 109 and quickly being made prisoner-of-war. His first escape attempt was made from Grizedale Hall. Every day, the prisoners-of-war were taken for walks outside of the camp, through the village of Satterthwaite and beyond. At a certain point along the way was High Bowkerstead corner, where the party was always brought to a halt for ten minutes. On Monday, 7 October 1940, von Werra made his Grizedale escape from fifteen prison guards over a dry-stone wall at High Bowkerstead corner, while a slow fruit cart – the driver was the local greengrocer – provided a lucky diversion. As the cart drew level, von Werra hoisted himself on to the wall, keeping as low as possible. He rolled over and dropped into the meadow, landing neatly on his hands and toes. No sound was heard above the loud chattering of the prisoners-of-war, all of whom had played a part in the plan. Not a stone was dislodged.

With the prison officer's permission, the mounted sergeant stopped the cart and bought some eating apples. Some of the other guards also bought fruit. By the time the transactions were completed and the greengrocer had moved off, there were only about two of the ten minutes rest period left. The sergeant ordered the column to re-form. As the order to march was about to be given, there were sounds of cries coming from a long way down the road to the south. Two women were trying to draw the guards' attention to the escaped prisoner-of-war, who was running bent double along the meadow-side of the wall. He skirted Cicely's Brow, Hob Gill, Low Fell, Higher Thorny Slack, Sale Moss, Green Hows, Ash Slack and Chamley Wood. To him, they were all the wood. For the next five nights and days, the rain was seldom to cease.

At about 11pm on Thursday, 10 October, two Home Guard soldiers – both shepherds by calling – found a man sheltering from the rain in a small stone hut used for storing sheep fodder near the village of Broughton Mills between Broughton-in-Furness and Torver. One of the Englishmen tied a cord around the man's right wrist and wound the other end several times round the palm of his own left hand. The other gripped the man's left arm firmly above the elbow. They set off into the blackness down a steep and slippery hill, the younger Home Guard carrying the lamp in his right hand and gripping the cord with his left. 'Your name's Werra, isn't it?' he asked. 'So? I see you know all about me.'

Satterthwaite, a village with around fifty dwellings in Grizedale, from Hob Gill Plantation, taken December 2006. (Michael Graham, geograph.org.uk)

'Hundreds of people have been looking for you.' 'I know. I've been watching them. What shall you do with me now?' 'Hand you over. There's police and troops down there on the road.' 'So? I'm sorry then, gentlemen, but – I – must – leave you!' As he spoke, von Werra pulled his right hand, to which the cord was attached, behind his back, throwing the Home Guard who was holding it off his balance. Then, wrenching his right arm free, he struck out at him. The man went sprawling backwards. The prisoner jumped out of reach of the other Home Guard and, at the same time, snatched with all his might with his bound wrist. The cord came free. The man had probably opened his hand as he fell.

Von Werra got away. Two nights previously, he had found an orchard. Most of the fruit had been picked, but there were still dozens of windfalls on the ground. He had lived on apples since then, and still had some left in his pockets. During the next two days, the hunt concentrated on the east side of the Duddon Valley. On Saturday, 12 October, the searchers reached the road running off west to Eskdale at about 2.30pm. After consulting with Lieutenant Blackburn, in charge of a party of about seventy troops from Ulverston, Superintendent W.S. Brown, in charge of a contingent of the Cumberland and Westmorland Constabulary, agreed to call off the hunt for that day. The searchers moved off down the hill from Hazel Head Farm in the Duddon Valley to the Traveller's Rest pub, Ulpha (now Old Traveller's Rest self-catering accommodation) before closing time.

While they were drinking, shouts were heard coming from a man on Bleak How, 350 feet above the road. The man was William Youdale, a sheep farmer of Hazel Head Farm. He had seen a man come out of the bracken and gorse on The Pike, overlooking the Duddon Valley on the west side. By the time the search party got up the hill, the man had disappeared. Mr Youdale said: 'Two minutes ago, he was walking round the side of the fell, about 25 yards inside the wall. He's simply vanished.'

The search party walked over a couple of fields to Hesk Fell, between the Duddon Valley and Eskdale, which reaches 1,566 feet. A movement was noticed along some turfs of coarser grass on a patch of damp ground. Von Werra was lying on his back, his body and arms sunk in the mud, with only his white, freshly shaven face showing between two clumps of coarse grass. A few minutes later he was handcuffed. At the Traveller's Rest, Superintendent Brown arranged for von Werra to be given a cup of tea. A soldier gave him a cigarette. He was taken to Ulverston Police Station and then to Grizedale Hall. After recapture, he was transferred to Camp 13 at the Hayes near Swanwick, Derbyshire. This was the scene of his second go at escaping.

After his second failed escape attempt, von Werra was sent to a prison camp in Canada. He managed to escape on 21 January 1941 and made his way

Hesk Fell from the cairn on The Pike, taken 2009. (Michael Graham.)

through the US, Mexico, South America and Spain to reach Germany on 18 April. He became a hero, and Hitler awarded him the Knight's Cross of the Iron Cross. He reported to the German High Command on how he had been treated as a prisoner-of-war, and this caused an improvement in the treatment of Allied prisoners-of-war in Germany. He wrote a book about his experiences, *My Escape from England* (*Meine Flucht aus England*), although it remained unpublished. He died on 25 October 1941 when his Messerschmitt 109 came down on a practice flight in the sea off Holland. Neither his body nor the aircraft were found.

Grizedale Hall also held General Field Marshall Gerd von Rundstedt (1875-1953), who served as a staff officer in the First World War, and Otto Kretschmer (1912-1998), Germany's most successful U-boat captain in the Second World War until his capture. His most successful patrol occurred in November and December 1940, when *U-99* sank HMS *Laurentic*, built by Harland and Wolff in 1927 (forty-nine people killed), HMS *Patroclus*, and HMS *Forfar* (the HMS *Forfar* memorial at Forfar Parish Church, Angus, Scotland gives the losses as 41 officers and 143 men). Albert Thelus Farlam Bell (1918-1940),

Above left: Knight's Cross of the Iron Cross (from 1 September 1939), awarded by the Führer and Reich president. (Public domain)

Above right: Otto Kretschmer was later an admiral in the Bundesmarine. Image, created in November 1940, from The German Federal Archive. Bundesarchiv, Bild 183-L22207 / Tölle (Tröller) / CC-BY-SA 3.0

son of Robert Farlam Bell and Lillias Smith Bell of Barrow, and Ordinary Seaman James Peter Earley (1919-1940), son of John William and Isabella Jane Earley of Barrow, were on board *Forfar*. Bell is on the Barrow Boys' Grammar School memorial. (Earley appears to be on no Barrow memorial.)

Maximilian von Herff (1893-1945), a high-ranking commander in the SS of Nazi Germany during the Second World War, was captured by British forces in 1945 and held at Grizedale. He suffered a stroke and died at Conishead Priory Military Hospital near Ulverston on 6 September 1945. He was later re-buried at Cannock Chase. He served with the Deutsches Afrika Korps in North Africa. He was promoted to *Oberst* (colonel) and commanded Kamfgruppe von Herff. On 14-15 May 1943, he was in Warsaw during the Warsaw Ghetto Uprising and supervised its suppression under orders from Himmler. On 20 April 1944, he was promoted to *SS-Obergruppenfuhrer* (SS General).

Above: Conishead Priory.
(Public Domain)

Right: Maximilian von Herff is buried at Cannock Chase Germany Military Cemetery. (Militaryimages.net)

13. Shap

(NB: referred to as 15 in some instances.)

The Earl of Lonsdale owned Shap Wells Hotel, which was requisitioned and turned into a prisoner-of-war camp in February 1941. It housed up to 200 prisoners on the top two floors of the hotel, these often waiting to be sent to Glasgow and then off to Canada. It took German army officers, with the camp leader at one point being a German prince who was related to Queen Mary. Conditions for officers were much more comfortable than that for their British counterparts and it is recorded that the hotel linen and crockery were used for the prisoners, hence its nickname 'U-Boat Hotel'.

There was an attempt, in 1940, by some Luftwaffe men to escape from Shap Wells. They got to Carlisle, where they stole a plane. They only got as far as Great Yarmouth, Norfolk, where they were arrested, according to *Cumbria at War*, a learning resource for secondary schools created by Guy Woolnough in 2009.

On 24 November 1941, two German pilots held at Shap escaped with flying jackets over their *Luftwaffe* uniforms and carrying forged identification documents that purported them to be Dutch airmen attached to the RAF. They were Lieutenants Heinz Schnabel and Harry Kurt Wappler (d1985). Without any apparent difficulty, they entered RAF Kingstown, Carlisle, and, with the help of an RAF ground mechanic, started up a *Miles Magister* trainer aircraft and took off. Short of fuel, they landed at another RAF airfield and refuelled. Setting off for the Netherlands, they suddenly realised the aircraft's range was insufficient and they turned back. Landing in a field near Great Yarmouth, they were recaptured and taken to RAF Horsham St Faith. Returned to the Shap prisoner-of-war camp to spend twenty-eight days in solitary confinement, both airmen were then shipped to more secure confinement in Canada. Their photos are in an album found in a Kendal archive building (*Westmorland Gazette*, 1 October 2010). The album, which was kept at Shap Police Station, contains pictures of 130 prisoners-of-war held at Shap between 1941 and 1942.

18. Featherstone, Haltwhistle

Featherstone prisoner-of-war camp was located near Featherstone Castle, Haltwhistle, Northumberland. It was originally opened in 1944 to accommodate American soldiers arriving for the Normandy invasions. Subsequently, it was used for Italian prisoners-of-war and then rehabilitating Nazi officers. 'PC

Wilson captured prisoners-of-war circulated as escaped from Featherstone Park POW camp about 9pm on 1 April 1945,' according to the Alston Police Station Occurrence Book at Cumbria Archive Centre, Carlisle. Alston is a small town in Cumbria on the River South Tyne.

They were Herbert Franzke, Luftwaffe; Josef Kirchdorfer, Luftwaffe; and Horso Osinksi, German Army. Kirchdorfer, an Austrian who in 2013 lived in Switzerland, penned his memoirs entitled *WW2 memories of a youngster* (2013). He was just 19 when he was captured in the Netherlands and brought to England. He told how, on his return to camp, he was stripped naked and beaten by British guards who wanted to find out where the other escapees were.

There is a plaque at Featherstone. It reads: 'Here was the entrance to POW camp 18 where thousands of German officers were held in the years 1945-48. The interpreter since January 1946 was Captain Herbert Sulzbach OBE who dedicated himself to making this camp a seed-bed of British-German reconciliation. Our two nations owe him heartfelt thanks. The friends and members of the Featherstone Park Association of Former Inmates of Camp 18. 1982.'

76. Merrythought, Calthwaite

Merrythought was a prisoner-of-war camp on the A6 just north of Plumpton. Re-educational surveys were conducted. The first visit for a survey was 7-10 May 1946. There were 781 prisoners-of-war at Merrythought. Hostels were at Alston (86 prisoners-of-war), Dalston (152), Hornick Hill (123), Brampton (175), Hethersgill (70), and there were 141 in billets. Werner Schramm, ex-USA, was appointed by the commander as camp leader.

Ex-USA men – prisoners-of-war taken by the Americans who, after the war had ended, were deliberately not returned to Germany immediately – were very depressed. Uncertainty about their repatriation, promise by the Americans that they would be sent to Germany, and better living conditions in the US were responsible for their low morale. Re-education had not yet been started. Morale was especially bad amongst the men who worked in the mines. They complained that work was heavy and unhealthy, food inadequate and that they had been doing this work for a long time without being exchanged. The hostel leader was Gert van Soellon, a Dutchman. The 15-20 August 1946 report said:

Since my last visit three months ago, 200 men have arrived from USA, and 150 have been posted to 189 satellite camp on medical grounds. Morale at Dalston hostel is very bad and barbed wire has been installed. At Brampton hostel, there is still a percentage of Nazi-minded men. Morale is very low at Hornby Hall hostel. The ex-USA men are dissatisfied and have brought unrest into the camp.

A visit for a survey was made 14-19 February 1947. Six hundred and sixty-four prisoners-of-war had been repatriated to date. Re-educational activities included a discussion group. Subjects included the route of the National Socialist German Workers' Party, and Problems of Youth. A survey conducted 6-10 May 1947 revealed that 50 per cent at Hethersgill and Alston hostels were youngsters. Sixty per cent were youngsters at Dalston hostel.

A visit for a survey was made 23-27 July 1947. One thousand seven hundred and sixty-five prisoners-of-war had been repatriated to date. Morale was slightly improved. One reason was improved entertainment (theatre and orchestra). Very bad news from Germany made many men despair of democratic ideas. Mr Parrot, headmaster of a school at Kirkby Stephen, was willing and highly qualified to act as official liasion between the camp and outside bodies. The library at Penrith was open to prisoners-of-war.

On 16-20 September 1947, the number of prisoners-of-war repatriated to date was 2,300. It was hoped to extend existing contacts with youth clubs in Carlisle. A further visit to Merrythought was made on 11-16 November 1947. There were 539 prisoners-of-war at the main camp, 49 at Appleby hostel, 41 at Alston hostel, 121 at Brampton hostel, 67 at Dalston hostel, 63 at Hethersgill hostel, 100 at Hornby Hall hostel, 124 at Hornick Hill hostel, and 248 in billets. Two thousand six hundred and eighty-six prisoners-of-war had been repatriated to date. Morale was fair but lower than two months previously. On 18-22 November 1947, 463 Germans were at Merrythought. It had five hostels, housing 792. Moota, Wath Head and Brougham hostels had closed. Brampton was the best hostel, where regular instruction was given. There were two teachers and some Germans attended science classes under the auspices of the Workers' Educational Association.The final visit to Merrythought for a re-educational survey was on 24 January 1948. Three thousand one hundred and forty prisoners-of-war had been repatriated to date. The survey reported that morale at Merrythought had deteriorated over the past few months. One reason was depressing news from Germany. At Hornick Hill, two-thirds were youngsters. Seven youngsters attended a course at 180 camp. One of these wished to return there for a further course. Alston and Hornby Hall hostels were without electricity. (Camp 180 was at Marbury Hall in Cheshire.) Merrythought camp is well preserved and still in government use. It is at grid reference NY 486 405.

103. Moota

'The Moota' was a prisoner-of-war agricultural campsite during the Second World War. German prisoners-of-war built a chapel at this 1,000-man camp near Cockermouth and filled it with some fine artworks, but it was all destroyed after the war. (Source *A Lake District Miscellany*.) German prisoners-of-war from the Moota camp were sometimes despatched to Scilly Banks and Moresby to work. A truck brought them to the village each morning to work on the farms and came back in the evening to collect them. (Source *News & Star*, 30 July 2009.)

Gloria Edwards, author of *Moota – Camp 103. The Story of a Cumbrian Prisoner of War Camp*, came across an 80-year-old lady during her research who said that her father used to cycle to St Bees and collect sea-washed pebbles with his friends (*Binsey Link* magazine, September 2017). Along with pieces of kidney ore/pencil ore, they took the pebbles in match- or cigarette-boxes and went for a ride on their bikes to Moota to see the prisoners-of-war. The boxes were thrown over the fence to prisoners, who made jewellery to pass away their free time. If cigarettes or sweets were taken on a later visit, they were rewarded with a brooch, a ring, earrings or necklace to take home to a girlfriend or wife.

Carl Pettendrup (1924-2004), a German prisoner-of-war at Moota, was sent to Low Nest Farm (it was called Pyatt Nest) to work with the Pepper family. He fell in love with the farmer's daughter, Elsie (1922-2006), and married her and stayed on for the rest of his life as a Cumbrian farmer. They had three children, Anthony, Angela and Alison. Both Alison True and Angela Healy live at Low Nest and Angela runs the bed & breakfast, as did her parents and her grandparents. Pyatt Nest and all the neighbouring farms are present in the registers of Crosthwaite Church, which began in 1562. Anthony Pettendrup now believes most of the farms, including Pyatt Nest along with the Manor of Castlerigg and Derwentwater to which they are subordinate, existed for many centuries before 1562, possibly from before the Conquest.

104. Milnthorpe

Bela River Camp is close to Milnthorpe. Locals recall that Italian prisoners-of-war appeared very happy to be staying there, and that guards spent more time keeping local girls out than the prisoners in. (Source *A Lake District Miscellany*.) After the war, the camp became an open prison until 1975. Wilhelm Hackly was a German prisoner-of-war at Bela. In 2005, he wrote an article for the *Westmorland Gazette*, in which he said: "Here we were treated as humans, free from threats and humiliation." He worked in a quarry near Coniston.

Prisoners-of-war working at Broadwater

As the war years passed, the workforce on Cumbrian farms was gradually boosted by the influx of prisoners-of-war. Broadwater, Bootle Station, was home of the author's grandparents Edwin (1906-1976) and Emily Mansergh (née Tyson) (1908-1972) and their children Dorothy, born in 1935, the author's father John (1937-1988), David (1940-1980s) and Teddy (1942-1991). Edwin was active with the coastguard during the war. (The coastguard hut has long since gone due to coastal erosion.)

Dorothy remembered:

Broadwater had both Italian and German prisoners-of-war working on the farm. The Italian prisoners-of-war were billeted near the Haverigg Aerodrome. I vaguely remember the Italian prisoners catching eels on our becks. One German prisoner-of-war, Ali, became very attached to Broadwater and did not want to return to Germany. But he was forced to be repatriated, much against his will. Mother wrote to him for ages – I do not know what happened to his letters. I think his last name was Mueller. *She added:* Regarding planes bombing Barrow, if they did not drop their bombs on Vickers they were too heavy to get back to Germany. So they'd swing out to sea and come back in over the coast. One time they dropped bombs on Broadwater fields – I don't know whether any livestock was killed.

The author's grandmother Emily Mansergh, née Tyson, on the family farm in Bootle. Emily had three brothers and three sisters. (Dorothy Adland Parker (nee Mansergh))

A prisoner-of-war miscellany

Three Dutch internees, who escaped from Ramsay, Isle of Man in a small yacht, were captured at Eskmeals at noon on Saturday, 17 October 1941 by members of Cumberland and Westmorland Constabulary and Military Police. PC Meylor, Bootle, and military men rushed into the water and caught the boat when it grounded, while the fugitives jumped into the water and waded ashore. The men were given a meal at a house near the shore and provided with a battle dress before being taken in a military car to the police station at Whitehaven, where they were detained awaiting an escort to take them back to the Isle of Man.

An Italian prisoner-of-war who worked for a farmer at Newlands Farm, Hesket Newmarket, Caldbeck, during the Second World War stayed in touch with the family after he went home, according to *A Second Dip into Calbeck's Past* by Evelyn M. Geddling (1988). Forty years later, the Newlands family visited the man, who was a bricklayer by trade and went back to it for a while, in Italy. He then bought a small farm and modelled everything on Newlands Farm. He came over to see the family in 1992 and they took him back to Newlands. The last major repatriation of German prisoners-of-war and German civilians who were used as forced labour by Allies after the war, in accordance with the agreement made at

The garden at Levens Hall from Morris's Country Seats (1880) PD-1923

the Yalta conference, was made in 1956. Most prisoners-of-war held by the US, France and the UK had been released by 1949.

The Levens Hall estate, 5 miles south of Kendal, was inherited by 7-year-old Oliver Robin Gaskell (1914-2000) in 1921, Sir Josceline Fitzroy Bagot's (1854-1913) grandson through his daughter Dorothy Gaskell (b1886). Levens was let to the Reynolds family, Lancashire cotton mill owners. In 1936, Oliver assumed the name of Bagot by Royal Licence and, in 1938, he married Annette Dorothy Stephens (1917-2003). During the Second World War, Oliver Robin Bagot, who was educated at Eton and Cambridge, was captured and sent to a German prisoner-of-war camp for much of the war (prisoner-of-war number 1060). He gained the rank of lieutenant in the 4th Battalion, Border Regiment. He was awarded the Territorial Decoration. He had four children and lived in 1999 at Levens Brow, Kendal. During the Second World War, his wife managed to change a potentially damaging billet of soldiers on Levens so the house was allocated to nuns instead.

David Usher Hodgson (1928-2010) attended Keswick School until moving to St Bees School. He later served in the Royal Army Service Corps in Egypt, looking after German prisoners-of-war. After completing his service, he returned to Keswick to join the family building business. He was one of Keswick Rugby Club's leading figures (*Cumberland & Westmorland Herald*, 12 March 2010).

Further research

Some 425,871 prisoners-of-war were taken by the Americans, of whom 371,683 were German, 50,273 Italian, and 3,915 Japanese. They were housed in 686 prisoner-of-war camps across the US, across all but four of the States. After the war had ended, many were deliberately not returned to Germany immediately because the country was shattered. They were gradually moved to France, Italy, Holland, Russia, the UK and other European countries to help to rebuild those countries, but also to re-educate them into the Allied frame of mind. They were seemingly often given false hope of exile in Allied countries, and were loathe to return home because they knew what had happened to Germany. Refer to the History Channel film *Nazi PoWs in America* for more details. (With thanks to Ian Stuart Nicholson.)

Contact Deutsche Dienstelle (*dd-wast.de*), the national information office in Berlin, for records of German prisoners-of-war. It also has around 1,500,000 files on prisoners-of-war in German custody. Contact Ministero della Difesa, Rome (*difesa.it*) for records of Italian prisoners-of-war.

CHAPTER 13

Barrow had not been Forgotten

Manchester-born Margaret Cairns White (1921-1972), whose father worked at Morton Sundour Fabrics of Carlisle, lived at Nelson Street, Carlisle, between 1915 and 1936 and worked at the same mill for some time. As a young woman, she joined the British Union of Fascists (BUF), a party in the UK formed in 1932 by Sir Oswald Mosley (1896-1980) who had identified Westmorland as a key seat. She became a regular speaker for the BUF to the crowds of shoppers outside Carlisle Market Hall and in nearby towns and villages. In 1935, she met William Joyce (1906-1946), who was born in America and whose family moved to Ireland when he was three, at one of the party's rallies at Dumfries. He proposed only weeks later, they married in March 1937, in Kensington, and they went to Germany on 26 August 1939. Joyce became a German citizen in 1940. There was a notable lack of evidence that she too had taken German citizenship, according to MI5 files released in 2000.

William Joyce, nicknamed Lord Haw-Haw, broadcast propaganda in English to British listeners on behalf of his Nazi masters. He was hanged at Wandsworth Prison, London in January 1946 for betraying Britain (Margaret was spared punishment). According to *eden.gov.uk*, Joyce, on German propaganda radio broadcasts, mentioned a small airfield at Whinfell, a few miles east of Penrith, where the planes were hidden by camouflage nets, to try and damage morale.

During the early days of 1941, Joyce, who introduced his Radio Hamburg programme with 'Germany calling, Germany calling', broadcast from Berlin to audiences in Britain that Barrow-in-Furness had not been forgotten. The Barrow Blitz took place primarily during April and May 1941. The difficulty of solely targeting Barrow's shipyard meant that many residential neighbourhoods were bombed instead. Eighty-three civilians were killed, 330 injured, and more than 10,000 houses were damaged or destroyed during the Barrow Blitz – about 25 per cent of the town's housing stock. It has been suggested that Barrow was poorly prepared for air attack as there were public shelters for only 5 per cent of the total population of 75,000.

Bombing during mid-April 1941 caused significant damage to a central portion of Abbey Road, completely destroying the Waverley Hotel as well as Christ Church and Abbey Road Baptist Church. The town's main public baths and Essoldo Theatre were also severely damaged. However, they were repaired within years.

On Wednesday, 16 April 1941, the *North Western Evening Mail* carried the headline 'Air raid on North-Western Town', with the sub-heading 'Church wrecked, cinema, houses and shops damaged, two killed while fire watching'. The report said seven were dead and others unaccounted for from the raids of the night before and early that day. It said: 'Among the bodies recovered was that of a minister who was fire watching at the church when the building collapsed. A member of the congregation who was with him was also recovered from the debris.' There is reference to the excellent work of the ARP wardens, Home Guard, police and others.

Hawcoat Lane is a street that is most noted for taking a direct destructive hit in early May 1941. Barrow Central Station was heavily damaged on 7 May 1941. A First World War memorial to sixty-eight men – of whom sixty-six were soldiers (the majority from the King's Own Royal Lancaster Regiment), one sailor (Royal Navy), and one airman – located within the station still bears the holes and gashes caused by the Second World War bombings. IWM record 4095 lists the 68 names.

Deaths in the period from 8 May to 10 May 1941 included an air raid warden, a first-aider and volunteer fire watchers – who would have taken turns on night

The First World War memorial inside the station shows damage from the Second World War bombing. (Taken by Author)

duty at public buildings to deal with incendiary bombs, armed with a bucket of sand and a stirrup pump. The age range of those falling victim to the bombing in that three-day period was 14 to 76.

There is a memorial to Vickers' fire watchers Thomas Martin Cooke (1887-1941), crane driver, and Christopher Fieldhouse (1921-1941), apprentice fitter, that was rededicated on 11 November 2010 and is located at Barrow Dock Museum. They lost their lives when on duty as fire watchers on the platform of a crane that was wrecked and brought down by enemy air attack on the night of 7-8 May 1941. On 8 May 1941, a bomb falling on the air raid shelter at Vernon Street killed husband and wife Richard (1896-1941) and Sarah Ann (1889-1941) Brocklebank. The family home was 11 Exmouth Street. James Halfpenny (1899-1941) and his mother Sarah (1878-1941), who both lived at 24 Vernon Street, and Sheila Mary Redman (1919-1941) of 22 Vernon Street were also casualties at the Vernon Street shelter. John W. Duxbury (1876-1941) died at 6 Hall Street on 8 May 1941 and John McManus (1876-1941) died at 228 Duke Street on 9 May 1941.

On 10 May 1941, Irene Biddulph (1918-1941) died at 6 Hall Street and William Harper (1886-1941) was killed at 1 Hall Street. George Brown (1888-1941) of

Bomb damage to the back of Vernon Street and Collingwood Street, Barrow, on the night of 7/8 May 1941. (Evening Mail Archive. 1941)

Vernon Street, Barrow, around three years ago. Newer houses have been built into the far end of the terrace. (Christine Johnstone, geograph. org.uk.)

The Strand, John James Higginson (1873-1941), a volunteer fire watcher of Hindpool Road, Robert William Mulholland (1889-1941), a fire watcher of Hindpool Road, Edward Simpson (1888-1941), Robert Smith (1914-1941), and Mary Ann Sawbrick (d1941) of Hindpool Road were killed at the Newland Street shelter. Robert (1865-1941) and wife Elizabeth Ann (1867-1941) Howie died at 8 Hall Street. Their home was 41 McClintock Street. Teenager James Rawcliffe (1927-1941) of 6 Hall Street and Edward Fisher (1869-1941) of 6 Hall Street died in the Hall Street air raid shelter. Ernest Edward Shipton (1874-1941), an air raid warden, died at his home in 33 Newland Street. The last bombs of the Barrow Blitz were dropped in January 1942, with no recorded casualties. The last air raid siren in Barrow was recorded on 25 March 1942.

Nella Last

Barrow housewife Nella Last (1889-1968), née Lord, wrote a diary of her everyday experiences on the home front during the war for the Mass Observation archive from 1939 until 1966. Mass Observation was a UK social research organisation founded in 1937. Its work ended in the mid-1960s, but was revived in 1981. The archive is housed at the University of Sussex near Brighton.

The daughter of local railway clerk John Lord, Nella was married on 17 May 1911, to William Last (d1969), a shopfitter and joiner, and had two sons, Arthur and Cliff (1918-1991). During the war, she worked for the WVS and the Red Cross. Her published writing describes what it was like for ordinary people to live through the Second World War, reporting on the bombing of Barrow in April 1941 (including her own home

Nella was not afraid to speak her mind. (Public domain)

at 9 Ilkley Road) and offering her reflections on a wide range of contemporary issues. Some critics see a proto-feminism that anticipates the post-war women's movement in her account of her own marriage and her liberation from housewifery through her war work. Her husband, William, died in 1969.

Nella ruminates on everything from euthanasia to the fate of the German people after the war. During the war, she wrote more than two million words recording events of international importance such as the German invasion of Holland, what she cooked every day, exactly how she spent her £3 10s 0d housekeeping allowance, and her work in the sewing room at the WVS Centre in Barrow.

Nella frequently mentioned goods given to the men on minesweepers and trawlers who were exposed to harsh weather. In April 1940, volunteers in Barrow were packing comforts for the men who were about to depart on the new aircraft carrier HMS *Illustrious*. 'A lot of the men who are coming into town to join her are from tropical service and to each the WVS and Mayoress together are giving a helmet, scarf, mitts and pullover,' Nella wrote on 20 April 1940. Nella was particularly proud of her imaginative ways with sparse resources. A typical entry reads: 'Lettuce were from 1s 2d to 1s 7d today and not as good value as my scrap of cress, costing 1d, at most ... My butcher laughs at me – says I shop like a French woman who demands the best even if it costs less.'

As well as documenting her own anxieties and feelings about the bombing raids on her home town and the news that her son Cliff had been hurt in action, Nella acts as a reporter, canvassing friends' and relatives' thoughts on the war. We learn that Cliff's friend Jack is far from enamoured of Churchill, of whom he says: 'He is not as popular as all that and he has a good press agent.'

CHAPTER 14

1941, Aside from Barrow Bombing

In January 1941, RAF Millom at Haverigg opened as No. 2 Bombing and Gunnery school later to become No. 2 Air Observer School, which was to be then re-designated No. 2 Observer Advanced Flying Unit and remain in that role until the station closed in 1945. A number of its aircraft crashed on the fells. The result was that Millom, like Llandwrog in North Wales, became home to one of the initial RAF Mountain Rescue Units (MRS) from 1943 to 1945, according to *Aircraft Wrecks: The Walker's Guide* (2008) by Nick Wotherspoon, Alan Clark and Mark Sheldon. An MRS was operational at RAF Cark from 1945 to 1946 and RAF Barrow in 1946.

Jack Park and Pete Langley with a model of a wartime Anson aircraft used to train wartime aircrew at RAF Millom, which forms part of an extended display being put together at the Millom Discovery Centre. (nwemail.co.uk, 2016, with permission from Millom Discovery Centre)

Nigel Hepper wrote:

Since the airfield at Haverigg was likely to be an aerial target, a decoy was built in a field of the Stangrah farm near Whitbeck. One could see it from the train between Bootle Station and Millom with its inflated rubber planes and mock hangars and heaps of inflammable stuff between them. The idea was that the latter would be ignited in the event of an air raid as a diversion from the true airfield, but it was never used in this way. Of course we did not discuss such things as we were constantly urged to be wary of careless talk – you never knew who might be listening and a poster warned us that 'Careless talk costs lives'. Another slogan was 'Be like Dad, keep MUM'.

Millom town was also a potential target, and a very obvious one too, owing to its blast furnaces being visible from many miles away. Hence, whenever there was an alert, the ironworks were shut down as quickly as possible.

The only enemy attack on Millom occurred at 12.20pm on 14 August 1942. A single enemy aircraft, thought to be a *Junkers Ju 88*, shot up the airfield with cannon fire. The airfield escaped with no casualties or damage.

Other bombing decoy sites in Cumbria were at Siddick, Pica (Moresby), Wylock Marsh, Lowsy Point, Westfield Point, Whicham Valley and Edderson for Silloth aerodrome. The Pica site was used to simulate 'permitted lighting' given off by Moss Bay Ironworks and Bessemer Converter. Permitted lighting was that which could not be successfully blacked-out during air raids, such as sparks from furnaces, coke-ovens and loco firebox doors.

HMS *Southampton*, launched in 1936, was hit by at least two bombs south-east of Malta on 11 January 1941. The resulting blaze spread from stern to stern and trapped a number of men below decks. Eighty-one men were killed (the casualty list can be found on *maltagc70.wordpress.com*), with the survivors being picked up by HMS *Gloucester* and the destroyer HMS *Diamond*, built at Barrow for the RN in the early 1930s. Writer Herbert Lewis of Thornhill, Egremont, who was severely burned, was rescued and taken to hospital in Egypt. Before joining the navy, Lewis was on the Whitehaven Town Hall staff. HMS *Diamond* was sunk by German aircraft on 27 April 1941 while evacuating Allied troops from Greece. HMS *Wyneck* was also sunk by German aircraft on 27 April 1941. HMS *Griffin*, built at Barrow and launched in August 1935, rescued fifty survivors from HMS *Wyneck* and HMS *Diamond*.

'St Bees School Lit Up "Like a Barrack Square",' read a headline in the *West Cumberland Times* on 1 February 1941. The headmaster, John Boulter, was fined for blackout negligence. Whitehaven Police Court described it as one of the worst blackout offences brought to the notice of the court since the regulations came into force.

In February 1941, women between 16 and 45 had to register as 'mobile' if they had no children living at home. This meant they could be directed to war work by the government. Many decided to work at Vickers. A warning to petrol retailers was issued at Cockermouth Police Court on Monday, 24 February 1941 after the justices had inflicted fines and costs amounting to more than £30 upon a defendant who obtained petrol without coupons. In March 1941, jam, marmalade, treacle and syrup were rationed.

Kids could get up to all sorts of mischief during the blackout and there was an increase in crime such as bag-snatching and reckless driving. Described by a police officer as 'a little devil', a 10-year-old evacuee was ordered by the magistrates at Cockermouth Juvenile Court on 17 March 1941 to be sent home to his parents. He was the ringleader of three boys, aged 10, 11 and 12, who admitted breaking into the county council office at Cockermouth and stealing biscuits, pencils, pen-nibs and rubber bands. The extensive damage caused by children on a Whitehaven farm since the Greenbank scheme for rehousing people from slum areas became completed was mentioned to Whitehaven magistrates on 21 April 1941. Great damage had been done to hedges, fences and a building, while stock had suffered by being chased about.

On 24 May 1941, HMS *Hood* was sunk, with 1,418 men aboard, by a powerful salvo from *Bismarck* in the North Atlantic. Those who died included: Henry Burgess (1897-1941), born in Carlisle and husband of Grace Burgess of Carlisle; John Corlett (1918-1941), one of four children of John and Nora Corlett of Barrow (he is remembered on the grave of his grandparents at the cemetery in Devonshire Road, Barrow); William Crellin (1915-1941), born in Wigton and husband of Helen Crellin of Wigton; Walter Donaghy (1922-1941), born to Walter and Agnes Donaghy of Barrow; Chief Petty Officer Writer John James Forrester (1899-1941), born in Great Broughton and husband of Margaret Forrester of Camerton, who was due to retire from service during summer 1941; John William Hayton (1919-1941), born in Carlisle; Able Seaman Albert Heaton (1912-1941), born in Harraby, Carlisle; Petty Officer Telegraphist Albert Allan Kean (1917-1941), born to James and Emily Kean of Workington; John Kelly (1920-1941), born in Carlisle to Thomas and Caroline Kelly; Able Seaman Wallace McDonald (1913-1941), whose family lived in Maryport; Marine Robert Stanley Neale (1905-1941), who was born in Workington; Stoker William Nelson (1905-1941), who was born at Frizington and moved to Carlisle; Thomas Francis Norris (1911-1941), husband of Isabel Norris of Carlisle;

Steward Gordon Parker (1918-1941), who was born in Workington; Petty Officer William Edward Reay DSM (1911-1941), born in Workington; Walter Little Routledge (1923-1941), who was born in Ambleside; Regulating Petty Officer John Henry Smith (1904-1941), born in Barrow; Ordinary Seaman Joseph William Steele (1923-1941), born in Bootle and whose family lived in Millom; Paymaster Sub-Lieutenant Stanley Watkinson (1919-1941), born in Barrow and whose family emigrated to New Zealand in the mid-20s; Stoker Charles Watt (1920-1941), whose family lived in Currock, Carlisle; Sub-Lieutenant Tom Willetts (1917-1941), who was born in Barrow; and Victor Marcus Winkfield (1919-1941), born in Barrow. Reay had been awarded a Distinguished Service Medal (DSM) and a Croix de Guerre during the Second World War. One was from the Battle of Narvik, 1940.

Writers were primarily clerical, being responsible for legal, pay, welfare and career issues for a crew. When the ship went into action, they could also be utilised with damage control parties, for instance, passing vital information to combat floods and fires. Each trade was broken down into numerous levels, similar to the Royal Navy's rank structure, but also denoting time in service and experience in a particular role. For example, writer could be broken down to: Chief Petty Officer Writer, Petty Officer Writer, Writer, Writer Probationer, and Boy Writer (Source: *Forces War Records*).

Only three men survived: Ordinary Signalman Ted Briggs (d2017), from Fareham in Hampshire; Able Seaman Robert Tilburn (1921-1995), born in Leeds; and Midshipman William John Dundas (1923-1965), born in Edinburgh. Briggs, who was president of the HMS *Hood* Association, described what he saw in the aftermath:

When I came to the surface, I was on her (the *Hood's*) port side ... I turned and swam as best I could in water 4ins thick with oil and managed to get on one of the small rafts she carried, of which there were a large number floating around. When I turned again, she had gone and there was a fire on the water where her bows had been. Over on the other side, I saw Dundas and Tilburn on similar rafts. There was not another soul to be seen. We hand-paddled towards each other and held on to one another's rafts until our hands became too numb to do so.

It is estimated that as many as 9,000 men served aboard *Hood* during the operational portion of her twenty-one-year career. These include James Kelly Moore (1923-1941), born in Kendal, whose parents Sidney Victor Pothecary Potter and Myrtle Moore married in Barrow in 1926. He is known to have entered

W. Donaghy

Above left: *Henry Burgess aboard Hood.* (hmshood.com)

Above right: *Walter Donaghy.* (hmshood.com)

Right: *Joseph William Steele, prior to joining the Navy, worked on the Whitaker farm at Arnside.* (hmshood.com)

J.W. Steele

the navy in 1938 or 1939 and is believed to have been injured in a fall shortly before *Hood's* final mission.

In June 1941, the distribution of eggs was controlled. The wartime newspapers were full of reports of people who had been caught in black marketeering. In January 1942, a Cleator Moor woman was caught selling eggs above the maximum price and fined £5 by Cleator Moor magistrates. (She sold six eggs for 11d.) Clothes rationing began on 1 June 1941. There was a shortage of materials to make clothes. Everyone was given a clothing book with coloured coupons in. Every item of clothing was given a value in coupons, according to how much labour and material were needed to produce it. Eleven coupons were needed for a dress (*iwm.org.uk*). To buy clothes, people handed over their clothing book to the shopkeeper, who cut out one of the coupons. They then handed over money to the shopkeeper to pay for the clothes. Children's clothes had lower coupon values in recognition of the fact that they would need more clothes as they grew. Coupons were also needed for school uniforms.

Extra coupons were available for manual workers and miners to buy working clothes. 'In the mining industry, underground workers are already receiving 60 supplementary coupons. Screen workers will receive 30 and a number of other categories of surface workers 20 supplementary coupons. Certain categories of iron and steel workers will receive 45, 25 and 15 supplementary coupons according to the nature of their employment,' the *Lancashire Evening Post* of 19 November 1941 reported. 'Children born on or after 1st January, 1925, and before 1st September, 1927, are entitled to extra clothing coupons,' the *Manchester Evening News* of 29 November 1941 reported.

The *Cumberland & Westmorland Herald* quoted the case of a young woman who used all but two of her coupons at one go, as she fitted herself out for a new job on a farm near Penrith. In this list of her purchases, the numbers of clothing points are in brackets: three black hose (six), two nightdresses (six), three overalls (nine), three pairs of knickers (nine), three cotton dresses (twenty-one), two ounces of wool (one), one pair of corsets (three), and three working aprons (nine).

The first aircraft arrived at RAF Crosby on 11 March 1941 and the airfield was then used as a training base by its first unit (59 Operational Training Unit – OTU) until August 1942. During this period, the aircraft was used by Bristol Beaufighter conversion squadrons. The airfield was also used for training in air and night firing. On 29 March 1941, the pilot of *Hurricane Mk 1 V6987*, Thomas Charles Smith, was ferrying the aircraft, along with Flying Officer John Wilfred

Seddon in *V7539*, from RAF Northolt to RAF Crosby. The two aircraft became separated due to the weather. *V6987* crashed on Birkhouse Moor above the village of Glenridding on the western side of Ullswater. *V7539* struck the upper most part of Scar Crags. Both men were killed.

On the night of 14 March 1941, a German plane dropped a bomb very close to Hugh's Crag Viaduct in Lowther Park. The pilot was probably aiming to destroy the main LMS railway line from London to Scotland. The following day, a group of boys from the Newcastle Royal Grammar School visited the site and collected a piece of shrapnel from the bomb, which is now in the Penrith Museum collection.

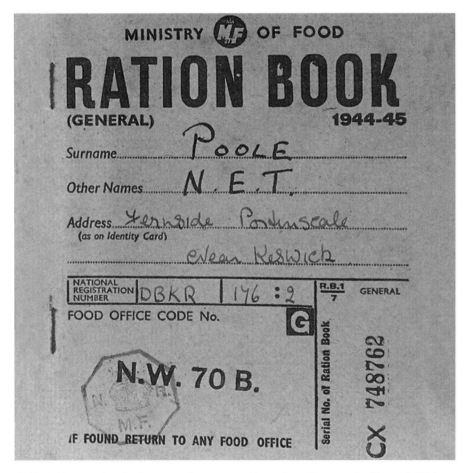

A 1944-45 ration book relating to the property Fernside in Portinscale, Keswick. With thanks to The Salisbury Review. (Permission to use from editor M. Harris)

The bombing of Cooper House, Selside

Cooper House, Selside near Kendal, was bombed in the early hours of 16 April 1941, killing eleven of its occupants, and one landmine fell on the hilly ground of Whinfell Beacon, located in the Howgill Fells area between the Lake District National Park and the Yorkshire Dales (the fells were originally shared by the West Riding of Yorkshire and Westmorland). Official opinion at the time was that the pilot of the German plane, returning from a bombing raid on Barrow shipyards, decided to jettison his load.

Those killed were five members of the Wood family, one housemaid, and five evacuees from London: Edith Hilda Wood (1906-1941), her husband Francis James Wood (1899-1941), Hannah Wood (1865-1941), Jean Dorothy Wood (1933-1941), Joseph Samuel Wood (1938-1941), and Agnes Lancaster Strickland (1925-1941), daughter of Maggie Strickland of Wads Howe, Longsleddale, Kendal, and of the late Thomas Henry Strickland. The evacuees were Annie Augusta Ambrose (1869-1941) of Haywards Heath, Sussex, Florence Louisa Moorhouse (1872-1941) of Hampstead, her husband John Edward Moorhouse (1863-1941) of Hampstead, Frank Bernard Walder (1896-1941) of Haywards Heath, and his wife Lucy Walder (1902-1941) of Haywards Heath.

Two farm men, who were sleeping in the opposite end of the house to where the landmine fell, survived, one sustaining several injuries from which he recovered. They were brothers, Norman and Brian, who lived in Staveley afterwards. Cooper House, where Christopher Gibson (b1839) farmed 210 acres in 1881, was rebuilt after the war to make it a complete farm dwelling once more.

Margaret Harper, whose father was a farmer and therefore exempt from joining the forces, was living at the time on a farm called Hill Fold near Burneside. She said:

After the bombing, we were all unsettled. We lived probably four miles as the crow flies from Cooper House and we all slept outside in the fields for the next two to three nights. Being in the farming area, we slept near another farm and cottage, laid down a big tarpaulin sheet and the ladies brought out blankets and rugs. I thought it was quite exciting to sleep outside and I slept near these trees for shelter. My neighbour's wife was extremely deaf so she couldn't hear the bombers going over low. She used to bring us out drinks at intervals and we said she mustn't risk going out of the house. We were two houses that didn't have cellars. People with cellars felt that they had somewhere safe to run but we didn't.

Bramwell 'Bram' Longstaffe (1885-1942), Labour Mayor of Barrow from 1934-5 and 1935-6, warned in August 1941 that many parents, faced with big bills for their evacuated children's keep, were bringing their families back into danger. He blamed government delay in collecting the money for the partial failure of evacuation. 'In many cases which have come before me as member of the War Emergency Committee and the Citizens' Advice Bureau, parents have received demands for several pounds after a lapse of months,' he told the *Daily Mirror* on 12 August 1941.

He said:

Presented with a bill for five, six, or seven pounds – in cases of large families considerably greater sums – the parents panic. They bring their children back to escape further charges. Their outlook is: 'There is always the chance that the bomb will miss us, but if it gets us we all go together'.

The shadow of court action looms greater than the bomber.

The money question, he thought, was at the root of the failure to keep old age pensioners evacuated. After fourteen days, public assistance authorities docked 5 shillings from their supplementary pensions because they were receiving the boarding allowance. 'It costs them more, they say, to live away from their homes,' Longstaffe said. 'So they go back. Five bob a week against their own lives.'

Satellite landing grounds (SLGs)

In 1940, Sir Archibald Sinclair (1890-1970), Secretary of State for Air, educated at Eton and the Royal Military College, Sandhurst, wrote:

There are many large private estates and huge parklands which, if the trees were taken down, would be suitable as landing grounds, if not aerodromes. We are out to win this war and should not be put off by a desire to maintain intact the stately homes of England or the future of horse racing and horse breeding.

An SLG is typically an airfield with one or two grass runways designed to be 'hidden' from the sky by using woods and other natural features to hide the presence of aircraft and associated buildings:

RAF Brayton Park (No. 39 SLG), east of Aspatria, should have opened during 1941, but it became active in May 1942. (Brayton Hall was practically destroyed by fire in 1918.)

RAF Hornby Hall (No. 9 SLG), 3 miles east of Penrith. Used as an SLG from June 1941 to August 1945.

RAF Hutton-in-the-Forest (No. 8 SLG) near Hutton Hall, Penrith. Used as an SLG from June 1941 to August 1945.

RAF Wath Head (No. 10 SLG), Wigton. Used as an SLG from 1941 until December 1945.

Sergeant Stanislaw Karubin, Polish Air Force, and Zygmunt Hohne, Polish Air Force, died on 12 August 1941 when their Hurricane aircrafts flew at high speed into a hill at Horn Crag, Scafell, crashing within 200 metres of each other. A memorial was erected at the crash site (the original plaque at the site, along with several pieces of wreckage, was moved to RAF Millom Museum). The men were based at RAF Usworth near Sunderland, now Sunderland Airport. Karubin had flown with 111 Eskadra Squadron in Poland and shot down a Bf110 German plane in September 1939. When France collapsed, he went to England and was enlisted in the Royal Air Force Volunteer Reserve (RAFVR). He joined 303 Squadron at Northolt, west London, at its formation on 2 August 1940. RAF Millom Museum closed in 2011. Many of the museum's exhibits were on loan and have been returned to owners.

On 2 November 1941, an *Airspeed Oxford Mk II* was being used for a navigation exercise from RAF Millom when it flew into Caw Fell near Ennerdale. Both crew members were killed: Sergeant RCAF Charles Andre Desbaillets, buried at Haverigg Churchyard, and Leading Aircraftman Henry Hodgkinson. Desbaillets, son of E.C. Desbaillets and Helene Desbaillets of Montreal, Canada, is listed on the Canadian Virtual War Memorial, *veterans.gc.ca*. Hodgkinson, husband of Margaret Olive Hodgkinson of London Road, Derby, was buried at Nottingham Road Cemetery, Derby.

On 25 November 1941, *U-331* sunk the battleship HMS *Barham* while covering Mediterranean convoys. An explosion resulted, probably the magazine going up, disintegrating the *Barham*, taking 841 men with her in three minutes. Stoker Wilfred Sidney Edgar (1920-1941) of Cowslow (farm), Wigton, Ordinary Seaman John 'Jackie' Hoggarth (1918-1941) of Barrow, and Cook John Westmorland (1921-1941) of Carlisle were killed. Edgar is commemorated at Westward Church, a few miles east of Wigton and the closest church to Cowslow. (Hoggarth and Westmorland are not commemorated anywhere in their home towns.) *Hotspur* and other escorting destroyers rescued 337 men, including Ordinary Seaman Douglas Palmer of Maryport, who died on 31 May 2013.

Above: *Impact site of V6565 with the new memorial to both men.* (Ian Stuart Nicholson)

Below: *The original memorial at the crash site, replaced in more recent years.* (Ian Stuart Nicholson)

He was a member of the HMS *Barham* Association and a photo of him can be found on *hmsbarham.com*.

On 14 December 1941, HMS *Galatea* was sunk by *U-557* off Alexandria, beginning a series of naval defeats for the Allies. Twenty-two officers and 447 ratings were killed. Some 100 survivors were picked up by the destroyers *Griffin* and *Hotspur*. The following day, HMS *Queen Elizabeth*, along with HMS *Valiant*, was mined and seriously damaged by Italian frogmen in the harbour at Alexandria, Egypt, with the loss of nine men of her complement. William Barman of Barrow lost his life on *Galatea*.

On 18 December 1941, a second National Service Act became law. It widened the scope of conscription still further by making all unmarried women and all childless widows between the ages of 20 and 30 liable to call-up. Men were now required to do some form of National Service up to the age of 60, which included military service for those under 51. The main reason was that there were not enough men volunteering for police and civilian defence work, or women for the auxiliary units of the armed forces.

The Women's Institute (WI)

The WI was a great thing during the war: preservation of food, making jams, jellies and marmalades, and knitting parties for the forces. And, in amongst all this activity, they sang, put on plays and organised parties to entertain their villages and keep their spirits up. Preservation centres were set up in villages or near where fruit was harvested. There were more than 5,000 of these, according to *thewi.org.uk*. The *West Cumberland Times* of 25 June 1941 reported:

> There are now three jam-preserving centres, in connection with North Westmorland Women's Institutes, 'on strike'. A week ago, it was reported that the Brampton and Long Marton centres had decided to 'down tools' – or whatever is the equivalent term in jam-making parlance – as a protest against the action of the Ministry of Food in appointing 'diplomaed' inspectors at £5 a week to supervise their work …
>
> Dufton centre has now thrown in its lot with the 'strikers' as evidenced by the following resolution passed at the June meeting: 'that the members are not prepared to carry on the scheme as a voluntary national service at a very busy time of the farmers' year whilst the appointed inspector is to receive £5 a week, plus expenses …
>
> 'Surely there are hundreds of women in Britain who would be honoured to do this work voluntarily'.

The year 1941 saw the formation of new WIs: Crosby (March 1941), Boltons, Allonby, Rosewain, Borrowdale, Hill-in-Millom, Welton (closed in 2007), Crosby Villa and Broughton Moor. And set up in January 1941 was the Keswick Townswomen's Guild (TG). The TG was formed in 1929 when women first won the right to vote and with the aim of educating women about good citizenship.

Top secret tanks

The fells around Walla Crag near Keswick and Bleaberry Fell, which stands between Borrowdale and Thirlmere, were used as a training area for tank crews. In 1941, Lowther Castle was requisitioned by the War Office to develop top secret anti-tank weapons.

The Canal Defence Light (CDL) was developed by the British Army with the intention of blinding the enemy. From a projector on a specially adapted tank, a fan-shaped beam of light lit up the area of attack and dazzled the enemy. A CDL school was set up at Lowther Castle, with the responsibility for technical development and basic and technical training in the CDL. Six

Lowther Castle and Gardens, August 2015. The castle's contents were removed in the late 1940s and the roof was removed in 1957. (Visitcumbria.com)

thousand officers and men attended the CDL school and 1,850 tanks were converted to the CDL role, according to *Come Back to Eden: Lakeland's Northern Neighbour*. In May 1942, Earl Mountbatten visited Lowther to see the CDL tank in action, and in December of that year King George VI, Eisenhower and Winston Churchill came to see a demonstration. As the war years passed and the secrecy melted away, the presence of CDL and the Royal Tank Regiment at Lowther became widely known. A team from the school played in a Carlisle football league.

CHAPTER 15

Three Unknown Merchant Navy Seamen

Whicham, neighbouring the Irish Sea, is a parish with three small villages, Silecroft, Whicham and Kirksanton, and some isolated farmsteads. In the churchyard of St Mary's, Whicham there are CWGC graves to three unknown merchant navy seamen. Two of the men were found washed up on the beach at Silecroft in mid-April 1941. The third, also washed ashore, was buried in July 1941. The currents are such that they could have been washed a long way. They were not in a state where visual identification of known missing seamen was possible, which made the coroner's task difficult.

The handwritten burial register entry for the men buried at the same spot on 17 April 1941 reads: '17.4.41 – On this day I laid to rest the mortal remains

Silecroft Beach where the bodies of the two sailors were washed ashore. (Perry Dark, thebeachguide.co.uk)

Two sailors of the Second World War buried at Whicham churchyard (north churchyard) on 17 April 1941.
(Taken by Author, summer 2017)

of two unknown males brought here after being found on Silecroft shore. R. Walker, Rector.'

The handwritten burial register for the man buried in July 1941 reads as follows: '10.7.41 – On this day I laid to rest the remains of an unknown male washed ashore. R.W.' The epitaph on both headstones is the same: Known Unto God.

Also buried at St Mary's, Whicham, are Corporal Clifford Oswald William Amos (1913-1941), Royal Australian Air Force, of Brighton, South Australia, and Aircraftman 1st Class John Charles Francis (d1941), Royal Australian Air Force, son of Charles Nicholas and Mary Violet Francis of New South Wales. Both were members of a Short Sunderland flying-boat of No. 10 Squadron that came down in the Irish Sea, killing six of its crew, on 28 April 1941. Their bodies were washed up at Silecroft some time later.

A sailor of the Second World War buried 10 July 1941 at Whicham churchyard (south churchyard). (Taken by Author, summer 2017)

Brier Rose, a small merchant vessel built in 1892, vanished in the Irish Sea on 26 March 1941 on a voyage between Belfast and Cardiff with a cargo of steel billets. There were ten casualties. It was assumed that she was sunk by enemy action, according to *wrecksite.eu*, though she may have sunk because of her age. Boyce Ethelbert Minton, an old boy of Bury Grammar School, of Roa Island, Barrow, was on board and never seen again. His name was added to a war memorial at Bury Grammar School in 2003.

On 13 June 1941, SS *St Lindsay* was torpedoed and sunk by *U-751* south-west of Iceland. The master and forty-two crew members were lost. Third Officer Gordon Hughes (1919-1941), born in Kendal, adopted son of Jane Hughes of Ulverston, died. His address on his Record of Death of Merchant Seamen is Witherslack Vicarage, Grange. He is named on the Tower Hill Memorial and the Witherslack War Memorial.

Witherslack War memorial, St Pauls Church, Witherslack. (Ian Stuart Nicholson)

CHAPTER 16

The Women's Land Army

The Women's Land Army (WLA) was created so women could work in agriculture, replacing men called up to the military. Women who worked for the WLA were commonly known as land girls. In effect, the WLA operated to place women with farms that needed workers, the farmers being their employers.

Land girls were paid directly by the farmers who employed them. The minimum wage was 28s per week. From this, 14s was deducted for board and lodgings (14s in 1940 was worth £27.54 in 2017). The basic working week for land girls was forty-eight hours in winter and fifty in summer.

In July 1939, Inez Jenkins (née Ferguson), who lived in an Oxfordshire village, was appointed chief of the WLA for England and Wales in the event

Above left: *Mary Watson was photographed on a tractor and this shot was used in recruitment posters for the WLA.* (Public domain)

Above right: *Mary Watson's husband James Watson in Home Guard uniform at Hill House, Salta, a hamlet in the parish of Holme St Cuthbert.* (Courtesy of Holme St Cuthbert History Group)

of war. Under her were seven regional directors, each in charge of one or more counties. Cumberland and Westmorland were administered as one region with county offices in Carlisle and Kendal. Cumberland and Westmorland had two chairwomen, Alison MacInnes of Rose Bank, Penrith (Cumberland), and Miss Christine May Elmslie (1900-1985) of Brathay How (a totally separate property from Brathay Hall), Ambleside (Westmorland). The secretary was Miss M.A. Soulsby, 11 Crown Square, Penrith. Mrs H.S. Cartmell, Heads Nook, Brampton, was appointed Cumberland organising secretary for the WLA (*Lancashire Evening Post*, 27 July 1939, which also reported that Millom Rural District Council had appointed ex-police inspector G.W. Wright as wartime food controller). Thirty applications had been received for service, and others were in training at Newton Rigg Farm School (now Newton Rigg College), Penrith. Mary Watson (née Nattrass) (1922-2005) left the Tomlinson Girls' Grammar School in Wigton in 1939 to become a boarder at Newton Rigg Farm School. She studied poultry and dairy management. She had to leave the college to help on the family farm, Hill House, Salta, Maryport, due to the severe labour shortage caused by the war. Her memories form an important part of the book *Plain People* by the Holme St Cuthbert History Group (2004).

Lumberjills

The *Land Girl* magazine of October 1940 referred to an influx of forestry workers in Cumberland and Westmorland, most of them being timber-measurers. The women, who made up the Women's Timber Corps, some only in their mid-teens, were known as 'Lumberjills' – and they played their part in the war effort in Britain's woodlands and forests, felling trees and working in sawmills. New home-produced timber was urgently required for industry and the war effort: for pit props and railway sleepers, telegraph poles, aircraft construction, shipbuilding, gunstocks for the troops, transport packaging for army supplies, charcoal for explosives and gas mask filters, and coffins. According to *crosthwaiteandlyth. co.uk*, girls in the Timber Corps worked alongside local men at the sawmill, which operated at Bridge End, in the Lyth Valley, during the Second World War. The building was made of timber and corrugated iron, and was established by the Ministry of Supply to prepare local timber. The wood was cut from plantations on Whitbarrow, a hill 6 miles south-west of Kendal, and the surrounding area. Stakes from the sawmill were sunk in the mosses to prevent enemy planes from landing there. Arrowsmith's Transport took the timber to Vickers in Barrow. The sawmill was shut after the war. According to *Snagging Turnips and Scaling Muck,*

Stripping tree trunks at Grizedale Forest for use as telephone poles. Taken in 1941 by Betty Kirkland, a past resident of Satterthwaite, a small village about 4 miles south of Hawkshead. (satterthwaitepc.org.uk)

The Women's Land Army in Westmorland, there were about ten members of the Women's Army Timber Corps based at Holker Hall.

The *West Cumberland Times* of 11 January 1941 said the WLA was in urgent need of new recruits and that a wireless appeal stated that 1,000 were needed immediately, and that number was likely to increase throughout the years. 'The local office at Penrith has a waiting list of farmers who need extra labour, and is experiencing difficulty in finding volunteers to fill the vacancies. Only a limited number of Cumberland and Westmorland girls have so far come forward, and about half of the 130 girls at present working in the district have come from other counties,' the *West Cumberland Times* said.

The following letter was printed in the *West Cumberland Times* of 9 August 1941 headlined 'Women in Trousers':

Sir – One day last week business took me to Keswick. In the course of a three minute walk up the main street I saw one young woman in a gaudy yellow silk pair of trousers and a flaming red short jacket without sleeves. Then came another of similar age with grass green wide slacks and a yellow jerseyette, a third had bright plum coloured bags and brilliant green jacket with short sleeves.

Their faces were fearfully and wonderfully got up. Lips and nails really gory. Eyes shaded, eyebrows plucked and pencilled, enamel powder and tan *ad lib.* What a commentary on our civilisation. Is this what our men are fighting for?

How do these vain creatures manage to evade Bevin's registration of young women for war work?

Is it not time some effort was made to sort out the parasites from the workers and let us take life in these tragic days a little more seriously? _ Yours, etc.

DISGUSTED No. 2

Keswick

The following letter of the same title was published in the *West Cumberland Times* of Saturday, 16 August 1941:

SIR – During the past few weeks I have seen, in your paper, evidence of the growing weight of public opinion against women wearing trousers. Despite all that has been said, these young women are still wandering round in these gaudy and unsightly garments. These hags in bags – you must agree that this is the best way to describe many of them – must realise that they are going against all the established traditions of womanhood. My grandmother used to say, "Since the bustle and crinoline went out of fashion women have lost that secret charm which was their greatest asset." I wonder what they would say now? Yours, etc.

"WOMANHOOD"

Cumberland & Westmorland WLA reported in April 1942 that it had a new hostel at Milnthorpe (closed 1948), built on the edge of the recreation ground in order to give its members a grandstand view of the local football matches. Girls came from cities such as Manchester, Liverpool and Newcastle in their new uniforms: brown breeches and hat with the badge of the WLA on it. As the Land Army was not a military force, however, uniform was not compulsory. The lorry that took the girls to the farms was kept in a garage of the Cross Keys Hotel, Milnthorpe.

Cumberland & Westmorland WLA told the *Land Girl* magazine (April 1942):

We have had a spate of Warship Week parades, with anything from 20 to 85 land girls at each, and are wondering how people who are never drilled manage to march as smartly as any girl in uniform. I hope this is not just our partiality, but quite a lot of impartial observers said the same thing. Perhaps the healthy life makes one naturally smart and erect. Nellie Jobson deserves special mention for walking six miles from an isolated farm beyond Kentmere in order to catch a bus to the Kendal parade, and did the same walk back at night; she is probably the most isolated member in our district, having to travel those six miles whenever she goes to town, except when she can catch the once-a-week bus which comes within three miles of her.

Cumberland & Westmorland's fifth hostel opened with thirty members on 15 June 1942 at Bolton Hall, Gosforth, home in 1912 of ironmaster Colonel James Robert Bain (1851-1913) and now a caravan site. The *Land Girl* of August 1942 reported: 'It is a delightful country house with a lovely view, a garden, four bathrooms and an Aga cooker. There will shortly be a sixth hostel at Appleby.'

The jobs our members do become more and more varied. A dozen are destroying rats and moles; some are driving tractors, despite the up-and-down character of the country; over 100 will be employed on threshing gangs in Cumberland during the winter, and six girls are to be trained to drive "Cub" excavators. Two forestry workers in an isolated district had an unlooked for excitement a few weeks ago when a British plane crashed into hillside, and they were first on the scene to help. Many dances and whist drives are taking place, mainly for the Benevolent Fund, and we hear of volunteers who intend to put the winter evenings to good use. One or two are studying for the RHS Examinations; a group of volunteers who want to run a farm after the war wish to read all they can about agriculture; one hostel is taking first-aid classes while at another a group is learning Esperanto. The WLA is now represented by Mrs Cartmell on the committee of the Girls' Training Corps in Carlisle – a welcome sign that our service is not always left out in the cold.

(*Cumberland & Westmorland County News*,
The Land Girl, December 1942)

There was a WLA hostel at Cliburn near Penrith. 'When the girls went on leave, they would cycle to Shap road and leave their bikes at a convenient farm and thumb a lift from the lorry drivers and military convoys passing by. Sometimes, the American convoys from a nearby American base would take them to their destination. There was also a camaraderie amongst the Services at that time and the girls never came to any harm, though they would never travel alone,' Martha Bates wrote in *Snagging Turnips and Scaling Muck* (2001). There have also been references to WLA hostels at: Appleby; Brampton, Carlisle; Bryon, a house in Sedbergh (a hostel until 1943); Geltsdale, Wetheral near Carlisle; Causeway Head, south-east of Silloth; Hawkshead (for forestry workers); Milgrove; and Scaleby Hall, Carlisle. Silloth hostel had been a vicarage. From Silloth, land girls went to work at Aigle Gill Farm near Aspatria, where there were German prisoners-of-war working. There was no trouble with the Germans, according to a former Land Girl interviewed by June Thistlethwaite (*Cumbria The War Years, Lake District Life during the 1940s*).

Every now and again, the Land Army split the girls up and sent them to different hostels. Some of the land girls, of course, were billeted on the farms where they worked – but they also came back to the hostels in the evening, or weekend, for a chat or a good old moan.

The *Land Girl* of February 1943 reported that about sixty girls in Cumberland & Westmorland were now employed on threshing. They found it a hard and dirty job. It reported in August 1943 that Miss Fletcher, warden of Bolton Hall, died in Whitehaven Infirmary. Milgrove and Scaleby Hall Hostels opened on 12 July and Causeway on 26 July. 'We can now issue our News Letter every two months only, owing to paper restrictions. Farm Sunday, July 4th, was reported in Carlisle,' it said.

There were some terrific feats of travel, the *Land Girl* of September 1943 reported. K. Gunning (Women's Land Army number 2923) of Lancashire bicycled from her farm in a remote part of the Lake District to catch the night-train to London, where she arrived in the early hours of the morning. On arrival at Euston Station, she was given a lift in a lorry and then travelled on to her destination in the Underground. After spending a day in London, which included sightseeing, the Buckingham Palace party, and a visit to a theatre, she took the night-train back to Ulverston and cycled back to the farm ready to start work again.

What did land girls do when outside work was held up by weather? In September 1943, R.W. Bell of Longtown, secretary of the National Farmers' Union (NFU) for Cumberland and North Westmorland from 1922, branded the land girls' no housework rule 'absurd'. He told a meeting of the Cumberland NFU Executive at Carlisle: 'Wet weather sometimes holds up work in the north for a week at a time.' A Whitehall regulation said they must not be asked to do housework.

The *Land Girl* of December 1944 reported that a new club had been formed at Wigton that met on the second and fourth Mondays of the month in the Congregational Hall. Cumberland and Westmorland's four other clubs were at Dacre, Keswick, Dalston and Kendal. The WLA canteen in Penrith, run by the Townswomen's Guild, was still much appreciated by all in the area. Geltsdale Hotel, Wetheral, gave a successful concert to the Garlands Military Convalescent Home.

Many women who had been in the WLA settled in the Milnthorpe area. A number of land girls married farmers. Laura Brunskill, who joined the WLA in 1947, was one of forty girls billeted to a hostel at Lazonby and put to work on farms around Eden. She stayed on a farm at Maughanby until the WLA was wound up in 1950. She went on to marry one of the sons of her employers, Bob Brunskill. (*Cumberland & Westmorland Herald*, 31 January 2008.) According to *crosthwaiteandlyth.co.uk*: Jean Kinstrey married Jim Smith from the Oaks, Cartmel Fell; Sylvia Holmes married Geoffrey Harrison of Woodside Cottage; Rose Fielden married Ernie Shepherd from Broad Oak; and Ivy Court married John Wilson from the Yews.

Jessie Woods

Jessie Rushton Woods (1920-1988) came from a slum area in Liverpool and lived in a house that was only held up by the buildings on either side. She was born in West Derby on 6 July 1920 and registered without the Rushton part of her name. She was the child of Thomas Rushton Woods, whose birth was also registered without the Rushton and who died without the Rushton, and Eleanor Frazer, born in 1876, who married in 1906. Jessie had one sibling, Thomas Rushton Woods (junior), born in 1908. There seem to have been at least three generations of Thomas Rushton Woods in Liverpool before her father. She lived with her mother according to the 1939 register, which shows that their address was 6 Buchanan Road, Walton on the Hill, Liverpool. (Her Service Record Card 03/06/42, at the National Archives, gives her address as 4 Weaver Street, Walton, Liverpool.)

Walton had a Dunlop factory where workers stood making wellies all day on a hard, concrete floor. Jessie's father was a railway goods porter, born in 1863, and had been in Prestwich Asylum, Manchester, for a time in 1887. Of the many who remained patients, a large number probably had no known mental problems. As with asylums up and down the British Isles, they were admitted by their family for a variety of reasons, including poverty, illness or because they were due to become unmarried mothers.

Jessie's father, who died in 1935, had lived at 6 Buchanan Road since at least 1901. Jessie, whose occupation was drying machine assistant, arrived via the WLA at Broadwater Farm, Bootle Station, on 26 June 1942. Jessie did rat- and mole-catching at Broadwater. Her Service Record Card reads that she went to the Isle of Wight on 28 October 1947, back to Lancashire on 1 May 1948, to East Sussex on 27 May 1948, and that her contract was completed on 30 November 1950. The author's grandmother, Emily, kept in touch with Jessie

Above: Great-grandfather George Albert Mansergh (1876-1941), born in Torver, who married Kate Gowan (1871-1940) of Hycemoorside in 1901. (They had two children. Author's own)

Below: Broadwater, the family farm, in the 1930s. (Author's Own)

and she visited Broadwater frequently, and went with Emily to visit Dorothy in California in 1969/1970. Dorothy kept in touch with Jessie, who did not have children.

Stop mucking around with Liverpool

Folk-song *Back Buchanan Street* (about Buchanan Road) was written by Harry and Gordon Dison for a BBC song-writing competition in the mid-1960s and was one of the entries selected to be performed on TV. It quickly found popularity around Liverpool, which was in the midst of a slum clearance programme moving people away from crowded conditions in the inner cities to the nearby towns of Kirkby Skelmersdale and Speke. Nineteen thousand people went to Halewood, which is where Jessie ended her days. In spite of the promise of improved living conditions, for many people there was a sense that communities were being broken up and that people were losing their homes and being torn from places they loved. Scottie Road was legendary for its forty pubs. It also housed Paddy's Market with the 'Two a penny, lemons' (*The Liverpool Blues*, a Liverpool folk-song). Not long after the publication of the song (below), Harry's son John became a town planner.

BACK BUCHANAN STREET
Original lyrics, written by Harry and Gordon Dison in the 1960s
A fella' from the Council, Just out of Planning School
Has told us that we're being moved right out of Liverpool
They're sending us to Kirkby, or Skelmersdale or Speke
Don't want to go from all we know in Back Buchanan Street

We'll miss a lot of little things like putting out the cat
For there's no back door on the fourteenth floor of a Unit-Camus flat
Don't want to go to Kirkby, or Skelmersdale or Speke
Don't want to go from all we know in Back Buchanan Street

We'll miss the fog horns on the river and we'll miss the ole' Pierhead
An' short cuts through the jiggers when we're rolling home to bed
Don't want to go to Kirkby, or Skelmersdale or Speke
Don't want to leave. We'll only grieve for Back Buchanan Street

We'll miss the pub around the corner, with the parlour painted red
Just like we miss the Green Goddesses and the Overhead

Don't want to go to Kirkby, or Skelmersdale or Speke
Just want to stay where we used to play in Back Buchanan Street

We'll miss the Mary Ellens, an' me Dad'll miss the Docks
An' Gran'll miss the washhouse, where she washed me Grandad's socks
Don't want to go to Kirkby … etc

They've closed down Paddy's Market, where me Ma once had a stall
And soon their picks and shovels, will be through our back yard wall
Don't want to go to Kirkby … etc

From Walton to the Dingle, you'll hear the same old cry
Stop messin' round with Liverpool at least until we die
Don't want to go to Kirkby, or Skelmersdale or Speke
Don't want to go from all we know in Back Buchanan Street

Speke, for example – where the new residents had hot running water and toilets inside – had later troubles, and by the 1980s some called it Beirut. In June 2017, Dorothy found a letter from Jessie with the address 73A Woolton Street,

Many of the small alleys: Bostock Street Court off Scotland Road, Liverpool, 1900

Woolton, Liverpool. Dorothy sent Christmas cards to Jessie in 1968 and 1988. The 1988 card came back 'deceased'. That part of Woolton Street is near the Halewood Range Rover and Land Rover Discovery car plant, originally opened by Ford in 1963 to build the Ford Anglia. Today it is difficult to imagine (Woolton is an affluent suburb) but Woolton had slum housing. Beer houses proliferated.

Woolton Street was in Prescot Registration District in the 1920s. It later moved into Liverpool South registration district and was in Liverpool Registration District by the 1980s. Prescot is now part of the Metropolitan

Borough of Knowsley. Many of the small alleys (courts/courtyards) in Prescot town centre, where people lived in small, unpretentious dwellings in appalling conditions, were demolished in the slum clearances of the 1930s when the large council estates at High Hill and Shaw Lane were built. Knowsley Council wrote in 2012: 'Prescot suffered from a certain amount of demolition in the 1960s and 1970s, which was usually associated with slum clearance or road widening schemes.'

Farm survey records

Every farm and holding of 5 acres and more was surveyed between 1941 and 1943 by the Agricultural Executive Committees in each county (County War Ags). Parish No. 53, Bootle, was surveyed between 1941 and 1943. Individual farm records in Parish No. 53, for example Hill Farm, Cross House, Langley, Kiskin, Stubb Place, Swallowhurst Hall, and Selker, can be accessed at The National Archives in Kew, west London, *MAF 32/170/53*. Broadwater was classified as Grade A under Management (including the condition of arable land and pasture). Water supply to the farmhouse, farm buildings and to the fields was by pipe. There was no electricity supply. A.E. Mansergh had fell rights and also occupied Baxter's Land, Waberthwaite (27 acres). By 1943, the Cumberland War Ag employed no fewer than 61 officers, supported by 114 clerks and typists and 4 mechanics, a part-time labour organiser, and a poultry instructress, according to *War Agriculture, and Food: Rural Europe from the 1930s to the 1950s. Snagging Turnips and Scaling Muck, the Women's Land Army in Westmorland*, said that the War Ag had a depot and offices in Oxenholme, and about fifty people worked from there.

Meanwhile, the Laura Ashley Belsfield Hotel at Windermere was used as a Women's Auxiliary Air Force (WAAF) training base. There are rumours that there may have once been a plaque to that effect. Mary Eleanor Lowthian (1920-2015) from Penrith joined the WAAF following the outbreak of the Second World War and served as a cook in the officers' mess, being stationed at places including Cheltenham, Stratford and Windermere. *Cumbria's Museum of Military Life* now has her WAAF uniform, her 1939-45 War Medal and documents including her RAF service and relief book, National Identity Card, and a notebook containing French phrases. Mary, who was a member of the WI branches in Addingham and Melmerby, died peacefully in a Penrith care home in 2015.

CHAPTER 17

Hiring Fairs

The textbooks will tell you that hiring fairs – a brutal and humiliating system – were supposed to have faded out after legislation in the 1880s to introduce compulsory schooling, and most will say they were finished by around 1930, so to be going as late as 1945 is interesting. Both male and female agricultural servants, as young as 12, would gather in order to bargain with prospective employers. In most cases, there was no money exchange until the end of the contract (often a six-month period). There was a Cockermouth Hiring Fair in May 1926. 'Farmers at Cockermouth hirings in their anxiety to secure female labour met women and girls alighting from trains and buses. First-class hands commanded £30, and experienced girls £17 to £22. Men were scarce, good horsemen nearby all having been re-engaged. First-class hands secured £39 to £45 and youths to £23,' the *Lancashire Evening Post* reported on 24 May 1926. Millom Hiring Fairs for farmers living within an easy distance of Millom were held in 1937 and 1938. At the Millom Hiring Fair on 16 November 1938, some of the farmers complained that men who would normally be returning to the farms for the winter months were putting down their names for work at the new tannery, nearing completion, at Haverigg.

The Cumberland Hirings at Carlisle were held on Saturday, 27 May 1939. The Whitsuntide hirings of farm labour were held at Appleby on the same day, covering a wide area of Westmorland. As anticipated, there was a great scarcity of men, and high prices were asked by those offering themselves for hire. At the Penrith hiring fair on Tuesday, 30 May 1939, farmers had great difficulty in securing men unless they were prepared to pay increased wages. Female servants had no difficulty in securing £30. 'There are more employers here than employees,' observed a farmer at the Martinmas hiring fair at Ulverston on 16 November 1939.

'Cabbages Wasting Away' read the headline in the *Liverpool Daily Post* on 11 November 1940. Mingling among hundreds of farm servants at Kendal on Saturday 9 November 1940 for the annual Martimas Hiring Fair were many city men and women, who were hoping to get farm work. The farm men and the prospective agricultural workers presented a strange contrast, the former in their rough Sunday suits, heavy boots, and the latter in patent leather shoes and bowler hats, while young women in smart slacks were among those seeking dairy work.

On Tuesday, 3 June 1941, the shortage of farm labour at Penrith Whitsuntide hiring was the acutest ever known, and minimum wages were greatly surpassed in cases where business was done. Many farmers with increased arable areas faced the coming harvest with concern, being much below the minimum staff required. Large numbers of farmers from outside districts were among those meeting trains and buses coming into Ulverston for the hiring fair on 5 June 1941.

The Ulverston Hiring Fair in May 1942 attracted three times as many farmers as servants. Well-known farmers were unable to find a girl or a woman who was available. Wages were tremendous, one local farmer remarked (*Lancashire Evening Post*, 28 May 1942).

There was scarcely any female labour available in Ulverston on Thursday, 1 June 1944. The supply of male labour was much less than the demand. At the hiring fair at Ulverston on Thursday, 16 November 1944, the demand well exceeded the supply. No girls were available at the Ulverston Hiring Fair on Thursday, 24 May 1945, but males were in greater supply than usual. The *Liverpool Daily Post* of 12 November 1945 reported: 'the Agricultural Wages Boards for agricultural workers' rights have made the old bargaining between employer and employed at the hiring fairs obsolete to a great extent, and the hiring fairs themselves have been shorn of most of their ancient glory.'

The Ulverston hiring fair at Whit in 1925. (North West Evening Mail)

CHAPTER 18

1942, Seeing it Through

January 1942, told to prepare to depart for Millom

In *World War Two, An Airman Remembers* by John Patterson, 2000, the airman writes about his introduction to England and the RAF. John joined the Royal Canadian Air Force after the outbreak of war. On 11 November 1941, aged 20, he began his train journey from Winnipeg to Toronto to start a new phase in his air force career. On 24 November, he boarded the train for Halifax (Nova Scotia) and on 9 December embarked on a troop ship called the *California*. It anchored in Greenock near Glasgow. After twenty-four hours on the train, he and other Canadian airmen arrived in Bournemouth on the south coast of England and that evening experienced their first city blackout. 'Christmas Eve found us in private billets,' he said. They were kept in Bournemouth until a training establishment could take them. Shortly after 3 January 1942, they were told to prepare to depart for Millom. Patterson writes:

> But it wasn't until 5 pm on January 5 (1942) after one train cancellation that we boarded a train that eventually would take us there. I say eventually because having to be routed through London, we did not arrive at Millom until 8.30 the following morning. On our journey we tried to have some WAAF members join us in our section but were not successful. They must have been forewarned against fraternizing with a virile group of Canadian airmen.
>
> Our introduction to life with the RAF was not exactly a bed of roses. We were quartered in Nissen huts, about twenty airmen to a hut with our cots lined up on each side with a small coal-fired heater in the centre for which we never had enough coal. There was not a warm location in the whole camp for us sergeants. We did not even have a canteen. The only time we really felt warm was when we had a bath.

The following was recorded in his notes:

> On being sent to a RAF training establishment, I had expected to find everything done efficiently and effectively. In this I was disappointed. Just as in Canada, we are often kept waiting, doing nothing. But that is not all;

planes are sent up unserviceable. One was not completely fuelled; another had a faulty engine and one landed with a flat tire. Sometime every night since we have been flying something seriously happens to one of our aircraft. A plane crashed in the Irish Sea near here. The crew is lost. Jamie's plane caught on fire last night. He managed to put it out but his map was burned. We fly tonight (January 11). Did not fly last night. Plane unserviceable. Observed my first German air raid. Saw anti-aircraft fire. Our A/C could not land but had to circle the aerodrome. Many A/C lost. All accounted for later. One crash landing.

He said that for the most part life at Millom was boring. Occasionally, a dance was held in camp where he could have an opportunity to dance with WAAFs and some of the local young ladies. He enjoyed the train rides to and from Barrow – which he later described as Barrie – because of the way some of the coaches were divided into separate sections so that they could be entered only from the outside of the train. 'Thus, as is normal for young people, we could be noisy without disturbing other passengers. Some coaches were first class. As sergeants we were expected to travel second class but when the coaches were overly crowded, we could occasionally occupy the more comfortable coaches,' he said.

Weather conditions made flying hazardous and, on 28 February 1942, an aircraft was reported missing.

All flying was scrubbed for days. There was nothing to do except hang around the sergeants' mess at Jurby or visit Ramsay, a small town nearby. On the sixth day, the weather cleared and in less than an hour Patterson was back on the Millom airfield. Life went on – more training, more visits to Barrow. With spring the weather improved, and they rented bikes, which were single speed, and toured the Lake District. On eight days' leave from 30 March, he visited a family in Scotland at Muirkirk who, though a relative in Canada, had invited him to spend his leave with them. Three days later, he received a phone call ordering him to return to Millom. He departed Millom on 6 April 1942 and Upper Heyford RAF station near Oxford was his new home for the following three months. Training went on much as it had in Millom. except that there was more of it. And the training was done in Wellington aircraft rather than the Ansons in which Patterson had done practically all his previous training, both in Canada and Millom. The Wellington, a two-engine bomber aircraft, was still being used on operations by a few squadrons. Life began for Patterson on a Bomber Command squadron after his eighteen months' training, and following a last evening in Windermere. His destination was Syerston, where he was to serve on 61 Squadron, 5 Group, Bomber Command.

Loss of all hands

HMS *Upholder*, a submarine built in Barrow (see page 255), was sunk on 14 April 1942, with the loss of all hands including Acting Leading Seaman John Edward Partleton (1908-1942), born in Wandsworth, husband of Edna Partleton of Barrow. He is listed on the main war memorial in Barrow and was buried at Chatham Naval Memorial, Kent.

Pigeons

It was not only vehicular methods of communicating that were utilised by the Home Guard. Pigeons were also a favourite, according to *Surrey Home Guard* by Paul Crook. Pigeon racing was suspended. Tommy the pigeon, bred by W. Brockbank of Barrow, received a PDSA Dickin Medal in February 1946 'for delivering a valuable message from Holland to Lancashire under difficult conditions, while serving with NPS in July 1942', according to the *Royal Pigeon Racing Association*. The PDSA (People's Dispensary for Sick Animals), the Dickin Medal is awarded to any animal displaying conspicuous gallantry and devotion to duty. Of the fifty-three Dickin Medals presented during the Second World War, thirty-two went to pigeons. On 8 January 1947, Pigeon NURP.43. CC.1418, bred by T. Markham of Kendal, was awarded a PDSA Dickin Medal 'for being the only pigeon to home from British Airborne Units and Paratrooops in Normandy operations in less than 24 hours in adverse weather after five days' detention in a small container'.

Air accidents, August 1942 to December 1942

Vickers Wellington Mk 1C T2715 of No. 25 OTY crashed on Dufton Fell near Appleby on 20 August 1942 while on a night cross-country exercise from Finningley. On 4 September 1942, the crew of *Wellington Mk 1C DV600* were tasked with a night cross-country flight. They departed RAF Finningley near Doncaster at 9pm. At 10.30pm, the aircraft flew into the wooded slopes on High Doat near Seatoller. Five crew died: Flight Sergeant William Bruce Sage of Canada, Flight Sergeant George Edward Derbyshire of Canada, Sergeant Jack Lionel Brovender of Canada, Flight Sergeant James Anderson of Canada, and Sergeant Henry Brown Burnett of Biggar, South Lanarkshire. Sage, Derbyshire and Anderson were buried at Silloth Cemetery.

On 1 October 1942, *Anson DJ410* crashed on Great Gable. Five crew died, including Pilot Frederick Orchard Cadham of Canada who was buried at Haverigg Churchyard. On 14 October 1942, *Beechcraft Model 18* crashed on the Old Man of Coniston, a mountain (2,634ft) that lies to the west of the village of Coniston. Three died. On 10 November 1942, *Spitfire AD554* crashed on Martindale between the lakes of Ullswater and Haweswater while on a training flight. Flying Officer Ryszard Josef Strozak (1916-1942) from Poland died and was buried at Silloth Cemetery. On 16 December 1942, *Wellington X3336* crashed on Ullock Pike, Skiddaw. Six men died. Flight Sergeant Reginald Victor Walker Bellew of Cheshire and Air Gunner Sergeant Richard Woffendale Lawton of Canada were buried at Silloth Cemetery.

Demand for tungsten

A tungsten shortage led the Ministry of Supply to reopen Carrock Fell Mine, Caldbeck Fells, for just over a year in 1942. Demand for tungsten increased rapidly with the development of alloy steels required for armaments manufacture. A detachment of sappers of the Royal Canadian Engineers Tunneling Company arrived at Carrock to undertake the work, under the management of employees from the Ministry of Supply. They drove a new crosscut into the vein and this has subsequently become known as the 'Canadian Crosscut'. In early 1943, most of the Canadians left Carrock Fell Mine to be assigned new duties in preparation for the D-Day landings. The workforce was supplemented with Spanish Pioneers and Italian prisoners-of-war.

On 2 November 1942, the merchant navy vessel the SS *Empire Leopard* was torpedoed and sunk in the Atlantic Ocean by *U-402* while attempting to bring supplies from North America to Britain, with the loss of thirty-eight of her forty-one crew. Most of the seamen on board the vessel were initially reported missing. Of those, four were from Whitehaven: Thomas Cradduck, William Truett, George Acton and William H. Acton. George and William were brothers. Mrs Evelyn Acton of George Street, Whitehaven, received a letter dated 19 May 1943 from the Ministry of War Transport to say her son George had been recorded as supposed drowned while on service with his ship. The names of George and William Acton are commemorated on the Second World War memorial inside the church tower of St Nicholas' Church, Lowther Street, Whitehaven.

The village of Anthorn, 13 miles west of Carlisle, was once home to a busy, thriving naval air station. The RN bagged the site in December 1942, building

Royal Navy Air Service (RNAS) *Anthorn*, eventually being commissioned in September 1944 and given the title HMS *Nuthatch*. Five test-firing butts were built, from Whitehaven bricks, around the perimeter of the site. In front of the butts stood a small hangar. Aircraft would harmonise their machine-guns by blasting into a bank of sand at the rear of the butts. The main aircraft types to pass through the unit were the *Grumman Hellcat* and *Fairey Firefly*.

Further research

Flight Sergeant Leslie Riddy Milner (1910-1942) of Kingston-upon-Thames, Surrey, was killed with Pilot Officer Richard J. Stevens when their plane crashed in flames near Blennerhasset, north-west Cumbria. But they avoided all people and buildings in the village as they crashed. On 30 June 1943, memorial photographs of the two men were unveiled at Blennerhasset School, presented by the parents of Stevens and Mollie Violet Milner, the widow of Milner. Milner is buried at Kingston-upon-Thames cemetery, where casualties from the First and Second World War were buried.

CHAPTER 19

1943, Turning the Corner

During the war, buses were overcrowded and there was an inadequate supply of parts for repairs. Ribble Motor Services printed the following in the *Penrith Observer* of 9 February 1943:

Whilst there is a rigid limit to the capacity of the bus services, there is no limit to the number of passengers who must be carried to and from their work on time. So we get overcrowding, disliked equally by us and you.

It is a wartime inconvenience which must be borne, but it can be lessened if only those who must travel do so. Think before you make a journey, and, if you can, travel when the workers do not need the buses.

In Scotby near Carlisle on 11 March 1943, a village dance was being held. When a bomb penetrated the hall roof, this resulted in a local farmer being killed. In the field on the opposite side of the Tyne Valley Line to All Saints Church, rubber tubes were laid out to represent railway lines to make the *Luftwaffe* think it was a major railway sidings of Carlisle. It is thought that the *Luftwaffe*, which was returning from a bombing raid on the munitions factory at Gretna, released their bomb-load on to the fake sidings in the hope of destroying them, and also to lighten their plane-load for the flight home. On the same night, a bomb also landed close to the war memorial in the churchyard. Although it did not explode, it did damage some of the church windows.

HMS *Beverley* was sunk by *U-188* on 11 April 1943. There were only four survivors out of a crew of 155. Engine Room Artificer 4th Class John Laing (1922-1943), son of Joseph and Esther Laing of Carlisle, and Leading Radio Mechanic Donald Muir (1923-1943), son of Stanley and Annie Muir of Workington, died.

From 6 April 1943, the accident rate at RAF Crosby rose to at least one *Beaufighter* crash per week. On 11 July 1943. *Beaufighter VIF X8036 'X'*, piloted by Sergeant M.M. Vinton, lost power and hit high tension cables in the ensuing forced landing at Harby Brown, an ancient residence, near Wigton. The navigator, Sergeant H.J. Shallow, was killed instantly in the crash. Sergeant Vinton died from burns in hospital twelve hours later. On 4 July 1943, *Bristol Beaufighter*

TF MkX JM223 of No. 9 (Coastal) Operational Training Unit dived into the ground on Croglin Fell to the east of Carlisle while on a training flight from RAF Crosby. Flying Officer (pilot) Herman Joe Carver and Flying Officer (navigator) Roderick Alfred Sedgley were killed. Carver and Flying Officer Sergeant James Bartholomew Spangler, Royal Canadian Air Force, were buried at Carlisle (Dalston Road) Cemetery, according to *The Foreign Burial of American War Dead* by Chris Dixon. On 15 November 1943, the two crew of *Beaufighter Mk VIC EL285* were on a night navigation training exercise from RAF Crosby. The aircraft flew into the grassy fell above Wolf Crag near Keswick, where it broke up killing both airmen. They were buried in Cheshire.

On Sunday, 23 May 1943, Sergeant Richard Jackson of Crofts Avenue, Penrith, a member of Penrith Company of the Cumberland Home Guard, was killed by the premature explosion of a bomb during Home Guard exercises at Watermillock, Ullswater. Some others in the vicinity were injured, including Lieutenant E. Hesketh of Fell Croft, Penrith, the battalion ammunition officer, and Captain Arthur Williams of Skirsgill Gardens, Penrith, the battalion bombing officer.

In the *West Cumberland News* of 10 July 1943, there is a piece about a German refugee of anti-Nazi tendencies being employed as an attendant at Workington Baths, having previously worked for the Forestry Commission. The decision was endorsed by the full council. Unfortunately his name is not recorded.

On 9 August 1943, the crew of *Anson Mk1 DJ275* were on a navigation exercise from Dumfries when they flew into the southern side of Scafell above Cam Spout, killing all on board: Pilot Stanislaw Kowalczyk, Sergeant Thomas William Pickering, Sergeant John Taylor Chadwick, Sergeant Robert Stanley Deason, and Sergeant Thomas Scorer Wheatley Lawson.

On 14 September 1943, the crew *of B-17E 41-9051* were on a cross-country navigation flight from Alconbury near Huntingdon to RAF Turnhouse on the edge of Edinburgh. While in cloud at 11.30am, the aircraft flew into the south-western side of Skiddaw. Five of the crew and one passenger died and were buried at Cambridge American Cemetery at Madingley near Cambridge.

A park bench with a metal plaque in the centre in Arrowthwaite Woods, Whitehaven is in memory of five Second World War airmen who died there on 14 October 1943 when their *Avro Anson*, on a training flight from RAF Millom, broke up in mid-air and crashed: Flying Officer Henry Joseph O'Gara, age 29, Glasgow; Sergeant Cyril Johnson, 33, Cheshire; Sergeant Vincent James Dunnigan, 26, USA; and Sergeant Rene Harold Murphy, 20, Canada. Frank Lewthwaite of Whitehaven remembered seeing the crash. He said:

There were bits and pieces of that aeroplane thrown all over Whitehaven. I would guess the crew knew something was about to happen, as when I looked up I saw a slightly open parachute tumbling to earth; someone had a go at bailing out.

A colour film dated *circa* 1943, which appears to have been made for training purposes, illustrates the work of the Home Guard in Kendal. Training activities included bayonet practice, night patrols, urban fighting and camouflaging a car. The transport used to enable rapid deployment in rural areas included cross-country motorcycling.

The Kendal Home Guard were subject to military discipline. The order pictured below, from a captain to one man, reads:

11th WESTMORLAND (KENDAL) BATTALION HOME GUARD.
You are posted to H. Company, 11th Westmorland (KENDAL) Battalion
Home Guard, and are hereby ordered to parade at Drill Hall, Kendal
at 09.30 hours on Feby 13th 1944, to receive Clothing & Equipment.

C Company, 9th Westmorland Battalion, relaxing off duty. From the Margaret and Percy Duff collection. (Cumbria Archive Centre, Kendal, collection WDMPD)

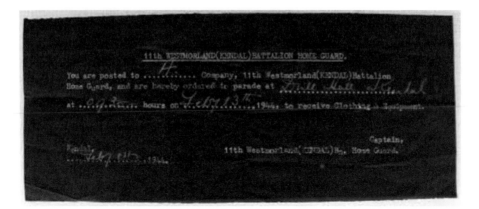

The Kendal Home Guard were subject to military discipline. From the Margaret and Percy Duff collection. (Cumbria Archive Centre, Kendal)

In Workington in 1943, numerous women auxiliaries enrolled with the Workington Home Guard battalion. Uniforms for women were difficult to obtain and so they were issued with Home Guard badges. They were largely employed on administrative duties and answering telephones on tactical exercises. Many proved to be crack .22 rifle shots and were trained as first-aiders, signallers and drivers. A company of army cadets was also attached to the battalion, consisting of three platoons: 1. attached to Workington Town Boys' Club; 2. attached to the Roman Catholic Boys' Club; and 3. a town platoon.

CHAPTER 20

1944, Outline of Key Events

In 1944, the threat of invasion had receded. The threat of air attack, however, remained as strong as ever. An instruction was received to the effect that all Home Guard in Workington were to actively assist the Civil Defence Service in the event of an air attack. In addition to the Home Guard, Workington was patrolled at night by air raid wardens.

On 18 January 1944, an explosion occurred at Royal Naval Armaments Depot (RNAD), Broughton Moor, north-west of Cockermouth, an armament depot

Workington's 'Marsh and Quay' ARP wardens. Back row: Mick Allister, Hughie Wilson, Mr McCoubrey, Kenny Halsall, Danny Thompson, Alf Davidson, Charlie Dadd, Buller Hall, unknown.

Middle row: Jack Gilchrist, Mrs Burrows, Kate Wise, Laura Vershur, Mr Murray, Mrs Ward, Mrs Riley, Lottie Thompson, Jackie Fry, unknown.

Front row: George Workman, Ronnie Pilate. Billy Cowman, unknown. (With kind permission from Keith Wallace)

dedicated to supply the needs of the RN. It appears to have occurred in one of the traverse laboratories and it resulted in the death of eleven people and left seventy injured. The depot was opened in 1939 on the site of Buckhill Colliery and, in 1944, was expanded from 800 to 1,050 acres. The depot continued to be used by the Ministry of Defence until 1963, at which point it was leased to the Federal Republic of Germany. The site closed in December 1992. The following lost their lives on 18 January 1944: Mary Katherine Barnes, Gertrude Fee (1919-1944), Jean Lister, Edward Lynch (1891-1944), William Morrison (1888-1944), Elizabeth Moses (1897-1944), Henry Rooke (1894-1944), Patricia Scutts (1915-1944), Mary Smith, Robert Swanston (1900-1944), and Ann Straughton Wilson (1913-1944). No remains have been found of Henry Rooke, who had been in charge of the room where the explosion occurred. Two of those killed were from Broughton Moor and are on the Broughton Moor war memorial.

On 24 January 1944, *Halifax Mk II JP182* flew into Eel Crag, which overlooks the valleys of Rannerdale and Coledale in the north-western part of the Lake District, just below its summit. The accident was quickly reported to the local police, who notified the RAF. The mountain rescue team from Millom set out but returned to base after being told by the police there were no survivors. Both crewmen died: Flight Captain Bernard Short (1911-1944) of Hull and Senior Flight Engineer Arthur Bird (1921-1944) of Canada.

In the early hours of 12 April 1944, *Halifax BB310* of 1674 Heavy Conversion Unit crashed on Great Dun Fell with the loss of all crewmen: Flight Officer Paul

A memorial plaque was placed at the Great Dun crash-site on 1 May 1994. (Alan Clark)

Bevan Stevens of Ohio, pilot; Flight Officer Sydney Brookes (1912-1944) of Halstead, Essex, second pilot; Flight Sergeant William Johnson of Gateshead; Flight Sergeant Frank Pess (1915-1944) of Canada; Flight Sergeant Harold Seabrook (1924-1944) of Canada; Sergeant Robert Littlefield (1923-1944) of Southampton; Sergeant William John Morrison (1923-1944) of Belfast; Sergeant Hugh Dunningham (1922-1944) of Hampstead; and Sergeant Dean Walter Swedberg (1923-1944) of Canada. The newly trained crew would have probably gone on to fly Liberators, patrolling the English Channel and looking for U-boats preparatory to the invasion of France, according to *aircrashsites.co.uk*. On 6 June 1944, British, American and Canadian troops landed on the beaches of Normandy, France. It marked the turning point in the Second World War when the Allied forces began to win their fight against the Axis powers.

HMS *Spartan*, a Dido-class cruiser built in Barrow for the RN, was launched in August 1942, and sunk on 29 January 1944 by a radio-controlled Henschel Hs 293 from a German aircraft off Anzio, western Italy. At the time of this attack,

The crew who died included Paul Stevens, pilot, who is buried at Blacon Cemetery, Chester, and Sydney Brookes, second pilot. (With thanks to Benson Parry, who took this photo of the crash site in 2014)

Spartan was anchored. Five officers and forty-one enlisted men were posted killed or missing presumed killed, including Ordinary Seaman George Lowry, son of Frederick and Dora Lowry of Currock, Carlisle. Forty-two enlisted men were wounded.

The following letter is dated May 1944 from Clementine Churchill, the wife of Winston Churchill, to Woodend WI, near Egremont:

May 1944, 10 Downing Street, Whitehall. I feel I must let you know the marvellous result which you are helping to achieve by your generous gift to my Red Cross 'Aid to Russia' Fund. During the past few months we have been able to keep up the flow of supplies that are to urgently needed for Russia; but this means that ever increasing demands made upon the resources of the fund. I thank you from my heart for your kindness and your help. Yours sincerely, Clementine S Churchill.

Salute the Soldier Week took place from 2 to 10 June 1944. The *Lancashire Evening Post* of 2 May 1944 reported that Barrow anticipated that its Salute the

Cartmel Gatehouse, Market Cross and Fish Slabs. (George Kitching, lakelandwalkingtales. co.uk)

Cartoon drawn by Lieutenant-Colonel Morton of the Westmorland Home Guard depicting him (the taller of the two) taking the salute at Windermere Salute the Soldier Week in June 1944. (With thanks to Cumbria Archive Centre, Kendal)

Soldier Week target of £400,000 would be reached. The target for Ulverston Rural Salute Week was £200,000. Cartmel opened its Salute on Saturday, 10 June 1944 with a parade around the village, Major Hibbert DSO took the salute at the Market Cross. In Cartmel Park, sports were held. The people of Cumbria showed their appreciation as soldiers marched through Windermere. The woman soldier on duty, marshalling the crowd, was serving in the Auxiliary Territorial Service

(ATS), the women's branch of the British Army. Their purpose was to do jobs in the army to replace men so they could go and fight. Penrith Local Savings Committee was awarded a plaque for success in Salute the Soldier Week. The plaque is in Penrith Museum.

The wording on the Salute the Soldier Week plaque at the Beacon Museum, Whitehaven, reads as follows:

FOR FREEDOM
War Savings Campaign 1944
Presented by the War Office
in recognition of
successful achievement in
SALUTE THE SOLDIER WEEK

A commemorative Salute the Soldier plaque at the Beacon Museum, Whitehaven. (With thanks to the Beacon Museum)

A Wellington bomber (*HZ715*) crashed into the near summit of Red Pike, near Buttermere, on 16 June 1944. Every bit of wreckage had to be carried down the mountainside from an altitude of more than 2,000 feet. Very little remains at the location today, just a few molten scraps. The crew were flying on a cross-country training exercise when they crashed into the hillside in cloud at around 1.30pm. The whole eight-man crew was killed. They were members of the RCAF and, as such, died a very long way from home. On 22 October 1944, *Handley Page Halifax LL505*, flying out of RAF Topcliffe, crashed into the summit of Great Carrs, above Wrynose Pass in the southern part of the Lake District. The crew, who were on a night navigation exercise, were probably descending under a cloud layer to try and get a navigation fix, but we will never know for certain as all were killed on impact with the mountain. An engine from the aircraft can be seen at the Ruskin Museum, Coniston.

On 17 November 1944, the crew of *Anson Mk 1 MG464* flew into Grisedale Pike above Force Crag near Keswick. Three of the four airmen survived. Within two hours of the crash, the RAF Mountain Rescue Team (MRT) at RAF Millom had been notified of the incident and set out for Keswick. The MRT at Millom notified RAF Silloth, who despatched their medical team and station engineering officer. The three survivors were brought off the mountain and taken to Keswick Cottage Hospital, while the body of Leading Aircraftman Elwyn Morgan was taken to Silloth before being returned to his family for burial.

Further research

During the Second World War, the Coniston Railway became a vital link to the 'outside world', according to *The Coniston Railway, Cumbria Railways Association*, 1985. Shops depended on the line for supplies, it said. Bread came from the Co-op bakery in Barrow, unwrapped, in wooden slatted boxes. After the Second World War, there continued to be around nine trains a day on weekdays on the line. The line, which opened in 1859 and ran for 8½ miles, closed in 1962.

CHAPTER 21

Kept Until 1944 to Celebrate a Special Occasion

A champagne bottle and a message can be found in *Cumbria's Museum of Military Life* at Carlisle Castle. During the Battle of Britain in 1940, officers of the 6th Battalion, Border Regiment bought a bottle of champagne. It was kept until 1944 to celebrate a special occasion. The 6th Battalion, as part of its Beach Group, embarked for Normandy on 5 June 1944 on board HMS *Empire Arquebus* (F 170). The officers decided that this was the occasion to celebrate by opening the bottle. A feeling of exhilaration having passed through all those who had participated in emptying the bottle, it was decided to write a message on a piece of regimental writing paper, place it in the bottle, re-cork it, and throw it overboard.

Philip Warner's *The D Day Landings* is a collection of personal accounts (the full texts are at the Imperial War Museum). Most of the contributors when the book (published 2004) was researched were over 80 years of age. Captain J.W. Triggs, Border Regiment, landed at 9.30m on D-Day. He contributed to Warner's book:

Except for fools and liars, I believe that everyone is afraid when going into action. I certainly was, although it is pretty easy to conceal it when you are sharing the experience with a mass of other people. As our LCA (Landing Craft Assault) approached the beach at Le Hamel, it was clear that the beach had not been completely taken by any means and when our craft blew up on a mine a few yards out those of us who were lucky enough to be thrown into the sea felt that death or capture was to be our fate. The understatement of D-Day came from my Cumbria batman, Lewis, from Shap Fell, who, being small, was up to his shoulders in water. 'This is a rum go, sir,' he said.

We managed to get ashore without loss and took cover until the fighting soldiers cleared enough space for us to start our beach activities. Two incidents are, I think, worth quoting. Firstly, as darkness fell on 5th June, several Border officers, myself among them, drank a bottle of champagne and then, with great effort, got a piece of paper with our names on it into the bottle, and a polite request that the finder would send it to the Border Regiment Depot at Carlisle Castle.

Secondly, in the late afternoon of D-Day, I went into a nursing home and found the officers' mess table with unfinished breakfast, including two exceedingly ugly but ornate sauce bottles. I 'liberated' them and they survived the rest of the war. They are also in the Castle Museum.

The bottle was found washed up on the coastline of the Isle of Wight later in June 1944 by a former sergeant with the Royal Artillery, who carried out the instructions on the message. Due to wartime restrictions, the bottle was not returned to Carlisle until September 1944. The message read: *5th June 1944. If found, please put this paper in the post (with bottle) to The Castle, Carlisle, Cumberland, England. Signed: HJ Bartholomew, J Westoll, C Askew, B Oliver, T Heath, JW Triggs, T Graham (MO), RC Troughton, T Mackie.*The only one believed to have been killed was Lieutenant Basil Oliver of Wallasey, Cheshire. Oliver died on 17 August 1944 and was buried in Ranville War Cemetery, a Second World War cemetery in lower Normandy, France, containing predominantly British soldiers killed during the early stages of the Battle of Normandy. The village of Ranville was the first to be liberated by elements of the British 6th Airborne Division on the morning of 6 June 1944 (D-Day) when the nearby Pegasus Bridge was attacked and captured. The cemetery contains the grave of Lieutenant Herbert Denham Brotherbridge (1915-1944), born in Staffordshire – considered to be the first Allied death on D-Day. He was shot in the neck during a fierce gun battle. He never met his daughter Margaret, who was born two weeks after his death.

Captain H.J. Bartholomew, who landed in Normandy on 16 June 1944, was wounded near St Odenrode on 30 September 1944 and subsequently posted to the 8th Battalion The Royal Scots (From *Normandy to the Baltic*, Advocate, *Pickle Partners Publishing*, 2017).

James Westoll (1918-1999), known as Tim Westoll, whose father James Westoll was a shipowner, was an English barrister, country landowner, politician, ornithologist, and racehorse owner. Brought up on a sporting estate in Cumbria near the Solway Firth and educated at Eton and Cambridge, he joined the Border Regiment at the outbreak of the Second World War and was posted to the Kent coast. He was commissioned as a second lieutenant on 11 February 1940. His battalion was part of 15th Scottish Division, who took part in the D-Day landings and the liberation of Europe, taking him as far as the Baltic Sea. He was Mentioned in Despatches on 4 April 1946 and retired the service at the end of the war with the rank of acting major. He became chairman of Cumberland County Council in 1958. J.W. Triggs (1911) was born in Southwark. His parents may be John William Triggs, born in 1879, and Margaret Emma Triggs (née

Message in a bottle. (Cumbria's Museum of Military Life, September 2017)

Noble) (1877-1946), who was born in Carlisle, lived in Newington, London in 1901 and died in Birkenhead.

Raymond Clarence Troughton (1910-1980) of 88 Main Street, Haverigg, whose father was iron ore miner James Troughton (1882-1945), emigrated to the British Honduras in 1952. He did not last long there farming as, in 1954, he sailed to Brisbane, then living at Darwen, Lancashire, now a rancher. By 1957, he was at Grey Lynn, Auckland, New Zealand, and retired aged 47. He was buried in a columbarium at Waikumete Cemetery, Auckland. A columbarium is a series of wall-mounted burial slots.

Stuart Eastwood of Cumbria's Museum of Military Life said in 2017: *The champagne bottle highlights how soldiers cope with the enormities of a unique moment in history. The bottle will be part of our D-Day display which will tell the story of the brave soldiers who went into Northern France as part of Operation Overlord in 1944.*

The Allied invasion of Normandy on 6 June 1944 was the largest amphibious assault ever launched. More than 75,000 British, Canadian and other Commonwealth troops landed on the beaches alongside the US and the Free French, in an Allied invasion force of more than 130,000. Another 7,900 British troops were landed by air. Supporting the invasion were more than 7,000 ships and smaller vessels off the coast (including the famous HMS *Belfast*, which today can be explored in London) and 11,000 aircraft. In total, British and Commonwealth casualties (killed, wounded or missing) on D-Day numbered approximately 4,300. The invasion established a crucial second front in the liberation of Europe from Nazi occupation, ultimately leading to victory for Allied Forces in 1945. HMS *Belfast*, built at Harland & Wolff Shipyard, Belfast, is one of only three remaining vessels from the bombardment fleet that supported the Normandy landings on 6 June 1944. Names of those who served with HMS *Belfast* can be found on *forcesreunited.co.uk*.

CHAPTER 22

1945, The Last Year of the War

On 2 January 1945, *Avro Anson LT741* took-off from RAF Walney Island on an Air Gunnery training exercise. Flying in cloud, the aircraft crashed into Black Combe near Millom. All four crewmen were killed: Flight Sergeant Arthur James Wood of Scarborough, Warrant Officer Thomas William Johnson of Liverpool, Sergeant Kenneth David Jenkins of Whitchurch, Wales, and Sergeant James Leonard Turner of Ormiston, Scotland. The bodies of the airmen were returned to their families for burial. An engine was removed from the crash site after 1982 and was kept for many years at RAF Millom Museum.

Anson EF935 was, on 8 January 1945, on a night navigation exercise from RAF Wigtown in southern Scotland when it crashed on Corney Fell above the village of Bootle. After failing to return, a search was started for the aircraft. A *Warwick* from No 281 Squadron at RAF Great Orton was tasked with following its route around the Irish Sea. It was later diverted to the Cumbrian coast when the missing *Anson* was spotted by another aircraft. The crash site was first reached by a farmer who was lower down the hill when one of the searching aircraft made a number of low passes over him heading in the direction of the wrecked aircraft before circling and then repeating the manoeuvre. The injured airmen were rescued by a mountain rescue team from RAF Millom and then transferred to hospital. One man of the crew, Warrant Officer Harold Biffen (1922-1945), died as a result of this accident. He was buried at Blacon Cemetery, Chester. Three others sustained broken legs.

On 16 January 1945, the crew of *Grumman Avenger Mk6 XB446* were on a night training flight from RNAS Inskip on the Fylde between Preston and Blackpool. They flew into the rock face close to Great Gully above Wastwater, killing all three airmen: Lieutenant Bernard John Kennedy (1921-1945), Midshipman Gordon Fell (1926-1945), and Leading Airman Phillip Royston Mallorie (1925-1945). In 2013, scuba divers from Keighley found the engine block of the *Grumman Avenger* while diving in Wastwater.

Ruth Margaret Bennet was in the WRNS, the women's branch of the navy. She came from Plumbland, Cumbria, but spent much of the war at Liverpool, where her work involved receiving and decoding messages from ships at sea. In February 1945, she went on a mission to Russia, as part of the British delegation going to meet the Russian and American leaders at Yalta. She wrote in her diary:

Wednesday 14th. Got up early for breakfast & at 9 o'clock. Mr Eden spoke to us all & then Sue & I went on to A Deck & watched the P.M. & his party leave. Mr Churchill was very sweet & waved to us all, Mr Eden too acknowledged our cheers & stood & waved. Am so glad we had such a good view of them all & were so often so close to Mr Churchill.

Poor weather conditions over East Anglia forced six *Lancasters* to divert to RAF Crosby after a raid on the city of Gelsenkirchen, a centre of coal production and oil refining during the Nazi era, on 23 February 1945. The bombers were from 186 Squadron at Stradishall and 195 Squadron from Wratting Common, both in Suffolk. These were the last operational aircraft to arrive at RAF Crosby before the end of the Second World War.

Although the fighting in Europe officially ceased on 8 May 1945 (VE Day), Britain was still at war with Japan. The country was still to a great extent under war conditions. Even so, everyone felt a powerful sense of relief. Kathleen Salrein, long-time resident of Burton in Lonsdale, 5 miles south-east of Kirkby Lonsdale, was 20 years old on VE Day. She contributed towards a Cumbria Archive Service learning resource for secondary schools created in 2009.

Celebrations erupted and, despite rationing, people managed to find enough food for a celebration. In Underley Avenue, Kendal, a street party featured 2 gallons of ice cream while at Calgarth Camp, Windermere, volunteer hostesses provided a feast for Jewish orphans undergoing rehabilitation. The Cumbria Archive Centre and Local Studies Library, Whitehaven, has a Gosforth School headteacher's log-book. The head reports that there were two days off for victory celebrations, followed by victory sports, and tea on the day school reopened. But overall, it seems that plimsolls and attendance were more important.

Ian McDonald from Coventry sent a letter, published on 11 May 1995, to the *Whitehaven News* recalling his wartime days in Cumbria:

SIR – The advent of VE Day 1945 has prompted me to reflect on this day, 50 years ago, as to my whereabouts and, for what it is worth, send you my own personal memories of my association with Whitehaven.

At that time I was a Technical Assistant II with the BBC and was working at a small medium-wave broadcasting station situated in the local brickworks on the outskirts of the town. The engineer in charge was Mr Jenkins.

The station formed part of the 'H Group' network; they served the local area with the BBC Home Service and would be used in the event of enemy occupation of main cities to broadcast instructions in the local populations.

In addition they were to be used to confuse enemy aircraft using certain broadcasting stations for homing and navigational purposes: whether this worked or was used in this respect – I do not recall.

Soon after VE Day the 'H Group' stations were all closed down and the staff dispersed.

During my stay in Whitehaven I joined the Whitehaven Rambling Club where I made many friends. Most Sundays (shifts permitting) were spent walking in the beautiful Lakeland countryside situated so conveniently.

To mark the VE celebrations the Rambling Club organised a celebration event at The Golden Lion, Whitehaven on May 14, 1945. We all danced to records of Tommy Dorsey, Glenn Miller and Benny Goodman, to name but a few.

Happy VE anniversary to you all. Ian H. McDonald.

Private John McKnight, youngest son of Mr and Mrs J. McKnight of Low Newton, and formerly Millom, arrived home after being a prisoner-of-war since the Battle of Arnhem (September 1944), the *Lancaster Guardian* reported on 25 May 1945. He was with a paratroop battalion. 'He is so thankful for the parcels sent to him by the Red Cross (without which, he says, he could not have existed) that one of his first acts will be to make a donation to the Society. On Whit-Monday, at a garden fete at Castlehead, Grange-over-Sands, he met James Simpson, a Lindale-in-Cartmel man, who was in the same prison camp in Germany,' the paper said.

Martha Bates, in *Snagging Turnips and Scaling Muck, The Women's Land Army in Westmorland*, wrote:

At last came Victory in Europe in June [sic] 1945 and Victory in the Far East in July [sic]. A grand victory parade was held in Windermere. Then came the most wonderful experience of all the rejoicing. Audrey Hutchinson and another girl from Penrith were chosen to represent Cumberland and Westmorland in the Women's Land Army contingent in the Victory Celebrations held in London on the 8th June the following year. There was at least one Land Army Girl representing every county.

RAF Hornby Hall was officially closed on 2 July 1945. The accommodation huts served as a temporary German prisoner-of-war camp from 25 July, and the last aircraft, an *Anson*, left RAF Hornby Hall on 31 July. *Auster I LB286* had to land at RAF Great Orton owing to a lack of fuel on 11 August 1945, becoming the last military aircraft to do so.

Six soldiers drowned in Windermere, July

On 20 July 1945, six soldiers aged between 18 and 21 drowned while on a training exercise on Windermere. The *Westmorland Gazette* of 28 July 1945 reported: 'An officer and five men of the King's Royal Rifle Corps were drowned crossing the 300 yards of water between Cockshott Point and Belle Isle. There were nine men on board when a sudden squall caused waves to swamp the boat. Three men were saved but six, wearing full battle kit, were drowned.' Members of the armed forces killed on exercise are no less worthy than those killed in action, said Don Lowis of Windermere in June 2015. The incident happened when he was a young boy.

In August 1945, 300 young survivors of the European Holocaust of the Second World War were airlifted from Eastern Europe to RAF Crosby. They were taken onwards by coach to Calgarth Camp. This group of children – 40 girls and 260 boys – became known as The Windermere Boys. Many were then found a home among the Jewish community in Manchester. In January 2015, Kendal was chosen as one of seventy locations to mark the seventieth anniversary of the liberation of the Auschwitz-Birkenau concentration camp on 27 January 1945. Kendal, as the main town in South Lakeland, was presented with a special seventieth anniversary candle because of the area's role in helping young Holocaust survivors. At the end of the war, the former army camp of brick-built and Nissen-type huts in Lowther Park, Penrith, was converted to accommodate 600 refugees from Poland. They had their own school, church, community centre and football club. Many of the refugees later integrated into the local community. As a displaced Pole, Danuta Kenyon (b1930) came to Britain in 1948 and stayed in Polish camps in various parts of England. She worked in Rugby and married there, in 1956, the Polish man she had met at Lowther Park. He had persuaded her not to return with her married sister to Poland, and helped her get onto a nursing course in Carlisle. (Source: *In War & Peace, Collected Memories of Birmingham's Poles,* 2011.)

Greystoke Castle, 5 miles west of Penrith, which at the outbreak of the war had been taken over by the army for tank-driver training, was later used to house about 2,000 Polish people. In 1984, Stafford Vaughan Stepney Howard (1915-1991) lived at Greystoke Castle. He fought in the Second World War, in North Africa, Italy and Burma, where he was mentioned in despatches. He gained the rank of captain in the Coldstream Guards.

Atomic bombs were dropped on Hiroshima and Nagasaki on 6 and 9 August respectively. On 2 September 1945, having agreed in principle to unconditional surrender on 15 August 1945, Japan formally surrendered, ending the Second World War throughout the rest of the world. On 15 September 1945, virtually every RAF station throughout Britain celebrated the ending of hostilities with a

Battle of Britain air display. RAF Crosby opened up to the public for the first time and more than 2,200 visited the show.

On 19 December 1945, the last aircraft left RAF Brayton Park, a single *Wellington* and a pair of *Vultee Vengeance* target tugs. A memorial to the site is the naming of Wellington Farm located near to the A596. In early 1946, *Dakota III KG502* was returning to RAF Crosby after a cross-country flight when, while descending through cloud, the aircraft crashed into the 2,400ft summit of Cold Fell, east of Castle Carrock, on 3 February. All six onboard stood no chance of surviving the impact, which scattered the *Dakota* over a wide area. Several small parts of the aircraft remain on the mountain today. RAF Longtown's flying days came to a close on 1 April 1946. In May 1946, the gunnery school (Walney Airfield) was moved to RAF Valley on Anglesey. By the end of 1946, there were no aircraft at Walney.

On 15 August 1947, there was an explosion at William Pit, Whitehaven. It claimed the lives of 104 men – the second worst pit disaster in the history of West Cumberland mining. Amongst the help that was sent to assist in the rescue was a team of RAF search dogs from RAF Staverton, Gloucestershire. One of these dogs was Jet of Iada (1942-1949) – a black pedigree German Shepherd. He had already done much work with the Civil Defence in the London Blitz, for which he was awarded the Dickin Medal for animal bravery on 12 January 1945. For his rescue efforts at William Pit, he was awarded the RSPCA's Medallion of Valour. There is a memorial to him at Calderstones Park, Liverpool, near his grave.

Sad end for Millom factory

The rationing of clothes and shoes ended on March 1949 (*iwm.org.uk*). By 1950, K Shoes employed 1,948 employees and production reached 20,000 pairs a week. More than three-quarters of all the shoes made went to independent shoe shops at home and aboard. K Shoe Shops were formed in 1961.

In the 1970s, K Shoes was under increasing pressure from cheaper imported shoes and they merged with Clarks Shoes in 1981. The last K Shoes to be made in Kendal came off the production line on 2 May 2003. 'Any industry that had once given employment to 20 per cent of the people of Kendal was no more,' wrote Keith Pauling in *Discovering the Dales Way* (2010). Clarks once had fifteen plants across the UK, but by 2005 only one small factory remained: Millom, with thirty-seven employees. The last pair of UK-made Clarks shoes were produced at the Millom works (the Doodles factory in Devonshire Road) in August 2006. Production was relocated offshore.

Further research

There is one interesting thing to come out of a 2017 book by Nicholas Leach on the lifeboats of Workington, Whitehaven, Maryport and Seascale. That is that the port of Workington had a naval officer during the Second World War, and that ammunition was shipped out, and the entrance to it was mined. This comes to light through the accounts of several wartime services of the Maryport lifeboat but especially the service of 7 February 1941. Briefly, a ship, the *Scottish Co-operator of Leith*, struck a mine off the port of Workington, while loaded with ammunition, and was badly damaged. The lifeboat and a government examination vessel towed the ship into port for repairs.

CHAPTER 23

Prisoners-of-War of the Japanese

During the Second World War, the Japanese Armed Forces captured nearly 140,000 Allied military personnel (Australia, Canada, Great Britain, India, Netherlands, New Zealand and the US) in the South-east Asia and Pacific areas. These people were forced to engage in hard labour. The most notorious use of forced labour was in the construction of the Burma-Thailand 'Death Railway', a 258-mile track route, from 22 June 1942 to 17 October 1943 – the most famous part being the 'bridge over the River Kwai', immortalised in the 1957 David Lean film of the same name. (The railway had been surveyed in the 1900s by the British, but the route was considered too difficult to construct due to the terrain of deep valleys and high mountains.) More than 180,000 – possibly many more – South-east Asian civilian labourers and 60,000 Allied prisoners-of-war worked on the railway. Twelve thousand six hundred and twenty-one Allied prisoners-of-war died during the construction. The dead PoWs included 6,904 British personnel.

Sidney Green (1931-2006), born in Newbiggin near Temple Sowerby, joined the Royal Air Force Volunteer Reserve (RAFVR) as a pilot officer and, within weeks of being commissioned, was posted to Malaya, to be taken prisoner-of-war by the Japanese at the fall of Singapore in 1941. He was later taken by his captors to work on the Burma-Thailand railway line, though later transferred to work as a dock labourer at Fukuoka, Japan. The only reading material he had in all his time in Japanese hands was a cutting from the *Whitehaven News*, which he carried with him everywhere, and which actually survived the war with him, much frayed, faded and sweat-stained. Mr Green joined Harecroft Hall School, Gosforth, staff in the 1950s. He had one daughter with Ann Lorraine Fitzsimmons, and he died in 2006 in Bedlington, Northumberland.

Most of the casualties of the Burma-Thailand railway are buried or commemorated in the cemeteries at Thanbyuzayat, Burma (1,651 casualties served with UK forces), Kanchanaburi, Thailand (3,585 casualties served with UK forces), and Chungkai, Thailand (1,373 casualties served with UK forces).

The Thanbyuzayat CWGC casualty list includes:

- Lieutenant John Alfred Disraeli Beaven (1909-1943), Royal Artillery, son of Alfred Disraeli Park Beaven and Phyllis Beaven, and husband of Eunice Margaret Beaven of Bouth. Cambridge-educated Beaven, a senior mathematical master at Wakefield Grammar School, died at Songkurai No. 2 Camp, Burma-Thailand Railway. He is named on the Queen Elizabeth Grammar School War Memorial, Wakefield, and commemorated at Holy Trinity, Colton, which is the church for Bouth. The task at Songkurai was to construct a large-span timber bridge, high above and across the River Kwai.
- Private Samuel Robert Beck (1918-1943), Royal Norfolk Regiment, son of Samuel and Ellen Beck and husband of Margaret Beck of Netherton, Maryport, died on 30 October 1943 at Burma. Beck is not on any Maryport memorial, even the one inside Netherton All Souls.
- Gunner John Ronald Cole, who died on 9 September 1943, Royal Artillery, son of John William and Rose Cole of Foxfield, is named on the war memorial at Broughton-in-Furness.
- Craftsman Joseph Patrick McAleese (1920-1943), Royal Electrical and Mechanical Engineers, son of James and Annie McAleese of Barrow, died on 6 November 1943 in Burma. He is on Barrow Cenotaph, and the memorial inside St John the Evangelist Church, Barrow Island.
- Driver Frank Vipond (1917-1943), Royal Army Service Corps, son of Joseph and Annie Vipond of Ireby, died on 11 June 1943. He enlisted in Carlisle TA as a driver on 7 September 1939. Overseas service: BEF September 1939 to June 1940; Far East October 1941 to February 1942; Japanese prisoner-of-war from 15 February 1942. On 11 June 1943, he was reported 'Died of Cholera whilst Prisoner of War at Sonkrai, Thailand'. He is not on the Ireby memorial, nor any other memorial in the area. Sonkrai, also known as Songkurai, was located close to the Thai/Burma border. The prisoners were forced to work on the construction of the Burma-Thailand railway.

Flight Sergeant Robert Bewsher, who died in 1944, RAFVR, the eldest son of Robert and Hannah Mary Bewsher of Thornhill, Egremont, is remembered on Column 434 of the Singapore Memorial. Known locally as the Kraji War Memorial, it stands over Kranji War Cemetery and was unveiled in 1957 by Sir Robert Black, a former prisoner-of-war of the Japanese. It bears the names of more than 24,000 casualties of the Commonwealth land and air forces who have no known grave. Many of them died during construction of the Burma-Thailand

ERECTED TO THE LOVING MEMORY OF THE MEN OF
THIS PARISH WHO FELL IN
THE GREAT WAR

ALSO THE WORLD WAR 1939-1945
THOMAS E. BELCHER   RICHARD H. FAWCITT
WILLIAM BROWNLEE   ERNEST HADWIN
J. RONALD COLE   THOMAS PARKER
RICHMUND G. CROSS   GEOFFREY St B. RABBIDGE
THOMAS B. DYKES   THOMAS SMART

"LEST WE FORGET"

John Ronald Cole is listed on the Broughton-in-Furness memorial. (Ian Stuart Nicholson)

railway, or at sea while being transported into imprisonment elsewhere. There was a prisoner-of-war camp at Kranji, established after the fall of Singapore.

Bewsher, a Whitehaven Secondary School old boy who was employed by the Egremont Co-operative Society, had first become interested in the RAF through the Scawfell [sic] squadron of the Egremont Flight Air Traffic Control (joined in March 1941), then joined the RAF in September 1941. His name is also on the Thornhill & Beckermet St John War Memorials. Bewsher's friend Sergeant Eric Speirs, who also joined the Air Training Corps (ATC), a volunteer-military youth organisation, and later the RAF and worked for Egremont Co-operative Society, was reported missing, believed killed, and Lieutenant Joseph V. Heaton, son of Mrs J.S. Unthank, Skelghyll Wood, Ambleside, was reported missing in Burma (*Lancashire Evening Post*, 10 March 1944). Speirs was born in 1921. Heaton, Duke of Wellington's Regiment (West Riding), died on 16 February 1944 and is remembered on the Rangoon Memorial, Burma, and on the Ambleside War Memorial. The Rangoon Memorial bears the names of almost 27,000 men of the Commonwealth land forces who died during the campaigns in Burma and who have no known grave. The Egremont Co-operative Society describe the business as grocers, drapers, butchers, coal merchants and dealers in earthenware in their entry in the *Directory of West Cumberland 1901*. Thomas Elliott of Bankfoot,

Above: Thanbyuzayat War Cemetery. (Phyo WP, CC BY-SA 4.0)

Below: Kanchanaburi War Cemetery. (Rdsmith4, ShareAlike 2.5 Generic (CC BY-SA 2.5))

Nenthead, Alston, was a prisoner-of-war. Some time after the war had ended, his mother Isabella Elliott learned that he had died in a Japanese prisoner-of-war camp in Java, Indonesia (then Dutch East Indies) in 1944. Cumbria Archive Centre, Carlisle, has a letter (undated) that Isabella received from her son while he was a prisoner-of-war in Japanese hands. It reads: 'I am now in a Japanese prisoner of war camp in Java. My health is excellent. The Japanese treat us well, so don't worry about me and never feel uneasy. Thomas.'

The Japanese camps in Java:

- Makasura (Celebes)
- Tanjung Priok PoW camp, Tanjung Priok (Java)
- Koan School, Batavia (modern Jakarta) (Java)
- Glodok Gaol, Golodok, a suburb of Batavia (modern Jakarta) (Java)
- Bicycle Camp, Batavia (modern Jakarta) (Java)
- Bandung/Bandoeng (Java)
- Tjideng
- Usapa Besar (Timor)
- Ambarawa (Java)
- Bangkong (Java)
- Lampersari (Java)

(Source forces-war-records.co.uk)

Gordon Harrison (d2001) from Harriston, a colliery village serving the Brayton Domain mine (closed 1942), near Aspatria, went to Blennerhasset School in Wigton and worked on the London, Midland and Scottish Railway, formed in January 1923, when he was aged 14. In 1939, he was called-up to the RAF. He was captured in 1942 by Japanese forces and spent three years in Japanese prisoner-of-war camps – Hiroshima (Mukaishima, Japan) and Osaka (Japan) – before he was freed following the end of the war. (Source *The Cumberland News*, 14 February 2018). From November 1942 until September 1945, 100 British prisoners-of-war who had been brought to Japan on the *Dainichi Maru* 'hell ship' were imprisoned in Mukaishima and forced to work at the Hitachi Zosen shipyard, Japan. In early 1945, Corporal Albert Etherington (1916-1981), Royal Scots, of Lancaster was a prisoner-of-war in Osaka camp. The *Lancaster Guardian* of 5 October 1945 reported that he was 'at present safe and well in Allied hands in Manila'.

Japanese 'Hell Ships'

After invading many countries in the Far East, Japan found itself with a large amount of prisoners. Japan decided to use them as slave labour to help their war effort, the majority being transported by ship to new destinations. These ships were not built for transporting the large numbers involved and were without correct markings, leaving them open to attack by the Allies as legitimate targets, the Allies not knowing what the ships contained. These ships became known as

Hell Ships. *Wikipedia* lists 200 Japanese hell ships used during the Second World War (it includes some variants that are different names referring to the same ship).

The submarine USS *Grouper* torpedoed *Lisbon Maru* off Shanghai on the morning of 1 October 1942. She was carrying, in addition to Japanese Army personnel, almost 2,000 British prisoners-of-war captured after the fall of Hong Kong in December 1941. Only 748 returned to Britain alive.

One torpedo exploded against the stern, bringing the ship to a standstill. *Grouper* immediately came under attack from patrol boats and aircraft, and departed the scene. Some prisoners who were up on deck were hustled and pushed into the ship's three holds. The Japanese partially closed the hatches. The Japanese destroyer *Kure* arrived at the scene during the afternoon of 1 October, and Japanese troops were removed to safety. Lieutenant Hideo Wada of the Japanese Imperial Army said that his twenty-five guards could not control the 1,816 prisoners-of-war under such circumstances. At 9pm, Lieutenant Wada ordered the captain to have the hatches closed. Canvas tarpaulins were stretched over them. A man with a knife managed to cut the canvas and get a hatch open. In all, 1,750 prisoners made it off the ship and into the water. Some men who climbed up on to Japanese boats were shot. For around 338 prisoners, rescue came in the form of Chinese fishermen, who risked Japanese fire to sail out from the nearby islands and pick them up. Fishermen took them to Dongji Island, where they were cared for. The survivors spent only a day on Dongji before a Japanese ship landed and recaptured them. They were taken to Shanghai.

Lisbon Maru ship. (Public domain)

On 23 December 1942, the War Office announced that it had received from the Japanese Government a list of British prisoners-of-war from Hong Kong who were on board *Lisbon Maru* and whose fate following the sinking of the ship was known. The *Hull Daily Mail* reported on 31 December 1942 that Lance Corporal Donald Joseph Grant of the Royal Engineers, youngest son of Mr and Mrs P. William Grant, of Penrith, had died after being rescued from *Lisbon Maru*. Mr P.W. Grant, who had not seen his son for more than four years, assumed that he died of wounds. 'He was a powerful swimmer, and should have been able to reach land safely,' he said.

Twelve months after the *Lisbon Maru* was torpedoed, Hilda Knowles of Windermere received official notification by the War Office that her husband, Captain Roland Ernest Knowles MC (1897-1942), Royal Artillery, and headmaster of Windermere Grammar School, went down with the ship, the *Liverpool Daily Post* reported on 12 November 1943. He is remembered on the Sai Wan Memorial, Hong Kong, and the Windermere War Memorial. Some British who were aboard the *Lisbon Maru* went she was sunk were detained in a camp at Shanghai, the *Hull Daily Mail* reported on 12 March 1943.

Donald Joseph Grant is named on the Queen Elizabeth Grammar School memorial, Penrith. He is also on the civic memorial on the park gates, and on the St Andrew's church memorial. (Ian Stuart Nicholson)

A reunion of *Lisbon Maru* survivors was held on board HMS *Belfast* on 2 October 2007 to mark the 65th anniversary of the escape. Six of the former prisoners attended. Dennis Morley, born in 1919, of Stroud, Gloucestershire, who was a private in the Royal Scots at the time, may be the last survivor of the tragedy. Tony Banham, a Hong Kong-based historian who has written an account of the sinking, told *The Telegraph* in September 2012: 'One by one, the others I was in touch with have all gone quiet. There could still be others. I am in touch with other prisoners of war who are older than Dennis.' Dennis was still with us in June 2017, Mr Banham confirmed. In July 2018, Morley, aged 98, said he did not back the idea of raising the Lisbon Maru for film-making purposes. Speaking to Emily Unia on the Today programme on BBC Radio 4, he said: 'It's a war grave, and should be left where it lies.'

Driver Thomas McGlone (1910-1943), Royal Army Service Corps, of Carlisle was sent overseas from Changi, Singapore, on 25 April 1943 as part of 'G party' on the *Kyokko Maru*. The hell ship, crowded with 1,000 Dutch, 300 British and 200 Australian prisoners-of-war, arrived in Moji, Japan on 23 May 1943. He was sent to Tokyo 7B camp, renamed Tokyo 7D and then renamed Tokyo 13B, where he was put to work in the quarry, cemetery and open hearth furnaces of the Denki Kagaku Kogyo Company. McGlone, who was born in Cockermouth, died around 2 October 1943 at the site. He was re-buried in Yokohama War Cemetery, Japan. (With thanks to Matthew Vernon, McGlone's great nephew.) On 15 November 1943, Lieutenant Commander Henry Munson's USS *Crevalle* torpedoed and sunk *Kyokko Maru*. Two crewmen and eight soldiers were killed in action.

The *Harugika Maru*, which left port on 25 June 1944 with 730 prisoners, was sunk on 26 June 1944 by a torpedo fired from HMS *Truculent*, just south of Balawan. A hundred and seventy-seven were lost. Most of the survivors were able to survive by clinging on to debris and lifeboats for hours. They were picked up by a tanker and remained one month at Singapore, before being put to work at the railway. HMS *Truculent*, of the third group of the T class, was built in Barrow and launched on 12 September 1942. The *Yorkshire Post and Leeds Intelligencer* reported on Friday, 24 March 1950:

The submarine *Truculent* berthed at Sheerness yesterday afternoon 69 days after she had sunk in the Thames Estuary in a collision which cost the lives of 64 men.

USS *Growler*, USS *Sealion SS-315* and USS *Pampanito SS-383* began a joint attack on Japanese ships (two convoys) on 12 September 1944, including *Rakuyo Maru*, which carried 1,300 prisoners taken after the fall of Singapore. She was bound for the Japanese mainland and was sunk around 6pm. USS *Sealion SS-315* rescued fifty-four prisoners-of-war on 15 September who had been on board *Rakuyo Maru* went it was sunk. Four of them died during the subsequent journey to Saipan, in the Marinas. The 159 survivors included Gunner C.M. Lowden, 88th Field Regiment, of Cornwallis Street, Barrow.

Japanese steamer *Hofuku Maru* was sunk by American carrier aircraft, 80 miles north of Corregidor in the Philippines on 21 September 1944, while carrying 1,289 British and Dutch prisoners-of-war. One thousand and forty-seven died, including Private Albert Catterall (1916-1944), 5th Battalion, Bedfordshire and Hertfordshire Regiment, and Private John Catterall (1919-1944), 5th Battalion, Bedfordshire and Hertfordshire Regiment. A display at Millom Discovery Centre confirms that the brothers had worked on the bridge over the River Kwai. Their mother was Mrs A.A. Catterall of Haverigg and father William, who died in 1940. Albert had a twin brother George, and they had a sister, Isabella, born in 1914. Both Albert and John are named on Haverigg War Memorial.

Lance Corporal Robert Salmon, Leicestershire Regiment, son of Joseph Thomas Salmon and Sarah Salmon of Aspatria, died when *Hofuku Maru* was

A. Catterall and J. Catterall are listed on Haverigg Village War Memorial to the First World War and Second World War. (Ian Stuart Nicholson)

sunk. He is remembered at Sai Wan War Cemetery and is on the Aspatria War Memorial Recreation Ground metal tablet. Of the names listed on the entrance gates, the bottom two lines list the twenty-eight names of Aspatrians who lost their lives during the Second World War. He is also named on the St Kentigern's Parish Second World War Memorial, St Kentigern's Parish Church, Aspatria.

Junyo Maru, built in 1913 in Glasgow, sailed from Batavia in Java to Sumatra with 6,343 prisoners – 64 British. On 18 September 1944, HMS *Tradewind*, a submarine built at Chatham, intercepted the *Junyo Maru* and fired torpedoes at her, sinking the ship with a loss of 5,620 lives, making it the worst maritime disaster of the Second World War. Leading Aircraftman Stanley Kellet, husband of Edna Kellet (1911-1983) of Morecambe, just to the south of Cumbria, died. Leading Aircraftman Arthur Wright (1914-1944), RAFVR, son of John Edwin and Agnes Findley Wright of Carlisle, died. Six hundred and eighty survivors were rescued, only to be put to work in conditions similar to those of the Burma Railway. They were employed on the 220km of Sumatra railway line between Pekanbaru and Muaro until 1945.

War Memorial, Aspatria. (Ian Stuart Nicholson)

CHAPTER 24

We Will Not Go to War

In 2016, a memorial plaque to those who refused to fight in the First and Second World Wars was unveiled in the peace gardens in Hardwicke Circus, Carlisle. Mary Savage, clerk of the Carlisle Quakers, said finding non-violent ways to peace was just as important today as 100 years ago. About forty people, Quakers and others, attended the short dedication ceremony, which has held on International Conscientious Objector Day on 15 May 2016.

A conscientious objector memorial plaque in Carlisle paid for by Carlisle Quakers. (Ian Stuart Nicholson)

According to *newsandstar.co.uk*, there were about thirteen conscientious objectors (COs) in Carlisle during both world wars. According to the *Peace Pledge Union* (PPU), the oldest non-sectarian pacifist organisation in Britain, there were 16,000 COs in the First World War and 60,000 in the Second World War. Three thousand Second World War COs went to prison.

Speaking at the annual conference of the North-Western area Council of British Legion at Kendal on Saturday, 4 February 1939, Major Sir Jack Benn Brunel Cohen (1886-1965), national treasurer for the British Legion, established after the First World War from four organisations of ex-servicemen, said: 'German people and ex-soldiers are not anxious to fight England. The next war, if there is one, will be considerably more unpleasant than the last.' The conference, by a large majority, rejected a resolution that compulsory service should be instituted forthwith. Cohen, who served as an army welfare officer for the Auxiliary Territorial Service in the Second World War, worked devotedly for the betterment of disabled ex-servicemen after losing both his legs in the 1914-18 war.

Who decided on exemptions? In the Second World War and after, the responsible government department was the Ministry of Labour and National service, now the Department for Work and Pensions. Local tribunals, as they were called, covered much wider areas. The members were appointed by the minister, and the chair was always a county court judge (without robes). These tribunals dealt only with COs, with other issues being taken care of by entirely separate bodies. The *Newcastle Evening Chronicle* of 25 July 1939 reported: 'The authorities are having difficulty in constituting the Tribunals to examine COs in Newcastle and Carlisle.' The delay in forming the tribunals in Newcastle and Carlisle was due to the reluctance of well-known public men to become members.

The Methodist church teaches that war is contrary to the spirit, teaching and purpose of Jesus Christ (*methodist.org.uk*). A Kendal newsagent and tobacconist, a Methodist local preacher, appeared before a tribunal to consider applications received in Cumberland and Westmorland for registration as COs at Carlisle on 24 November 1939. He said he objected to any form of war service, and he was given exemption on condition he took up St John Ambulance, a first-aid charity, work. A water engineering student with South Westmorland Rural District Council, whose father was a CO in the previous war, told the tribunal that he would help a wounded soldier, but as a human being and not in a military capacity. 'If I did so,' he added, 'I should feel it necessary to lecture him on the error of his ways to such an extent that he would probably leave the ranks and I should find myself before the law.' He was registered as a CO on condition he continued his present work for a local authority.

A farmer of Gatebeck, Kendal, told the tribunal that he was a Methodist church member and a pacifist, as his father and his four brothers were in the last war. He was a member of the PPU and given conditional exemption. An agricultural worker of Wigton also appeared before the tribunal. He said he was 'just an ordinary Christian'. When he was asked if he would resist the Germans if they came over here and ill-treated his mother and others as they had brutally ill-treated Czechoslovaks and Poles, he said that he would allow them to be ill-treated. The chairman said the tribunal was not satisfied with the grounds of his application. His name would be removed from the register of COs without qualification.

A Carlisle surveyor told the Cumberland and Westmorland COs' tribunal at Carlisle on 24 November 1939 that he would rather be ruled by Hitler than have war. He said: 'I will be quite prepared for Hitler to come over here. It will be better to give up a few of our liberties than to be subject to the miseries of war.' He was registered as a CO on condition he undertook first-aid training. A forestry student of Windermere said he thought the Society of Friends (Quakers) was morally

President of the PPU, British composer Sir Michael Tippett (1905-1998), himself a CO during the Second World War, unveiled a memorial to COs in Tavistock Square, London, in 1994, a 450-million-year-old Cumbrian rock. (Vernon White)

wrong to recognise the existence of war by sending ambulance units to the front. A member of the tribunal said: 'In the Spanish War, foodstuffs were sent out from this country to save children from dying from hunger. Would you say that the people who sent out those ships were morally wrong to recognise the existence of war?' He was registered a CO on condition he remained in forestry work.

A Penrith man told the Cumberland and Westmorland COs' tribunal at Carlisle on 12 March 1940 that he joined the army five years before and did not like it. He deserted and was punished with a sentence of twenty-one days' imprisonment, later obtaining his discharge. The tribunal told him that dislike of the army was not a conscientious objection. His name was removed from the register.

A 21-year-old French polisher of Allison Street, Barrow, appeared at the first Lancaster COs' tribunal on 14 March 1940. He stated that he was a member of the Catholic Church, objected to taking part in warfare, either directly or indirectly, because it was against the teaching of God and the Catholic Church. He could not join the RAMC because he felt that in so doing he would be giving moral support to the war. He was registered as a CO without conditions.

A gardener from Arnside was sent for non-combatant duties. He was a Quaker of a family of many generations in the Society of Friends. (*Lancashire Evening Post*, 1 May 1940). A journalist of Hawkshead said to accept conscription would, to him, be moral suicide. He was registered for service on non-combatant duties, the *Lancashire Evening Post* reported on 14 June 1940.

The *Whitehaven News* of 9 May 1940 reported on a West Cumberland COs' tribunal. The men, both aged 24, were offered alternatives in Air Raid Precautions (ARP) or in the emergency medical services. A 28-year-old Workington assistant solicitor and managing clerk appeared before the CO tribunal at Carlisle on 31 July 1940 and was granted exemption. He said he objected to all forms of service under the Act, as well as being an absolute pacifist. Asked by Judge Peel what would be the effect on civilisation if the Germans invaded this country, he replied that the things for which England stands would never be defeated by war or by another country ruling it. A 27-year-old coke oven labourer of Hensingham handed the members of the tribunal a poem he had composed, which Judge Peel said showed no relevancy to the question of conscience. He said he was a Roman Catholic but left the church because of its attitude to the war.

An unsuccessful applicant before the Cumberland CO tribunal, a 33-year-old of Egremont, was charged at Whitehaven on Saturday, 5 October 1940 with being an army absentee. Evidence was given that he was called-up for duty with the Auxiliary Military Pioneer Corps (AMPC) on 12 September but failed to report. He told the police: 'I am going to be a conscientious objector.' He was remanded to await a military escort.

A 20-year-old arms worker living at Brougham, Penrith told the CO tribunal at Carlisle on 20 December 1940 that he could never have anything to do with the destruction of mankind. In a reply to the chairman, Judge Peel, he said he would not defend his parents if the Germans came to the house to kill them in cold blood. A member of the tribunal asked: 'You would just leave them to die, would you?' The reply was 'Yes, if it was God's will that they should die.' The case was adjourned. Conditional exemption was given to a 20-year-old metal machinist, setting up his own machine in Workington. The condition was that he remained in his present occupation. The applicant stated that he was acting superintendent of the Derwent Mission, Workington. A 20-year-old of Rowrah was removed without qualification from the register as he failed to satisfy the tribunal of his ground of objection. The applicant stated that he did not know much about the Old Testament, but he based his objection on the commandment 'Thou shalt not kill'. Non-combatant duties were ordered for a 30-year-old from Newlands, Keswick. He was a Quaker. A general routine clerk of Ambleside was registered without qualification. He said he was now a joiner in Windermere and had given up a remunerative job because of his convictions.

A 23-year-old of Cockermouth told the Cumberland COs' tribunal at Carlisle on 21 December 1940 that he was negotiating for a confidential post with the government. Judge Peel asked what was the nature of the work. The applicant said he was not in a position to say. He was told to write it down. On examining the written statement, Judge Peel said: 'I don't see anything secret in this.' Later it was stated that the work was with the Ministry of Information. The applicant had also been taking a course of study to qualify as a milk recorder. The tribunal decided to register him for non-combatant service, this to be either in agriculture or with the Ministry of Information.

The *West Cumberland Times* of 26 April 1941 reported on a number of West Cumberland appeals heard at the North of England Division Appellate Tribunal on 24 April 1941. The appeal of a 23-year-old iron-mine haulage hand of Cleator was allowed conditional upon his obtaining full-time land, hospital or ambulance work. He was asked by the chairman: 'Should you not do something to protect your country from invasion?' Appellant: 'Not brutally.' The chairman: 'You cannot deal with brutes except brutally, can you?' Appellant: 'Yes. By speaking to them and letting them see your point of view.' A 20-year-old quarry worker of Rowrah said it would be impossible for him to kill a man. The tribunal registered him as liable to be employed only in non-combatant duties. The tribunal dismissed the appeal of an unemployed 31-year-old of Cleator who said: 'The country doesn't help me, so I don't see why I should help the country.'

The International Voluntary Service for Peace (IVSP) was acknowledged in Spring 1939 by the Commons during a debate on an alternative form of national service for COs, such as reconstruction work. Four members of the IVSP at Holmwood, Hensingham, Whitehaven, objected to military service when they appeared on Monday, 8 December 1941 before the local tribunal for COs in Carlisle. One was ordered to take up non-combatant duties, while his twin brother was registered as a CO on condition he undertook civil defence service.

Donald Pleasance (1919-1995), an English actor, initially refused conscription, and spent six months as a CO in Cumbria working in lumbering for the war effort. He changed his stance in 1940 and volunteered with the RAF. On 31 August 1944, *Lancaster NE112*, in which he was a crew member, was shot down during an attack. He was captured and imprisoned in a German prisoner-of-war camp, Stalag Luft 1, where he produced and acted in plays. In 1945, he was returned to England. He played The Forger in *The Great Escape* film (1963).

By 1942, all male British subjects between 18 and 51 years old and all females 20 to 30 years old resident in Britain were liable to be called up, with some exemptions:

- British subjects from outside Britain and the Isle of Man who had lived in the country for less than two years
- Police, medical and prison officers
- Northern Ireland
- Students
- Persons employed by the government of any country of the British Empire except the UK
- Clergy of any denomination
- Those who were blind or had mental disorders
- Married women
- Women who had one or more children 14 years old or younger living with them.

Conscientious objector John William Skelly (1913-2002), born at Plumblands Lane, Whitehaven, started work when he was 14, firstly as a coal miner at Wellington Pit. He registered as a CO on religious grounds during the Second World War, even though he was already working in an exempted occupation, and worked as a fire watcher at Haig Pit, Kells. He had become a member of the Christian Brethren as a young boy, and remained so for the rest of his life. His younger brother George, who worked in farming, also registered as a CO. They appeared at Carlisle Tribunal and were allowed to be COs. George Skelly left

This mosaic memorial was unveiled on 15 August 1988. John Skelly took part in the service. It commemorates those who have died in Cumbrian mining accidents. (Courtesy of Joseph Ritson)

farming and joined the army as a non-combatant, firstly in the Pioneer Corps and then in the Medical Corps. Private George Skelly, RAMC, went on to parachute into Normandy on D-Day and was decorated with the Military Medal (MM) for gallantry (*Lancashire Evening Post*, 23 August 1944).

Ernest Bevin, Minister for Labour, introduced a scheme whereby young boys – 'Bevin boys' – were trained as miners instead of being sent to fight. They were conscripted between December 1943 and March 1948. Bill Pratt from Mirfield, West Yorkshire, interviewed by the *Yorkshire Post* in 2013, grew up on his father's farm near Appleby. He was a Bevin Boy in Durham from 1944 to 1947.

CHAPTER 25

Victoria Cross Winners

The Victoria Cross (VC) is the highest and most prestigious award for gallantry in the face of the enemy that can be awarded to British and Commonwealth forces. Of the 181 recipients for action in the Second World War, 85 were awarded posthumously.

Flying Officer Kenneth Campbell VC (1917-1941) was educated at Sedbergh School and gained a chemistry degree at Clare College, Cambridge. Campbell, born in Ayrshire, was posthumously awarded the VC for an attack on 6 April 1941 that damaged the German battlecruiser *Gneisenau*, moored in Brest, France. The attack had to be made with absolute precision. The *Gneisenau* was moored only 500 yards from a mole in Brest's inner harbour. For the attack to be effective, Campbell would have to time the release to drop the torpedo close to the side of the mole. That Campbell managed to launch his torpedo accurately is testament to his courage and determination. The ship was severely damaged below the waterline and was obliged to return to the dock from whence she had come only the day before. She was out of action for six months, lessening the threat to Allied shipping crossing the Atlantic. Generally, once a torpedo was dropped, an escape was made by low-level jinking at full throttle. Because of rising ground surrounding the harbour, Campbell was forced into a steep banking turn, revealing the Beaufort's full silhouette to the gunners. The aircraft met a withering wall of flak and crashed into the harbour. The Germans buried Campbell and his three crew mates, Sergeants J.P. Scott DFM RCAF (navigator), R.W. Hillman (wireless operator) and W.C. Mulliss (air gunner), with full military honours. His valour was only recognised when the French Resistance managed to pass along news of his brave deeds to England. A memorial stands to him in Sedbergh School.

George Ward Gunn VC (1912-1941), educated at Sedbergh School with his three brothers – collectively known as 'The Gunn Battery' – and at Mostyn House, Cheshire (closed 2010), was born at Calf Hall, Muggleswick, Durham, at the home of his grandparents, and grew up in Neston, Cheshire. His father George Gunn (d1946), born in Australia, worked for a while in Cairo where he met his future wife, who came from a distinguished Durham family. He was a senior GP at Neston, Cheshire from 1911 to 1945. After leaving school, Ward Gunn trained as an accountant in London and Liverpool, passing his final exams in 1938. At the outbreak of the Second World War, Ward Gunn joined the Royal Horse Artillery. He was part of the 7th Armoured Division (The Desert Rats) and was involved in the successful campaign from Egypt in 1940 and early 1941, winning the Military Cross at the Battle for Bardia (just inside Libya). On 21 November 1941, Ward Gunn was helping to defend the airfield at Sidi Rezegh, in the Libyan desert. After three of his guns and all but one of his men had been put out of action, he continued to fire accurately at a large number of enemy tanks, until he fell dead. For this act of conspicuous courage, Ward Gunn was awarded the VC. A memorial to Ward Gunn stands in Sedbergh School, where he did well at cricket and cross-country

Campbell was born in Saltcoats, Ayrshire. (Public domain)

running. His VC is displayed at the Royal Artillery Museum in Woolwich, and he is buried at Knightsbridge War Cemetery, Acroma, Libya. There is an oak board at Parish Church, Muggleswick, Derwentside, Durham in memory of George Gunn (senior) and of his sons, George Ward Gunn and Major Philip Maclean Gunn of Muggleswick, accidentally killed on 9 December 1944.

Frank Jefferson VC (1921-1982) was born in Ulverston. He was 22 years old, and a fusilier in the 2nd Battalion, Lancashire Fusiliers when the following deed took place. On 16 May 1944, during an attack on the Gustav Line, Monte Cassino, Italy, the leading company of Fusilier Jefferson's battalion had to dig-in without protection. The enemy counter-attacked, opening fire at short range, and Fusilier Jefferson on his own initiative seized a PIAT gun (the PIAT was a spigot mortar – a powerful spring inside held back a long steel spigot) and, running forward under a hail of bullets, fired on the leading tank. It burst into flames and its crew were killed. The fusilier then reloaded and went towards the second tank, which withdrew before he could get within range. By this time, British tanks had arrived and the enemy counter-attack was smashed. Jefferson later achieved the rank of lance corporal. He was buried at Overdale Crematorium, Bolton. His VC was stolen in January 1982 from his mother's home at Luton Street, Bolton, and has not been recovered. A list of VCs reported stolen can be found on *victoriacross.org.uk.*

William Basil Weston VC (1924-1945) of Ulverston, a Market Street tailor and outfitter, was a lieutenant in the Green Howards, British Army, attached

Above: *Frank Jefferson with his parents after receiving his medal.* (Lancashire Fusiliers)

Left: *Painting of Jefferson by Rushton, 1962, at The Fusilier Museum, Bury.* (It was a gift to the museum from Lieutenant KA Hill)

Right: *Depiction of Jefferson holding a PIAT gun at the Fusilier Museum, Bury, 2016.* (Chemical Engineer under ShareAlike 4.0 International (CC BY-SA 4.0))

Below: *Lieutenant William Basil Weston VC Window at St Mary of Furness Church, Ulverston.* (Ian Stuart Nicholson)

Above*: Weston's medals displayed at the Green Howards Museum, Richmond, North Yorkshire.* (Andrew Swan, *vconline.org.uk*)

Below*: Taukkyan War Cemetery.* (RegentsPark, under ShareAlike 3.0 Unported (CC BY-SA 3.0))

to 1st Battalion, West Yorkshire Regiment during the Second World War when the following deed took place. On 3 March 1945 during the attack on Meiktila, Burma, Weston was commanding a platoon which, together with the rest of the company, had to clear an area of the town of the enemy. In the face of fanatical opposition, he led his men superbly, encouraging them from one bunker position to the next. When he came to the last particularly well-defended bunker, he fell wounded in the entrance. Knowing that his men would not be able to capture the position without heavy casualties, he pulled the pin out of one of his grenades as he lay on the ground and deliberately blew himself up with the occupants of the bunker. He was buried at Taukkyan War Cemetery, Rangoon, Burma. His medal was placed on permanent loan at the Green Howards Museum at Richmond, North Yorkshire by his nephew Basil Weston of Ulverston.

CHAPTER 26

What's that Medal for?

CBE, OBE and MBE

Twice a year, honours including the CBE, OBE and MBE (Commander, Officer and Member of the Order of the British Empire) are bestowed upon individuals. William Hanlon (1896-1956) from Roper Street, Whitehaven, a member of the Manchester City Police War Reserve, was awarded the OBE for gallantry and devotion to duty during a raid on Manchester on 22 December 1940, aged 44. Bringing into effect his experience as a miner, Reservist Hanlon tunnelled for two-and-a-half hours through debris to rescue people trapped in a cellar and afterwards did continuous duty for forty hours, taking part in rescue work until he was exhausted.

Major General Desmond Alexander Bruce Clarke (1912-1986) CBE CB (Order of the Bath), who in 1984 lived in Caldbeck, was Mentioned in Despatches four times, awarded the Belgium Croix de Guerre, and appointed an OBE and a Chevalier of the Order of the Crown of Belgium. He served throughout the Western Desert Campaign both on regimental duty and on the staff and was briefly captured at the Fall of Tobruk in June 1942. He then served in India, briefly taking part in the Burma campaign, before returning to England early in 1943 and joining the planning staff for the Normandy landings. In August 1943, as a young lieutenant colonel, he was appointed adjutant and quartermaster general of the 59th (Staffordshire) Division and later, in the same role, with the 43rd (Wessex) Division. He fought with these divisions from Normandy to the Baltic and the surrender of Germany in May 1945. In 1961, he was appointed CBE and, in 1965, CB (Order of the Bath). His portrait by Hay Wrightson Ltd in the 1960s, was transferred from the Imperial War Museum to the National Portrait Gallery in 1993.

Commander Hugh William Falcon Steward OBE (b1907), who in 1984 lived at Newton Manor, Gosforth, was educated in 1921, aged 13 years 6 months, at Royal Naval Colleges Osborne, Isle of Wight and Dartmouth, Devon and retired in 1957. He was an anti-submarine specialist. He was awarded an OBE (Military Division) in 1957. From 1959, he was president of Whitehaven Unit Sea Cadet Corps.

According to *Wikipedia*, the award was made on 4 June 1957 as part of the queen's birthday honours. According to *U-boat.net*, that was also the day he retired after thirty years' service. Given that the award was in the military division, rather than the civil division, it probably would have been for his thirty years of illustrious service to the Royal Navy.

Documents YDX 659/1 & 2 at Whitehaven Archives are his own hugely detailed log books during his training as a midshipman – a rank of officer in the Royal Navy, above naval cadet and below sub-lieutenant – from 1924 to 1927. These were standard documents for any midshipman in training. As well as giving details of the minutiae of life on board ship, they detail the movements of the whole Mediterranean fleet and give huge detail of the plans of each of his ships, and detailed plans of each cruise.

Awards

- 1939-1945 Star, a military campaign medal, instituted by the UK on 8 July 1943 for award to subjects of the British Commonwealth for service in the Second World War.
- Western Approaches Star Medal
- North Africa Star Medal
- Defence Medal, a campaign medal instituted by the UK in May 1945, to be awarded to subjects of the British Commonwealth for both non-operational military and certain types of civilian war service during the Second World War.
- Mentioned in Despatches for action against a U-boat, 1942
- OBE, 1957

Career

- 15 June 1921, Royal Naval College Osborne
- 15 August 1921, Royal Naval College Dartmouth
- 6 September 1924, HMS *Malaya*, promoted to Midshipman on 13 September. Remained on HMS *Malaya* to September 1927. *Malaya* became an accommodation ship for a torpedo school at the end of 1944.
- 29 September 1927, Royal Naval College Greenwich
- 30 August 1927, *Brydal* then HMS *Vernon*
- 19 September 1928, HMS *Excellent*
- 8 October 1928, HMS *Victory*
- 8 November 1928, promoted Lieutenant

- 31 March 1930, HMS *Osprey*. HMS *Osprey*, Portland was an anti-submarine training establishment established at the Isle of Portland, Dorset between 1924 and 1941.
- 12 April 1930, HMS *Vidette*. *Vidette* took part in the destruction of *U-413* in August 1944. *U-413* sunk *Warwick Castle*, the British troop warship, on 14 November 1942 (96 died and 366 survived), *Wanstead* on 21 April 1943 (two died and forty-eight survived), HMS *Warwick* (sixty-seven died and ninety-three survived) on 21 April 1944, and *Saint Enogat* (four died and thirty-seven survived) on 19 August 1944.
- 31 December 1931, Royal Naval College Greenwich
- 24 March 1932, *Osprey*
- 3 October 1932, HMS *Thruster* at Portsmouth, an R-class destroyer broken up in 1937
- 12 January 1933, *Osprey*
- 25 October 1934, HMS *Escapade*. The ship saw service before and during the Second World War.
- 30 April 1935, HMS *Echo* (H23). The ship saw service in the Atlantic, Arctic and Mediterranean theatres during the Second World War, before being transferred to the Royal Hellenic Navy in 1944.
- 15 August 1938, *Osprey*
- 21 August 1940, promoted to commander. He was commander of HMS *Venomous* from 3 July 1941 to 26 March 1942 and from April 1942 to 18 December 1942.
- 30 December 1942, HMS *Egret*. She was sunk by a guided missile on 27 August 1943 (198 died).
- 15 March 1945, HMS *Helmsdale*. *U-484* was sunk in the North Atlantic north-west of Ireland by depth charges from HMS *Portchester Castle* and HMS *Helmsdale*.
- 3 February 1946, HMS *President*. During the Second World War, *President* was converted to a gunnery training ship.
- 8 September 1947, HMS *Defiance*
- 16 March 1950, HMS *Drake*, Plymouth
- 11 September 1952, HMS *President*
- 30 August 1954, HMS *Drake*, Plymouth
- 4 June 1957, retired

Brigadier Paul Hopkinson MBE (1906-1991), whose father John Henry Hopkinson (d1957) eventually retired as Archdeacon of Westmorland, lived in Thurstonfield, Carlisle, in 1984. He commanded the only Indian Parachute Battalion (152) which, in March 1944, bore the brunt of the Japanese assault east from the River Chindwin. After the first eight days of action – during which nineteen of his thirty-one officers were killed and seven wounded, and the battalion was reduced to 40 per cent of its original strength – he himself was badly wounded leading a counter-attack. Undaunted, his lower leg and ankle in plaster, Hopkinson led what was left of his battalion across mountainous jungle territory, teeming with enemy units, to Imphal, India, where the battalion was re-formed at less than half strength. As soon as he could discharge himself from hospital, he returned to his command, briefed to harass the Japanese as they began to fall back. He received the MBE in 1945.

The 9th Battalion, the Border Regiment was formed in June 1940. By April 1942, it was officially recognised as an efficient Service Battalion and was one of the few newly formed wartime units to be selected for Service Overseas. The following month, it sailed for India on HMT *Orcades*, troop transport that was completed at Vickers in Barrow in 1937 and was known from 1937 to 1939 as RMS *Orcades*. Lieutenant Colonel John Petty (b1920) MBE MC, who lived at Wetheral, was awarded the MC when major of B Company 9th Border at Pyawbwe, Burma. HMT *Orcades* departed Cape Town on 9 October 1942. On the next day, she was sunk by *U-172*: 45 died and 1,022 survived. Fourth Engineer Officer Gilbert Foggin (b1907) of Barrow and Senior Assistant Engineer F. McKenna (b1908) of Barrow were on board. They survived.

During the Second World War, Ronald Irving Porter MBE (1912-2005), a native of Ulverston and educated at Ulverston Grammar School, was commissioned in the King's Own Royal Regiment (Lancaster), being seconded for service in the radio location and anti-aircraft gunnery, attached to AA Command. In 1943, he became personal scientific adviser to the General Officer Commanding in Chief of AA Command, Sir F.A. Pile, and remained so until the end of the war, holding the rank of major. In 1945, he was awarded the MBE (Military Division). He was headmaster of Penrith Queen Elizabeth Grammar School for twelve years from 1961. He lived at Margate Cross, Tirrill, a small village between Pooley Bridge and Eamont Bridge, and died at Penrith hospital aged 93.

Distinguished Flying Cross (DFC) and Distinguished Flying Medal (DFM)

The DFC was established in 1918 and is awarded to officers and warrant officers for 'an act or acts of valour and courage or devotion to duty performed whilst flying in active operations against the enemy'. During the Second World War, around 1,000 DFCs were awarded.

Above left: *Distinguished Flying Cross. Permission to re-use given by Crown Patent Officer* (Thomas Jenkins)

Above right: *Distinguished Flying Medal.* (Researcher1944, under ShareAlike 4.0 International (CC BY-SA 4.0))

Acting Flight Lieutenant Cecil Ford Bedell (1912-1944) completed a large number of sorties and won his DFC in January 1944. The *Liverpool Daily Post* of 6 June 1944 reported that he was born at Alderley Edge, Cheshire, and lived at Silecroft. It said: 'He took part in the Battle of Britain and in numerous attacks on vital targets. The success of these attacks has been due in no small way to the courage, calmness and devotion to duty displayed by this officer, and the methodical preparation he has invariably made both in the air and on the ground.' He died on 14 August 1944 at Brest, Finistere, Bretagne, France (Brest fell to the Allies on 19 August 1944), and is remembered on the War Memorial, Wilmslow, Cheshire. He is not on Silecroft War Memorial.

On 29 June 1944, the *Whitehaven News* reported the death of John Edward 'Jack' Blair DFC DFM (1912-1944), an Egremont airman. He was the son of John Edward Blair (d1948) and Elizabeth Blair (1880-1953), and married Selina Cook Braithwaite (1915-2005) in December 1937. His brother was George Woodburn Blair (1904-1986), who died in Entwistle, 6½ miles north of Bolton, Lancashire. According to the newspaper, he was originally from the village of Bigrigg, about 2 miles north of Egremont, had lived in Egremont and then the village of Thornhill, south of Egremont, and volunteered to serve with the RAF at the outbreak of war in 1939. The article stated that he was initially awarded the DFM as a sergeant and then the DFC as an officer. He was in the RAF Volunteer Reserve and was flying with 156 Squadron lost while on a mission to Duisburg, Germany on 22 May 1944.

His remains were buried in the Netherlands, in Molensgraaf Protestant Churchyard, along with another five airmen. (The grave dedicated to the airmen can be viewed on *edp24.co.uk*.) However, he does not appear on the Egremont war memorial. A framed photograph of him is displayed on the wall inside Egremont Royal British Legion. The DFM citation for the award is displayed below his photograph: 'Recommendation for the award of the distinguished flying medal to 984600 Sergeant JE Blair of No 103 Squadron.' The DFC citation for the award is also displayed below his photograph: 'Recommendation for the award of the distinguished flying cross to Flight Lieutenant JE Blair DFM of No 97 Squadron.' Ian Stuart Nicholson has added Blair to the Imperial War Museum's War Memorials Register (report 67603). He is now commemorated at national level.

The other members of the crew were Sergeant (pilot) Sidney Smith of Norwich, Flight Sergeant Raymond George Watts of Liverpool, Flight Sergeant Raymond Keating (1917-1944) of Monmouthshire, Sergeant John Thomas Eardley McCaffery of Plean, Scotland, and Flight Sergeant Evan Ephraim Roberts (1918-1944) of Barry, Wales. Flight Sergeant William Ward (d1993) was thrown clear of the aircraft, landed with the aid of his parachute and, although badly wounded, managed to survive. He became a prisoner-of-war in Stalag Luft 7 located in Bankau, Silesia, Germany. The camp was opened on 6 June 1944 for RAF NCO (non-commissioned officer) flying crews and, by July, held 230 prisoners. By 1 January 1945, it held 1,578 prisoners. Ward returned to Britain in April 1945.

Fighter pilot Michael Christopher Bindloss 'Bodd' Boddington (1914-1977) of Hawkshead, who married Lola Alan (1899-1978) in 1939, joined the RAFVR in December 1936 and was called up to the RAF on 1 September 1939. He was

Left: *Jack Blair.* (With thanks to David Fell)

Below: *Jack Blair is on the extreme left, with 103 Squadron.* (With thanks to David Fell)

Gravestone in memory of John Edward Blair (d1948), his wife Elizabeth (d1953) and his son John Edward Blair DFC DFM, at Egremont Cemetery.
(Ian Stuart Nicholson)

awarded the DFM and the DFC, and released from the RAF in February 1946 as a squadron leader. In operations against Sicily, he led his squadron with great skill contributing materially to the successes obtained. Within the first three days of the invasion of the island, Boddington shot down three and shared in the destruction of another enemy aircraft. 'This officer, who has displayed fine fighting qualities, has destroyed 12 hostile aircraft,' reported the *London Gazette* of 7 September 1943.

He is reputed to have become somewhat eccentric (*Aces High: A Further Tribute to the Most Notable Fighter Pilots in WWII*). In 1947, he lived at Ramsteads, Outgate, Ambleside, a caravan site. Planning permissions show that he built company offices from Nissen Huts at Ramsteads in 1947. These were demolished in 1972 and a house built on the site. The present chalets and caravan site must be subsequent to 1974 after Ulverston Rural District Council (RDC) was subsumed into South Lakeland. By 1948, he is described as an exporter when he goes on a business trip to Montreal and, by 1949, as a company director when he goes on another business trip to Montreal. The 1948 trip was with his wife Lola. Interestingly, in 1922, a Major Boddington had an ex-army hut converted into a bungalow at Outgate. This was his father, Humphrey West Boddington DSO JP, of the Border Regiment.

Michael Boddington emigrated to New Guinea in the 1970s. He returned to the UK, but died in Manchester in January 1977. Bindloss was his mother's maiden name. Her family had amassed a fortune from their business as Kendal clothiers. Brian Mansergh (d1529) and his son George (1490-1571) lived at Borwick Hall. George Mansergh (1596-1636), born at Borwick Hall, married Rebecca Redman (b1613) in 1623. Borwick Hall was inherited by his brother William Mansergh (1589-1640), and was sold to the Bindloss family - probably a son of Sir Christopher Bindloss (d1589) - in 1650 (house re-built). Borwick Hall was used by the military in the Second World War. However, there is nothing tangible there about its war use – no plaque, for example. Boddington's father died at Hawkshead on 27 April 1938 and his mother Alice Maud on 25 October 1949. His sister Zaida died at Hawkshead in 2001. Borwick Hall now belongs to Lancashire County Council and is a conference venue.

According to local legend, King Charles II fathered a child with Lady Dashwood at Borwick Hall. (Lancashire County Council.)

William Sholto Douglas (1893-1969) GCB MC DFC, a Sedbergh old boy, was a senior commander in the RAF. Douglas, who was born in Headington, Oxford, served as a flying instructor during the inter-war years before becoming director of staff duties and then assistant chief of the air staff at the Air Ministry. During the Second World War, he clashed with other senior commanders over strategy in the Battle of Britain. He argued that RAF fighters should be sent out to meet the German planes before they reached Britain. He went on to be air officer commander in chief of RAF Middle East Command. He became commander of the British Zone of Occupation in Germany after the war.

Acting Flight Lieutenant Austin Drinkall (1915-1944) DFC, born at Allithwaite, Grange-over-Sands and educated at Ulverston Grammar School and Skerry's College, Liverpool, enlisted for air-crew duties in 1941, trained in Canada and the US and, commissioned in 1943, died on 6 August 1944 when his Lancaster bomber was shot down trying to bomb V2 rocket sites in France. He was posthumously given the DFC and buried at Pontoise Communal Cemetery, France. Pontoise

Slate plaque at St Mary's Church, Allithwaite in memory of the men who fell in the First World War and the Second World War. (Ian Stuart Nicholson)

Above: World War Two burials, Pontoise Communal Cemetery, France. (With thanks to photographer Johan Pauwels)

Left: Austin Drinkall's grave. (With thanks to Fiona Rogers)

Communal Cemetery contains the graves of sixteen Commonwealth airmen of the Second World War – one of them unidentified – and one First World War burial.

Squadron Leader John 'Jake' Kennard DFC (1919-1943) was born in Ipswich, attended Ipswich School, and was stationed at RAF Millom. On 3 March 1941, he married Joan Reading, also stationed at RAF Millom, at St George's Church in Millom. They were married by the RAF chaplain. Her father was Cecil Charles Thomas Reading (1891-1955), an army officer. His own wedding was at St Saviour's Church, South Hampstead on 21 August 1919 when he was a lieutenant in the Machine Gun Corps. Joan may have been a British overseas army birth. In 1938, Joan arrived back from Burma on a ship with her mother, sister and brother, going to live at 19 Queens Crescent, Haverstock Hill, London.

John and Joan had one daughter, June Kennard (b1942). Cecil died on 1 January 1955 at 31 Copse Hill, Wimbledon, but his home was at Bognor Regis, Sussex.

Kennard, who was with 103 Squadron, was awarded the DFC on 6 October 1942. The *London Gazette* of 6 October 1942 reported:

One night in September, 1942, Flight Lieutenant Kennard was captain of an aircraft detailed to attack Bremen. When about 15 miles from the target the bomber was attacked by an enemy fighter, the fire from which stunned the rear gunner and caused the bomber's aileron controls to jam. Displaying commendable courage and flying skill, Flight Lieutenant Kennard eventually evaded his attacker and flew on to his target which he bombed and photographed. While in the target area his aircraft was hit by fire from the ground defences which caused damage to the port fuel tanks. A serious amount of petrol was lost but despite this and the difficulty of controlling the aircraft, due to the jammed aileron, Flight Lieutenant Kennard reached this country and made a safe landing. His courage and determination to complete his allotted task were worthy of the highest praise.

Kennard died on 27 September 1943, was buried in Hanover War Cemetery, Germany, and is remembered on the Ipswich School Chapel war memorial.

The *Barrow News* reported on 19 April 1941: 'Amongst those recently decorated by HM the King was Acting Flight-Lieutenant Thomas Smart who was awarded the DFC in January last.' Thomas Smart (1919-1943) was awarded the DFC for destroying a bomber at night. He was given command of 229 Squadron at Ta Kali, Malta, in November 1942 and led it until he was killed on 12 April 1943. His Spitfire EP716 was shot down. Smart bailed out too low for his parachute to fully deploy. He is commemorated on the memorial at Broughton-in-Furness and on the Malta Memorial.

John, Joan and baby June outside Buckingham Palace, 9 December 1942, after his DFC investiture. (David Fell, ipswichwarmemorial.co.uk)

Squadron Leader George Taylor of Brampton, who won the Air Force Cross (AFC) in September 1941, was awarded the DFC for his attack on oil refineries at Donges, western France (*WCT,* 25 October 1941). He descended to 200 feet to press home his attack, skillfully evading large fires. Two nights later, he dropped high explosives and incendiaries from a low level on the docks at Nantes. He joined the RAF when he was 16. He afterwards served nearly four years at Singapore.

Distinguished Service Cross

The Distinguished Service Cross (DSC) is a third-level military decoration awarded to officers, and (since 1993) other ranks, of the British Armed Forces, Royal Fleet Artillery and British Merchant Navy and formerly also to officers of other Commonwealth countries. It is granted in recognition of gallantry during active operations against the enemy at sea. Commander William Spooner Donald (1910-2002), the son of a mayor of Carlisle, Lieutenant Colonel W.N. Donald, was born in Keswick. He proved himself one of the most successful small ship commanders during the Norwegian campaign in 1940, and then served at sea continuously throughout the rest of the Second World War (*telegraph.co.uk*, 10 May 2002). For his services in Norway, Donald was awarded the DSC. He returned to live at Keswick, where he ran Castle Fisheries.

Paul Norman Wilson, Baron Wilson of High Wray OBE DSC KStJ (1908-1980), was a British engineer, Lord Lieutenant of Westmorland (1965-1974) and of Cumbria (1974-1980) and Governor of the BBC. He served in the Second World War with the Royal Naval Volunteer Reserve, most of that time being spent at sea in capital ships. He was awarded the DSC and retired as a temporary lieutenant commander, to return to Gilbert Gilkes & Gordon, water turbine manufacturers, of Kendal. He was awarded an OBE in 1959.

Distinguished Service Medal

Until 1993, the Distinguished Service Medal (DSM) was a military decoration awarded to personnel of the Royal Navy and members of the other services, and formerly also to personnel of other Commonwealth countries, up to and including the rank of chief petty officer, for bravery and resourcefulness on active service at sea. Leading Gunner T.M. Lee, of Maryport, who was educated at Cockermouth Secondary School, was awarded the DSM for distinguished service in North Norwegian waters.

Distinguished Service Order

Brigadier George Hyde Harrison DSO, colonel of the Border Regiment 1936-47, has a wooden communion rail in his memory at Carlisle Cathedral. After the war, he retired to Surrey.

Hyde Harrison Communion Rail. (Ian Stuart Nicholson)

Military Cross

The Military Cross (MC) is the third-level military decoration awarded to officers and (since 1983) other ranks of the British Armed Forces and used to be awarded to officers of other Commonwealth countries. The MC is granted in recognition of an act or acts of exemplary gallantry during active operations against the enemy on land to all members, of any rank in our armed forces.

Sir Alfred John Ainley MC (1906-1992), the son of the Reverend A. Ainley, former vicar of St Bees, was educated at St Bees and at Corpus Christi College, Oxford. During the Second World War, he served as a lieutenant in the Gold Coast Regiment, active in the African theatre, and was awarded the MC in 1941. After the war, he was appointed as a puisne judge in Uganda before spending a term as Chief Justice of the Eastern Region of Nigeria. He was knighted for his services in 1957. In 1959, he was appointed Chief Justice of the United Judiciary of Sarawak, North Borneo and Brunei, but then transferred back to Africa to be Chief Justice of Kenya. He retired in 1968 and moved to live with his wife Mona Sybil in Watermillock, a village on the western shore of Ullswater.

Drigg Officer Lieutenant W.M. McFarlen, serving with the Gordon Highlanders in the Middle East, was awarded the MC and promoted to the rank of captain, the *West Cumberland Times* reported on 6 February 1943.

Military Medal

Until 1993, the Military Medal (MM) was a military decoration awarded to personnel of the British Army and other services, and formerly also to personnel of other Commonwealth countries, below commissioned rank, for bravery in battle on land.

Private William 'Billy' Harker Lee (1920-1947), the son of Jacob and Margaret Lee of 16 Thwaiteville, Arrowthwaite, Whitehaven, was born at 2 Bridson's Court, Bardy Lane, Whitehaven, close to the West Strand of Whitehaven Harbour. He enlisted in the 5th Battalion the Border Regiment before the war while working as a miner at William Pit. After the withdrawal of the BEF to the Dunkirk area, at the beginning of June 1940, Lee was seriously wounded by enemy machine-gun fire. While he was in hospital, the Germans arrived at Dunkirk and Lee was taken to a prisoner-of-war camp at Tournai, Belgium. At the end of August 1940, he managed to escape from the camp, and made his way back to the UK via France, Spain and Gibraltar.

Lee told the *Whitehaven News* (12 December 1940):

During the fighting I was wounded in the back and stomach by shrapnel and had four machine-gun bullets in my legs. I was taken to the British Hospital and was there when the Germans came. When I was able to get about I was put into prison uniform and sent to a prison camp. The food was awful – cabbage soup, black bread, rice and potatoes – so I determined to escape at the first opportunity. I managed to pinch a key out of the guard room and made my way out of the camp with a lad from Birmingham.

We got some civilian clothes, money and food, and then set off for Switzerland. We made our way through Holland and Luxembourg but we were told we had no chance of getting through. We then made our way back to Belgium, swimming through canals as the bridges were guarded by 'Jerries', and crossed into France. Here civilians helped us and we set off for Spain, which we eventually reached though it was pretty tough going over the Pyrenees. In Spain we were arrested and put into gaol, but after 60 days our release was effected and we got on board a ship for England.

Altogether, it took us about five months to get home. Now I have to go back to hospital to have the remains of the bullets and shrapnel extracted – what will happen after that I don't know. I can tell you I am more than glad to be home again but I rather miss my pals.

Miner Billy Lee. (Joseph Ritson)

In 1941, he was awarded the MM. After being treated for his wounds, he returned to his pre-war occupation as a miner. At that time, mining was regarded as 'work of national importance'. In 1945, he married Julia Fleming of Cleator Moor. Her brother, Private Hugh Fleming, also of Cleator Moor, had served with Lee in the 5th Border Regiment in France but was killed in the German spring assault of 1940.

On 15 August 1947 at 5.40pm, Lee was one of the 104 men who died in a gas explosion underground at William Pit. In a quiet corner of Whitehaven Cemetery is a family headstone made of pink marble in memory of Margaret H. Lee (1894-1943), wife of Jacob, and their sons William Lee MM and Albert Lee. Lee was one of

Private Joseph Lister.
(Whitehaven News)

two Military Medallists to die at William Pit that afternoon. The other was John Henry Doran MM (1897-1947), who had gained his award in the First World War. Doran, of Low Harras Moor, Whitehaven, was married with eight children. A memorial service to remember the lives of the 104 men who died was held in August 2017 at the head of the former pit.

Private Joseph Lister, a native of Lowca near Whitehaven, who had worked in the lamp room at Harrington (Lowca) No. 10 Colliery, was one of the few people to receive the MM for an action that took place on British soil. One of the *Luftwaffe's* chief targets during the Battle of Britain was Manston Aerodrome, Kent. In September 1940, as the number one machine-gunner, Lister was helping to defend Manston against twelve Heinkel bombers. He returned fire and continued doing so despite being hit eight times by enemy machine-gun fire. These serious bullet wounds were to his face, left arm and left thigh, while another bullet exploded two rounds of his ammunition pouch. Subsequently, he was hit in the right leg below the knee – an even more serious wound that led to amputation of the lower part of his leg. Nevertheless, the defenders managed a successful defence of Manston aerodrome. Following a period in hospital, Lister, on 28 March 1941, returned to Lowca where the officers and men from the Lowca and Parton platoons of the Whitehaven Home Guard battalion turned out in tribute to one of their home-grown heroes. This was also the occasion when Lister was presented with the MM by Whitehaven Battalion Adjutant W.C. Sumner MM. Lister thanked everyone present and stated that what he had done was in the course of his duty. In 1941, Lister's parents were living at 24 West Croft Terrace, Lowca, while his wife and child were living near Dumfries.

Mentioned in Despatches

A member of the armed forces Mentioned in Despatches (MiD) is one whose name appears in an official report written by a superior officer and sent to the high command, in which his or her gallant or meritorious action in the face of the enemy is described. David Angus Donald (b1915), educated at Sedbergh, was wounded in 1945 and twice MiD. In 1984, Donald, who was headmaster of Cressbrook Prep School, Kirkby Lonsdale, from 1946 to 1976 and a Justice of the Peace from 1961, lived at Kirkby Lonsdale.

William Morgan Fletcher-Vane Inglewood (1909-1989) lived, in 1984, at Hutton-in-the-Forest, Penrith. Inglewood, who was the son of Lieutenant Colonel the Hon William Lyonel Vane (1859-1920), served in the Second World War in France and the Middle East as lieutenant colonel in the Durham Light Infantry, and was MiD. He was elected at the 1945 General Election as Member of Parliament (MP) for Westmorland. On 30 June 1964, he was ennobled as Baron Inglewood of Hutton-in-the-Forest.

Cyril Wilkinson Jackson (1915-2006), born in Carlisle and educated at Carlisle Grammar School, lived, in 1984, at Stanwix, a district of Carlisle. During the Second World War, he served with the RAF Volunteer Reserve, becoming a squadron leader, and was MiD for his distinguished services in administration in Africa. After the war, he returned to the Cumberland Building Society where he eventually succeeded John Middleton as general manager.

Brigadier John Durnival Kemp, 1st Viscount Rochdale OBE TD (Territorial Decoration) DL (1906-1993), served in the Second World War with US Forces in the Pacific and the British Army in India, where he was MiD, and achieved the rank of brigadier. He was deputy lieutenant of Cumbria from 1948 to 1983. In 1984, he lived at Lingholm. The TD was a military medal of the UK awarded for long service in the Territorial Force and its successor, the Territorial Army.

Signaller William McKendry, son of Gunner and Mrs George McKendry of Nelson Street, Maryport, was MiD for distinguished service in the field from March until the evacuation of Dunkirk, and his name appeared in the *London Gazette* on 20 December 1940. He had been in the army three years and prior to that was employed in the lead mines at Penruddock. Two of his brothers were also serving in the forces and his father, who was in the Artillery, served throughout the Great War.

Michael Weaver KC, prospective Conservative candidate for the Workington Parliamentary Division, served with the 1st King's Dragoon Guards and lost his life on 17 October 1941 during the desert campaign in the Middle East, and was buried in the Tobruk War Cemetery, Libya. In 1938, his engagement to the Honourable Jacqueline Vereker (1914-1962), only daughter of Field Marshall John Standish Surtees Prendergast Vereker, 6th Viscount Gort VC GCB CBE DSO & Two Bars MVO MC (1886-1946), was announced. But five weeks later, it was stated that the marriage would not take place. Weaver, an old Etonian who attended Trinity College Cambridge, had been MiD and was also a barrister by profession. Because of the war he never actually stood for election in the Workington constituency.

CHAPTER 27

Carlisle's War Memorials

The Carlisle City Centre Cenotaph, in the area of the Greenmarket in the city centre, commemorates the men who died in the Second World War and was dedicated and unveiled by the Bishop of Carlisle on 16 November 1990. The original Cenotaph, unveiled in 1922, is to be found in Rickerby Park, Carlisle.

In Carlisle Cathedral is a bronze plaque in memory of five old choristers who gave their lives in the Second World War. There is a sandstone tablet set into the floor in the south aisle to remember the Burma Campaign 1942-1945. There is also a simple tablet set into the floor, unveiled in 1997, to remember those who gave their lives in the Normandy Campaign 1944, and a wooden communion rail, now in use as a prayer desk, in memory of all ranks of the 9th Battalion the Border Regiment who died serving their country during the Second World War. It was presented by their friends and relations in 1988.

The Beaumont & Grinsdale Roll of Honour, previously at St Mary's Church, Beaumont, Carlisle, is at Carlisle Archive Centre, Petteril Bank Road, Carlisle. There are forty-five names on the Roll of Honour. Thirty-nine served and returned, and six died. Eight on the Roll of Honour have the surname Beattie. The Charlotte Street Congregational Church memorial is lost. However, the Roll of Honour, with forty-eight names, is at Carlisle Archive Centre. A Book of Remembrance in

The War Memorial of the City of Carlisle. (British Legion)

wooden lectern at St Aidan's Church, Warwick Road, Carlisle, records eleven names. The Carlisle Corporation Employees Second World War Roll of Honour is inside the Civic Centre, Carlisle (twenty-two names).

There are forty names on the Holy Trinity Church, Carlisle Second World War memorial, a bronze plaque. The Fisher Street Presbyterian Church Roll of Honour is at Carlisle Archive Centre (seventy-two names). A window at St Cuthbert's Church, Carlisle, is in memory of three worshippers who died in the Second World War. Three men who gave their lives in the Second World War are commemorated on a brass plaque memorial at St Peter's Church, Carlisle. There is a simple white marble tablet for the Second World War at Carlisle St John the Evangelist Church. The Carleton and District Second World War Roll of Honour is at St John the Baptist Church, Carlisle (sixty-eight names), and the Denton Holme Second World War memorial is at St James' Church, Carlisle.

A window at Lowther Street Congregational Church, Carlisle, is in memory of Sergeant (Air Bomber) Tom Lawrence Ormerod, RAF Volunteer Reserve, who gave his life while on active service on 29 July 1943. He was buried at Ohlsdorfer Friedhof Cemetery, Hamburg. Also at this church is a brass plaque in memory of three men who died in the Second World War: Gordon Fettes, Allan Little, and Tom Lawrence Ormerod. A brass cup dedicated to Flight Lieutenant James Alan Lamberton (1924-1944) used to be at St George's Church, Carlisle, but the current location is unknown. Lamberton, son of James and Jessie Miller Lamberton of Carlisle, went missing *en route* from le Bourget, Paris, to RAF Tempsford, Bedfordshire, with two RAF passengers. He was buried at Runnymede, Surrey.

At Creighton School, Carlisle, in 1949, a light oak memorial, with the school blue badge and ribbon with crosses and lettering decorated in the school colours at the top of the board, was unveiled at a ceremony. Eighty-one names are on the memorial, which is currently located at Trinity School, Strand Road, Carlisle. A Celtic cross with wheel surmounting tapered plinth and base, all in granite, can be found in the churchyard at St John the Baptist Church, Westlinton, in the City of Carlisle district. There are four First World War names and three Second World War names on the memorial.

Carlisle Grammar School

Captain Joseph Cornelius Tobin's son Squadron Leader James Richard Tobin (1915-1945) was killed on active service in March 1945 near Brough Airfield, East Yorkshire. He was by then living at Bedford (CWGC), but is commemorated on the Carlisle Grammar School memorial (eighty-eight names).

Carlisle Grammar School Second World War Memorial, Trinity School, Strand Road, Carlisle. Tobin's name is to the far right. (Ian Stuart Nicholson)

Irthington

Aircraftman 2nd Class George Barrow Hodgson, son of Thomas Andrew and Isabel Hodgson of Carlisle, died on 10 May 1940 and is commemorated on Irthington War Memorial, St Kentigern's churchyard, within the City of Carlisle district. He is actually buried at Irthington. There is an additional Second World War casualty buried in the churchyard but not listed on the war memorial, Basil Willoughby Vickers.

Dedication and Second World War names on Irthington War Memorial, St Kentigern's churchyard.
(Ian Stuart Nicholson)

CHAPTER 28

Memorials, a Selection A-L

Barrow

The Barrow Park Cenotaph is the main war memorial in the town. It was built in commemoration of the 616 Barrovian men who lost their lives in combat in the First World War. Since then, 274 more locals have been added (268 of these being fatalities of the Second World War). There is a stone of remembrance to the Barrow Blitz on Abbey Road parkland on the west side of the road between the Holker Street junction and the law courts. It is an irregular-shaped piece of local slate.

Boot

There is a wooden memorial bench in the churchyard at St Catherine's Church, Boot, to Captain Dudley Hows, church warden there for many years. While the bench commemorates his civilian life, not his army life (and therefore is not a war memorial), he fought in both the First and Second World Wars and was an author.

Bootle

The Bootle memorial, in the new churchyard across the road from St Michael's Church, lists eighteen men who lost their lives in the First World War and three in the Second World War, including Leading Aircraftman George McClellan of the RAF Volunteer Reserve, who died on 20 May 1943. McClellan, the son of Samuel Sydney and Margaret Jane McClellan of Carlisle but living in Bootle at the time of his death, was buried in Heliopolis War Cemetery, Cairo. When George was at school, the family lived at Nethertown Station House, Nethertown, near St Bees. His father was a railwayman, probably stationmaster.

Borrowdale

A memorial bridge in the Langstrath Valley, Borrowdale was erected in memory of Flying Officer John Derek Brearley Rigby (d1942), son of John Kay Rigby and Grace Annie Rigby of Dartmouth.

Bridekirk

There is a brass plaque with engraved laurel above eight names at St Bridget's Church, Bridekirk, Allerdale, unveiled in 1949 at a service attended by Neville Gilbert Barraclough (1882-1961) of Tallentire Hall, Cockermouth. Pilot Officer Thomas Lunson Hayston, only son of Mr and Mrs T.L. Hayston of The Schoolhouse, Dovenby, Cockermouth, lost his life in a flying accident during coastal command operations on 16 August 1941. Some months earlier, Hayston, in his Hudson, flew above the parish church and waved farewell to worshippers leaving a Sunday morning service. He was educated at Dovenby, where his father was headmaster, and Workington Secondary School.

Broughton-in-Furness

The memorial at Broughton-in-Furness is generally considered to include the Duddon Valley, where there are no memorials. However, there is at least one man missing: Driver Colin Sheldon Amos (1914-1940), Royal Army Service Corps. Amos, the only son of Sir Percy Maurice Maclardie Sheldon Amos (1872-1940) and Lucy Scott-Montcrieff (1881-1958) of

The memorial at St Mary Magdalene Churchyard, Broughton-in-Furness, bears ten names for the Second World War. (Author)

*St John's Church,
Ulpha.* (John Holmes,
under CC BY-SA 2.0)

Ulpha, died at Oxford on 4 August 1940. Amos, who was born in Cairo, was buried at St John's New Churchyard, Ulpha, and listed on the Cambridge Trinity College War Memorial. Sir Percy Maurice Maclardie Sheldon Amos died on 10 June 1940 in Ulverston.

Camerton

St Peter's Church, Camerton, on the bank of the River Derwent, has served the parish since around the eleventh century, but has been rebuilt at least twice, in 1694 and again in 1796. The churchyard gate is in memory of Stoker First Class James Lowden Kendall (1917-1941) of Camerton, who lost his life on HMS *Thracian*. She was bombed and damaged in Hong Kong by Japanese aircraft and was beached. *Thracian* had a near miss, killing a few. She was subsequently salvaged by the Japanese and entered service in 1942 at Patrol Boat No. 101. The battle for Hong Kong lasted from 8 December until 25 December 1941 when the British forces surrendered to the Japanese.

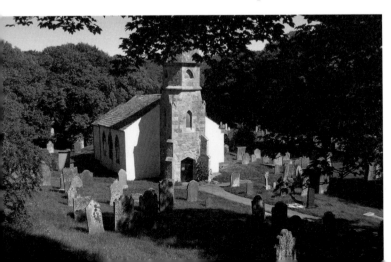

*St Peter's Church
Camerton.*
(PC Bloke 1971 at
English Wikipedia
(CC BY 3.0))

*Headstone of former
soldier James McAvoy.*
(Joseph Ritson)

Cleator

Two names were added to the Second World War roll of honour at St Mary's Church, Cleator in 2010: Ella Rossi Eldon (her correct name is Ella Esterina Eldon) and Michael Toman. There are now two women's names remembered. William Darby of Bowthorn Road, Cleator Moor is also listed. He was a civilian who was killed in an explosion at the Drigg Royal Ordnance Factory.

The photograph shows the headstone at St Mary's Churchyard of Second World War casualty James McAvoy, who died on 23 September 1942. However, he has never been counted as an official casualty of war. He is among the many 'missing' war casualties not officially recorded and rarely, if ever, considered as casualties of war.

Cleator Moor

Catherine Williamson (1923-1944), whose mother lived at Ehen Road, Cleator Moor, was a supply assistant for the WRNS. She was based at HMS *Ferret*, a shore establishment for the anti-submarine naval training base at Derry, Northern Ireland. On 3 January 1944, she was found unconscious beside a railway line near the River Foyle ferry. The inquest decided that she had been struck by a train during the blackout, on her way to the naval barracks to report for duty. She had only been in the WRNS for two months and had previously worked as a clerk at the Cleator Moor food office. She is on the Cleator Moor roll of honour.

In addition to being commemorated at Cleator Moor, Catherine Williamson is one of forty-five Old Boys and Girls remembered on the Whitehaven County Secondary School Second World War roll of honour. This tablet – which also lists the names of two other West Cumbrian women casualties of the Second World War – can now be found inside St James' Church, Whitehaven.

Grasmere

There is an interesting gravestone at Grasmere Cemetery – behind the Chance houses, not the church graveyard. It reads: CHARLES HESTERMAN/MERZ/ BORN 1874/PAULINE BYRNE MERZ/BORN 1919/ROBERT DE SATUR MERZ/BORN 1916/KILLED TOGETHER DURING THE BOMBING/OF LONDON, 1940

It is interesting as Dr Charles Merz (1874-1940) was of Gateshead and London, and he owned Heugh Folds, Grasmere, in 1921 and bought Alcock Tarn,

Gravestone to Charles Hesterman Merz at Grasmere. (Ian Stuart Nicholson)

Grasmere (converted into a reservoir by the Victorians), and Brackenfell, Grasmere, in 1936. His children Pauline Byrne Merz (1919-1940), an air raid warden, and Robert de Satur Merz (1916-1940) – and two of the family's servants, 'Hetty' and 'Jackson' – died at 14 Melbury Road, West Kensington, on the night of 14-15 October 1940. It is most unlikely that they were brought to Grasmere for burial and this may be a 'blind' gravestone.

Dr Charles Merz – the eldest son of John Theodore Merz (from a German Quaker family) and Alice Mary Richardson – was a British electrical engineer. Anna Deborah Richardson, a prominent writer, had built Heugh Folds, Grasmere, in 1862. Charles pioneered the use of high-voltage three-phase AC power distribution in the UK, building a system in the North-East in the early twentieth century that became the model for the country's National Grid. In 1940,

DR. C. H. MERZ

Dr Charles Hesterman Merz. During the First World War, he was director of experiment and research at the Admiralty, dealing especially with anti-submarine warfare. (Grace's Guide)

he designed the electric drive equipment for the TOG 1 tank, a prototype British heavy tank produced in the early part of the Second World War. No. 14 Melbury Road, which he and his wife Stella (1883-1974) moved into in 1914, was completely demolished with only Stella Merz escaping (14 Melbury Road is now a block of flats). Nobert Merz, born in 1877, Charles' brother, owned Heugh Folds in 1941, and Teresa Merz (1879-1958) owned Heugh Folds in 1942. Stella Merz, born Stella Alice Pauline Byrne de Satur, died in Bournemouth in 1974 at the age of 90.

The *Yorkshire Post and Leeds Intelligencer* of 2 April 1943 reported:

New Lakeland acquisitions announced by the National Trust include Alcock Tarn, Grasmere and nearly 70 acres of adjoining land. The property had been bought to prevent the lapse of privileges granted by the late Mr CH Merz, the electric traction engineer, the residue of whose estate passed to the Trust.

Richard William Rollason is named on the stained-glass window at Millom Discovery Centre. (Ian Stuart Nicholson)

Haverigg

Pilot Officer Richard William Rollason was one of four crew (three Australian, one Canadian) of *Hudson AM 794* that took-off on an operational navigational exercise training flight on 24 May 1942. The aircraft did not return to base from the exercise. His remains were recovered from the Irish Sea on 24 June 1942. Rollason, from New South Wales, Australia, was the only one recovered and was buried in the Haverigg (St Luke) Churchyard. Ian Stuart Nicholson from Whitehaven Archives found a stained-glass window at Millom Discovery Centre in June 2017 (subsequently logged as Imperial War Museum memorial 72735). The window was made for RAF Millom Museum in the 1990s by the lady who tended the war graves plot at Haverigg Churchyard. Rollason's name is on that window.

The Whicham parish burial register for the war years also records the burial of an unknown male washed ashore on 2 September 1944. There is no official CWGC memorial for this individual. This indicates there was nothing found on his body to suggest he was a member of the armed forces or served with the merchant navy.

Holme

At Holme, behind the pulpit of Holy Trinity Church, there is a wooden cross bearing a brass plate for each man killed during the First World War, and a plate for the two men killed in the Second World War. This memorial is what is semi-officially called a Westmorland Cross. These are in most churches in the old county of Westmorland and are unique to the area. They are very good as the little brass plates give rank, regiments, date and sometimes place of death, sometimes age. But they are impossible to photograph to read the detail, as the plates are so small – normally 4in by 2in.

Kells

St Peter's Church, Kells, Whitehaven, opened at the very beginning of the war, on 16 September 1939. Although most of the population of Kells were employed in the reserved occupation of mining, many voluntarily chose to fight for their country instead. There are twenty names on the memorial, two metal plaques, one on the end of each choir stall. There are known to be at least three names missing – William Lithgow, a soldier who died in an off-duty boating accident, plus two civilians who died in an accident at the Royal Ordnance Factory, Drigg, on 25 July 1941: William Steele and Richard Ashburne.

Kendal

There are 316 names for the First World War and 168 names for the Second World War. (Ian Stuart Nicholson)

Penrith, Queen Elizabeth Grammar School

The Keswick School of Industrial Art designed the Second World War memorial at Queen Elizabeth Grammar School, Penrith. Thirty-six old boys are named on the copper plaque that was unveiled on 24 July 1948.

CHAPTER 29

Memorials, a Selection M-Z

Millom

A Millom memorial at the town's Discovery Centre on Station Road is a plaque in the form of a fouled anchor to commemorate the adoption of HMS *Loosestrife* during warship week 14-21 February 1942. Warship weeks were British national savings campaigns during the war, with the adoption of a RN warship by a civil community. A level of savings would be set to raise enough money to provide the cost of building a particular naval ship. The aim was for cities to raise enough to adopt battleships and aircraft carriers, while towns and villages would focus on cruisers and destroyers.

Scene from inside Millom Discovery Centre. (With thanks to Millom Discovery Centre)

Smaller towns and villages would be set a lower figure. Once the target money was saved for the ship, the community would adopt the ship and her crew.

Parton and Moresby

There are fifty-two names on the Parton and Moresby memorial, Village Green, The Square that remembers those who fell in the First World War (forty-five) and Second World War (seven). Sergeant Pilot Robert Brady, son of Parton Boy's School headmaster Mr Brady of 'Braemar', Hill Crest, Parton, was Parton's first casualty. His parents received a letter from A.C. Farquarson, group captain, commanding RAF Station:

> It is with deep regret that I have to confirm my telegram. Your son left the ground at 1.45pm in a Spitfire aircraft to carry out camera gun exercises. He found himself, after half-an-hour's flying, above the clouds and apparently came down to ascertain his position. And the aircraft struck the top of a hill which was obscured by cloud.

He was at home the weekend before the accident and in another week would have received his wings. Squadron Leader Borthwick, RAF Chaplain, accompanied the remains, which were brought home on Monday, 8 September 1941, and in the afternoon assisted Rev T.W. Coles at the funeral at the Moresby churchyard.

Penrith

Penrith's memorial to the Second World War (100 names) is on the north wall of the nave at St Andrew's Church. In June 1940, a headline in the *Herald* said: 'Missing, believed killed... Penrith's first victim on active service.' James Henry Kitching, formerly a baker in Penrith, volunteered for the navy at the outbreak of war. He died while working as a cook aboard a minesweeper and minelaying vessel. Information about his death was sparse but the newspaper was able to publish the message of sympathy which the king sent to his parents, Mr and Mrs William Kitching, Holme Riggs Avenue, Penrith:

> The Queen and I offer our heartfelt sympathy in your great sorrow. We pray that your country's gratitude for a life so nobly given in its service may bring you some measure of consolation.

Setmurthy Church

Reverend Daniel Harrison (1862-1940) of Dunthwaite, Setmurthy, a civil parish in Allerdale, died on 18 September 1940. He was the last of the Harrison family of Dunthwaite, who had lived there since 1696. After his death, as he had no family, the Dunthwaite estate was bequeathed to the National Trust.

He owned two private communion sets. One was given to St Barnabas Church, Setmurthy, and the other to the chaplain of HM Hospital Ship (HMHS) *Vasna*. His only sister, Mary Elizabeth (1857-1933), had married Reverend Herbert Awdry Mais, born in Jamaica.

St Bees School

Among the works of sculptor Josefina Alys Hermes de Vasconcellos (1904-2005) is *The Hand*, carved in Honister green slate as a memorial to a friend who died in the Second World War and placed in St Bees School as a war memorial. De Vasconcellos, whose father was an atheist Brazilian diplomat and mother an English Quaker, married the artist Delmar Harmood Banner (1896-1983) in 1930. They adopted two orphan boys, Brian Hugh Banner (1934-2009) and William Banner (1935-1986), who had been rescued from wartime bombing in London, and the family settled in a farmhouse at The Bield in Little Langdale. All four are buried in Langdale Cemetery, Chapel Stile. The cemetery is behind the village school away from the church.

On the south wall of St Bees School Chapel is a brass plaque with the school coat of arms at the top in memory of the Old Boys of St Bees who lost their lives in the Second World War, in Malaya in 1946 and Korea in 1951. There are eighty-five names on this memorial (listed on *iwm.org*).

The Hand, carved in Honister green slate. (Visit Cumbria)

Tebay

A table with two china flower holders and rectangular tablet at St James' Church, Tebay, Eden, is in memory of six men who gave their lives in the Second World War. Airman John Scaife Sanderson (1923-1945), son of Mr and Mrs Sanderson, farmers of Row End Farm, Tebay, was buried at Hotton War Cemetery, Belgium. He was educated at Penrith Grammar School and was employed in the accounts department at the County Hall, Kendal. A collection of family papers is held at Cumbria Archive Centre, Kendal. His last letter home, from his RAF base in Norfolk, was to his brother. The full letter extends to ten pages in which he mentioned comrades who had been lost. He described a dangerous operation over Germany, from which they were lucky to return safely. He described looking forward to being on leave in the following week. That week never came. He died in a plane crash in Belgium in January 1945. The official letter from the Air Ministry telling his father that he was missing presumed dead was received several months later. The wreckage had been located but Sanderson's body had not been identified. A few weeks later, another official letter told his family that his body had been found 'some little distance away from the wrecked aircraft'. He was buried in a Belgian Military Cemetery.

Troutbeck

There is a plaque inside Jesus Church, Troutbeck, giving thanks for the safe return of all parishioners from the Second World War. But outside is a private gravestone for the war burial of Flight Lieutenant Alec Paul Dixon, who died on 19 July 1943 (the stone says 1944).

In memory of Louis James Beagley and his wife Janet Annie. (Ian Stuart Nicholson)

*In memory of John
Leonard Dixon.*
(Ian Stuart Nicholson)

There is also a gravestone for a Home Guard called Louis James Beagley (d1942) who died on duty on 12 April 1942, aged 60. He was of the 9th Westmorland (Lakes) Battalion. Therefore, there are two casualties – rather than none.

Ulverston

Peter Birkett Hague (1917-1942), a Cambridge-educated barrister-at-law whose home address was Woodside, Kilner Park, Ulverston, served on HMS *Kingston* (built in the Isle of Wight) from 27 November 1939 to 4 April 1942. He died of wounds after the ship was bombed by German aircraft in Malta drydock. He was buried at Imtarfa Military Cemetery, Malta, and is on Ulverston Cenotaph and Ulverston St Mary's Parish Church memorials.

Whitehaven

At the time of the German invasion of Denmark during the Second World War, part of the Danish fishing fleet was at sea. Rather than return to occupied Denmark, many of the fishermen decided to sail to British ports, offering their services to the Allied war effort. From June 1940 onwards, a number of these free Danish seamen relocated to ports such as Fleetwood, Lancashire or Whitehaven. In the Irish Sea area, it was less likely they would be attacked by German U-boats. At least three of these Danish fishermen based at Whitehaven passed away before the end of the war: Andreas Frederiksen (1899-1944), Severin Bolther Pedersen (1910-1945), and Harald Hertz (1901-1943). Frederiksen was found drowned, lying in the mud, in the West Harbour, Whitehaven at 6.30 am on 20 September 1944. It is believed he fell into the dock, a victim of the blackout. He was buried at Whitehaven Cemetery. Pedersen was found drowned off Parton, 40 yards south of the Tanyard arch, at the high water mark at 11.35am on 10 February 1945 and buried at Whitehaven Cemetery on 14 February 1945.

Pillar to First and Second World Wars, with relief carving of a female figure, at Castle Park, Whitehaven. The names are on a scroll in a lead casket buried in the foundations.
(Ian Stuart Nicholson)

The war memorial in the side chapel at St James' Parish Church, Whitehaven, commemorates the fallen of the First and Second World Wars. (Ian Stuart Nicholson)

Hertz died at Eden Mount Nursing Home, Carlisle and was buried at Whitehaven Cemetery on 30 December 1945.

Pederson was lodging at Mount Pleasant near Whitehaven Harbour and was single. He was mate on a fishing boat skippered by Peter C.A. Andersen, and had last been seen at 6.30pm on 9 February 1945 at the Golden Lion Hotel, Whitehaven by Inan Neilson, another Danish skipper. Pederson's stomach contained fluid smelling strongly of alcohol, and he was believed to have fallen in the docks and then been washed north by the tide. Following a request at the

Gravestone at Whitehaven Cemetery to one Danish skipper and three Danish fishermen with reference to the Whitehaven-based Kutter ASBO ship, but the mystery of her loss persists. Traditionally, a cutter (kutter) is a smaller sailing ship with a single mast. (Ian Stuart Nicholson, November 2018)

Gravestone at Whitehaven Cemetery to two Danish fishermen. (Ian Stuart Nicholson, November 2018)

inquest by the Danish Vice-Consul, John Singleton (d1957), the lighting on the docks was improved. When last seen, Pederson had £40 to £50 in his pocket. When recovered, he had just 10 shillings. It was not resolved if he had been robbed before or after death. Pederson had planned to become engaged to a local girl.

Gravestone at Whitehaven Cemetery to Danish fisherman Harald Hertz. (Ian Stuart Nicholson, November 2018)

Singleton was appointed Danish Vice-Consul in 1932 and transacted all legal business for the fleet at Whitehaven in World War Two, which was eighteen boats at the peak. A solicitor who practised on his own at Lowther Street, Whitehaven and later formed the firm of Sumner & Singleton in Scotch Street, Whitehaven, he died in 1957, aged 81, at his home in Distington.

On 23 December 1943, a pleasing ceremony took place in the Mayor's Parlour, Whitehaven when skippers J. Jorgensen, C. Carlsen and C. Nielsen, accompanied by Singleton, presented the Mayor, Councillor H. Harrison, with £70 to be distributed amongst old age pensioners with the best wishes of the following donors (all skippers of Danish boats in Whitehaven): C. Carlsen, C. Nielsen, H. Stage, J. Noer, A. Andersen, G. Jorgensen, V. Jensen, L. Sorensen, E. Josefsen, and A. Thinnesen. Another £70 was being sent to them by the Mayor of Grimsby for the same service, and another £70 to the Welfare Committee for the Danish Volunteers in the Services.

On 19 March 2010, a bronze plaque was unveiled at Marina View, New Lowther Street, Whitehaven by Birger Riis Jorgensen (b1949), the Danish Ambassador to Britain, to remember fishermen who came to Whitehaven when Denmark was occupied during World War Two. The inspiration for the memorial plaque, funded by the Nuclear Decommissioning Agency, came from Henry Wormstrup, Mayor of Copeland 2009-2010. His father, Eskild Wormstrup (1909-1977), a fisherman, came over to England during the war after being sent to fish out of the Irish Sea. He married Frances Priestley (1923-2003) in Whitehaven in December 1943.

Workington

On the bottom of the white CWGC gravestone of Able Seaman J. Hendren (d1946) at Salterbeck Cemetery, Workington, is an extra citation: 'also his sister

Although the names of the townsfolk who lost their lives during the First World War (554) and Second World War (170) have not been engraved on Workington War memorial, they are sealed within the memorial.
(Ian Stuart Nicholson)

Lillian/served with ATS/in the 1939-1945 war/died 11-1-48 age 21.' Due to the date of death, she is not on the CWGC. They both lived at 15 Byron Street, Workington. She died 'after a long illness', so it seems as though this may have been due to the effects of war. Both had a 'service at home' before burial. They were members of the Salvation Army (*Workington Star & Harrington Guardian* 22 November 1946).

Wythburn Church

Sergeant Harry Stephenson of Bridge End, Thirlmere, was a flight engineer with 218 Squadron RAF and failed to return from operations against Germany on 19/20 May 1942. There is a dedication, with the 218 Squadron Air Force emblem at the bottom, at Wythburn Church, Allerdale, in memory of Stephenson:

Wythburn Church, early 20th century postcard. It is still standing today.

In Memory of
Sgt Harry Stephenson
of Bridge End
Thirlmere
Harry was a Flight Engineer with
218 Sqn Royal Air Force and failed to
return from operations against Germany on the
night of 19th 20th May 1942.
You may be "missing" Harry
but you are always in the
thoughts of your family.

All that now remains of the otherwise submerged village of Wythburn is Wythburn Church, which is located on the A591. The villages of Armboth and Wythburn were flooded to create, in 1894, Thirlmere reservoir (Thirlmere was originally two smaller lakes, Leathes Water and Wythburn Water) to augment Manchester Corporation's water supplies.

Further Research

Count Anthony Jackson-Ossalinsky-Jackson-Harrison (b1961), a Polish prince, has announced that he supports the creation of a memorial in Hyde Park to celebrate the actions of Polish pilots in the Battle of Britain. Count Harrison descends from his grandfather, Wing Commander Anthony Cecil Boris Harrison CBE MC (b1898), through his father Captain Boris Anthony Michael Jackson-Ossalinsky-Harrison MC (b1922). Wing Commander Harrison administered the Polish pilots in the RAF during the Second World War. The Anthony Harrison who was mentioned in Dorothy Wordsworth's diary for August 1801 is Count Anthony Harrison's immediate ancestor. The Jackson-Ossalinsky-Jackson heritage of both Armboth and Thirlmere descends to him today, according to the *Harrison of the North Limited*, the enterprise of an ancient family of Cumberland (*harrisonofthenorth.com*). Countess Boris Ossalinsky's extract from *The Nobilities of Europe* (2000) is as follows: 'The Countess Boris Ossalinsky, widow of a Polish nobleman who lived for many years at Musgrave Hall, Penrith, died at Pembridge Square, Bayswater in 1901, aged 81. She was the daughter and heiress of a Yeoman landowner of Cumberland who owned Thirlmere Lake and some 850 acres of adjoining land on Armboth.'

CHAPTER 30

Defence Architecture

Walney Island was home to two of Britain's many coastal artillery installations: the Hilpsford Fort on the south of the island, and Fort Walney to the north, now lost beneath Barrow's golf links. The Second World War battery at Fort Walney was preceded by coastal defences constructed in July 1911. Hilpsford Fort was constructed during 1914 as a First World War emergency battery, and was dismantled in the 1920s, providing a source of much-needed labour to this employment-starved area. The artillery was reinstated in 1940, with new construction work undertaken.

Barrow Dock was surrounded by pill-boxes – defence against a potential western invasion via Ireland. There are two pill-boxes at Fort Walney. Lowsy Point also accommodated one of the Admiralty's decoy sites for the dockyard and works of Barrow. A 'Cumberland Machine-Gun and Anti-Tank Rifle Emplacment' pill-box is at Brampton, just south of Hadrian's Wall, and another at Grune Point near Silloth. The 'Cumberland' pattern pill-box at Newby East stands elevated above the north-west bank of the River Irving, just to the south of the village of Newby East.

The Carlisle (Brampton Road) pill-box can be found guarding the exit from Rickerby Park, Carlisle. There is a pill-box at Greymoorhill, when exiting the M6 North at Junction 44. Hadrian's Camp – a large wartime training establishment – was around a mile south from here, though it may have had something to do with the Kingstown aerodrome. The Dunmail Raise pill-box, Grasmere, was strategically placed on the main A591. The Gummers How pill-box was elevated slightly from the A592 Bowness to Newby Bridge Road. The Haverthwaite pill-box is located off the A590. The Kirkby Lonsdale pill-box can be found high above Devil's Bridge near the A65. The Kirkby Stephen one overlooks the A685. The Levens Hall pill-box gazes down on Levens Hall, on the opposite side of the A6. And the Stainmore pill-box sits high upon Bowes Moor, where the A66 crosses the Pennine chain. There are pill-boxes at Lindale (two) and High Newton. A pill-box at Haverigg was part of the airfield defences at RAF Millom. Camouflage in the form of earth and grass on the roof was provided to restrict observation from the air. There are pill-boxes sited at Kirkbride aerodrome, including one with an anti-tank loophole.

A pill-box nestles in a prime defensive position above and behind the bus station in Whitehaven. It would have covered the road to the dock, the road from the railway station, the bottom of Bransty, and the entrance to William Pit and the 'Waggon Road'. It is now used to support an oil tank.

Loopholes were built into the wall at Eamont Bridge to enable rifle and possibly machine-gun fire down Pooley Bridge Road. Nearby Ullswater was patrolled in boats by the Home Guard in case of enemy landings there. The gun pit at Lazonby had an artillery piece trained on the bridge between Lazonby and Kirkoswald, a vulnerable crossing point over the River Eden, a natural north-south divide line.

An old tower at Millom – perhaps a lighthouse of some sort – had a concrete extension and steel balcony fitted in 1941 and was the wartime Royal Observer Corps (ROC) post. The post was moved to another site in 1950. St Bees RADAR station was built at the lighthouse in 1941, going off-air for the last time at 11pm on 4 February 1944, after which, RADAR coverage for the area was handled by the Hawcoats site near Barrow.

At Whitehaven (Bransty), two gun casements on the cliffs were demolished in the 1980s. A similar coastal-defence arrangement existed 8 miles up the coast at Workington. As well as guns, battery observation post and camp up on the clifftops, the Whitehaven battery consisted of two concrete and steel searchlight emplacements and a generator building. A miniature range was provided for training purposes and was located about halfway between the searchlight emplacements and Parton, just off the 'Waggon Road'.

CHAPTER 31

Barrow-Built Vessels

HMS *Indomitable* was commissioned on 10 October 1941 and returned to the UK from the Far East in November 1945. In addition to her crew – she carried a normal complement of 1,600 – she brought home 40 ex-internees of Japanese prison camps, including twenty-nine women.

Bombed in the Mediterranean, torpedoed off the Isles of Scilly, and hit by a suicide plane off Okinawa, the 23,000-tons Fleet aircraft carrier HMS Indomitable returned from the Far East to Portsmouth, her home port, late last night.

(Western Morning News, *1 December 1945*)

HMS Inconstant in 1941. (Public domain)

John McLeod Kennedy (1920-1944), son of Norman McLeod Kennedy and Winifred Hardwick Moss of Windermere, was, from 11 October 1941 to August 1942, pilot, 827 Squadron Fleet Air Arm (FAA), HMS *Indomitable*. From 19 November 1943 to 11 April 1944, he was pilot, 848 Squadron FAA, HMS *Sparrowhawk*. He was missing, presumed killed, during a navigational exercise. Gerald A. Hancock (1916-1979) from Dundee served on HMS *Indomitable* from September 1941 to August 1942, and his wartime diary can be found on *royalnavyresearcharchive.org.uk*.

HMS *Inconstant* was an I-class destroyer laid down for the Turkish Navy in May 1941, as *Muavenet*, but was purchased by the RN in 1939. The ship participated in the assault on Madagascar in May 1942 and attacked and sank *U-409* in the Mediterreanean north-east of Algiers on 12 July 1943, and *U-767* while in company with the destroyers *Fame* and *Havelock* in the English Channel south-west of Guernsey on 18 June 1944. *Inconstant* was returned to Turkey on 9 March 1946 and discarded in 1960.

Four U-409 prisoners-of-war in US Army custody on 7 September 1943. (uboatarchive.net)

TCG *Gayret*/HMS *Ithuriel*, an I-class destroyer, was laid down Gayret for the Turkish Navy by Vickers in May 1939, but taken over by the RN on the outbreak of the Second World War while still under construction. She took part in Operations *Harpoon* and *Pedestal*, the escorting of convoys to Malta in June and August 1942. She was attacked by German aircraft at Bone in Algeria on the night 27-28 November 1942 and damaged beyond repair.

HMS *Jamaica*, a Crown Colony-class cruiser, was built for the RN, launched in 1940, and decommissioned in 1960. She was named after the island of Jamaica, which was in British possession when she was built in the late 1930s. The light cruiser spent almost her entire wartime career on Arctic convoy duties, except for a deployment south for the landings in North Africa in November 1942.

Kongo, the first battlecruiser of the Kongo-class (among the most heavily armed ships in any navy when first built), was completed and commissioned into the Japanese Navy in August 1913, and patrolled off the Chinese coast during the First World War. She fought in a number of major naval actions of the war in the Pacific during the Second World War, before she was torpedoed and sunk by the submarine USS *Sealion*, while crossing the Formoso Strait on 21 November 1944.

HMS *Hurricane* was a destroyer built in 1939 and torpedoed by *U-415* on 24 December 1943. Three of her crew were killed and nine wounded. HMS *Hurricane* is also remembered for picking up survivors of the *City of Benares*, a ship transporting children to Canada, sunk in 1940.

HMS *Urchin*, a U-class destroyer, was built for the RN and launched in 1943. She formed part of the British Pacific Fleet – an RN formation that saw action against Japan – during the latter part of the war. HMS *Urania*, a U-class destroyer, was built for the RN, launched in 1943, and saw service during the war as part of the British Pacific Fleet.

HMS *Wizard*, a W-class destroyer, was built for the RN, launched in September 1943, and decommissioned in 1967. During the war, she was adopted by the borough of Wood Green in London as part of Warship Week. After trials, while in the North Western Approaches, she suffered major structural damage from an explosion of her own depth charges on 9 June 1944. Six members of her crew died.

HMS *Wrangler*/SAS *Vyrstaat*, a W-class destroyer, was built for the RN/ South African Navy, and launched in 1943. She saw service during the war. After the war, in January 1946, she was the chemical warfare training ship based at Devonport.

Submarines

Sir Leonard Redshaw (1911-1989) recalled an experience during the Second World War, saying 'We were struggling to build submarines as fast as we could. We wanted to weld them in part or in full,' according to *The British Economy Since 1700: A Macroeconomic Perspective* by C.H. Lee (1986). Sir Leonard, son of Joseph Stanley Redshaw OBE (1888-1957), was educated at Barrow Grammar School and Liverpool University. Like his father, he became an apprentice ship draughtsman at Vickers at the age of 16. He became the shipbuilding manager at the yard in 1950. In 1984, he lived at Ireleth, close to Barrow.

According to the *Dock Museum*, 112 submarines were built at Barrow in the Second World War. The British U-class submarines (officially War Emergency 1940 and 1941 programmes, short hull) were a class of forty-nine small submarines built just before and during the Second World War. The initial three U-class boats entered service in the latter half of 1938: HMS *Undine*, HMS *Unity* and HMS *Ursula*, all built at Barrow. Initially designed as training vessels, they were effective enough to persuade the Admiralty to expand the class. Only *Ursula* would survive the war, however. Roger Brockbank, born in 1923, of Kendal, served on HMS *Undine* from 10 November 1944 to April 1946. He joined the family firm of Staveley Wood Turning, Kendal. Michael Dent Tattersall (1919-2004), who lived in Kendal, was commanding officer, HMS *Ursula* from 7 May 1943 to July 1943.

The second group of the U-class consisted of twelve submarines. Ten were built at Barrow, including HMS *Upholder*. She was laid down in October 1939 and launched in July 1940 by Doris Thompson, wife of a director of Vickers. The most successful British submarine of the Second World War, she completed twenty-four patrols, sinking around 12,000 tons of enemy shipping, including Italian destroyer *Libeccio* (9 November 1941) after the Battle of the Duisburg Convoy, and the 18,000-ton Italian liner SS *Conte Rosso* (24 May 1941). Of the 2,729 soldiers and crew aboard, 1,300 were killed. *Upholder* was lost with all hands on her 25th patrol, which was to have been her last before she returned to England. She left for patrol on 6 April 1942 and became overdue on 14 April. On 12 April, she was ordered – with HMS *Urge* and HMS *Thrasher* – to form a patrol line to intercept a convoy, but it is not known whether she received the signal. The most likely explanation for her loss is that, after being spotted by a reconnaissance seaplane, she fell victim to depth charges dropped by the Italian *Orsa*-class torpedo boat *Pegaso* north-east of Tripoli on 14 April 1942, although no debris was seen on the surface.

The group three boats formed the largest group of U-class submarines, comprising thirty-four vessels ordered in three batches, ten on 11 March 1940, all built in Barrow, twelve on 23 August 1940, all built at Barrow, and a final twelve on 12 July 1941. Five of these were built at Barrow, including HMS *Vandal* (P64). She was laid down on 17 March 1942, launched on 23 November 1942, and, on 20 February 1943, she sailed out of Barrow. The submarine probably had the shortest career of any RN submarine, being lost with all thirty-seven on board on 24 February 1943 (north of the Isle of Arran), just four days after commissioning. She was lost while carrying out a three-day-long working-up exercise. According to *clydemaritime.co.uk*, the cause of her loss remains a mystery to date.

George Lawson and the *Narwhal*

HMS *Narwhal* was built in Barrow, launched on 29 August 1935 and lost on 22-23 July 1940 in the North Sea, carrying fifty-eight crew. She was probably sunk by German aircraft, according to *Wikipedia*. (The *Barrow Submariners Association* has an online *Narwal* Roll of Honour and *wrecksite.eu* lists people on board). George Clandon, a retired plumber from Burscough in west Lancashire, is the nephew of George Lawson, an engineer on the *Narwhal* who hailed from Burscough, who was lost. He told the author that he had received a reply, in 2017, from a Polish deep-sea exploration dive team, the Santi Odnalecz Orla Expedition. 'They informed me that my uncle's boat had inadvertently been found (on 24 May 2017) in the North Sea south of Norway, whilst searching for their own boat, the ORP *Orzel*.

'I won't dwell but I'd truly like to say that after 77 years, my uncle and the crew of the *Narwhal* can truly rest in peace, now we know where she is. The families of the *Narwhal* are having a reunion next month with the dive crew in London,' he said. The *Narwhal* is one of the submarines commemorated on the plaque at Ramsden Square roundabout, Barrow.

George Clandon said:

Something else has come to light – the position of the boat. The submarine was on its way to a position south of Norway about 150 miles east of Edinburgh, more or less in the middle of the North Sea when the boat was attacked.

The German coastal command knew the approximate course and just waited their time and sank the boat when she was on the surface.

Codes apparently had also been intercepted.

It was a scalp the German hierarchy had been waiting for after the *Narwhal* had been involved in the sinking of a German troop ship at some stage on the way to the invasion of Norway.

Something I'd also found out later was the crews of these boats called at Blyth in Northumberland for R and R after a mission.

I went to London in January (2018) to meet the Polish dive crew and the other families from the *Narwhal* that managed to make it. It was a nice discussion along with a video instruction as to how the boat was found. Little sad really.

Having been on a couple of submarines in my time in the Royal Navy, I can only say that I have complete admiration for the bravery of the crews.

The same cannot be said about the defensive quality of these submarines. You joined them and there was more than a good chance you'd be lying dead on the seabed before the war ended. Forty-five British boats didn't make it, with well over 100 German U-boats. This is what makes the discovery of this particular boat so special to members of my family. It was a complete fluke.

In February 1940, *Narwhal* helped HMS *Imogen* and HMS *Inglefield* to sink *U-63* south of the Shetland Islands. One man died; there were twenty-four survivors.

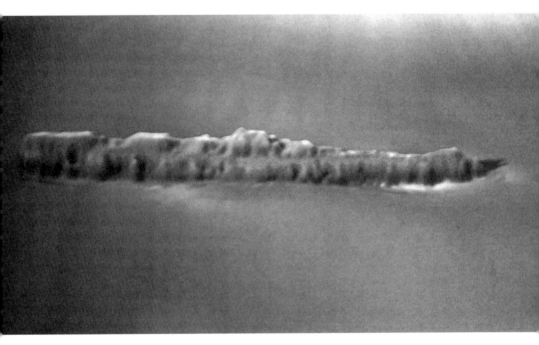

The Narwhal on the seabed encrusted with sea life. (George Clandon)

Above: The CEO of the Polish dive team, Mr Strachura, gazing over the side. (George Clandon)

Below: The Polish dive team celebrating. (George Clandon)

Those who survived, including Kapitanleutnant (captain lieutenant) Gunther Lorentz (1913-1989), spent the remainder of the war as prisoners-of-war in British hands. (Lorentz at Featherstone Park Camp, Haltwhistle, Northumberland). In May 1940, *Narwhal* torpedoed and sank the German troop transport

Above: The Polish historian presenting the story. (George Clandon)

Below: Four of the dive team that came to the meeting in London. (George Clandon)

Above: *George Clandon by the cenotaph in Burscough holding a photograph of his uncle George Lawson.* (With thanks to George Clandon)

Below: *Tamara Lo is the daughter of the commanding officer of the Narwhal, Lieutenant Commander Ronald James Burch (1907-1940), son of a farmer. She is 83 and only has vague memories of her father.*

Buenos Aires. Most of *Narwhal's* sinkings were caused by her mines. A mine laid by *Narwhal* may have sunk *U-1*, which disappeared on 6 April 1940 west of Heligoland, a small German archipelago in the North Sea. *U-1* may have also been sunk by the British submarine *Porpoise*. *Porpoise* was built at Barrow and launched in 1932. She was sunk by Japanese aircraft in the Malacca Strait, a stretch of water between the Malay Peninsula and the Indonesian island of Sumatra, on 11 January 1945, and was the last Royal Navy submarine to be lost to enemy action. Also on 11 January 1945, the British cargo ship *Normandy Coast* was torpedoed and sunk in the Irish Sea west of Anglesey with the loss of nineteen of her twenty-seven crew.

The North Sea is littered with submarine wrecks – There are 150 sunken German U-boats as well as 50 British submarines, several French, two Dutch and one Polish – the long-lost *Eagle* (*Orzel*) that Poland has been searching for over the last decade, according to an article in the *Telegraph* of 17 December 2017.

George Clandon's son-in-law David and a young lady called Emma Ballard. Emma is the daughter of Robert Ballard (b1942), the man whose dive team found RMS Titanic (sank 1912) in 1985

Barrow-built civilian ships attacked during the Second World War

The civilian ship *Awatea* was built for the Union Steam Ship Company of New Zealand, and launched in February 1936. She was attacked near Bougie by German bombers and sank during the night (November 1942). RMS *Carinthia*, a passenger liner, was built for the Cunard Steamship Company, launched in 1924, and sunk by *U-46* off the coast of Ireland on 7 June 1940; four people died during the sinking. *U-46* sunk *Phidias* on 9 June 1941; fifty died, including Ordinary Seaman Robert Hill (1923-1941), son of John and Jennie Hill of Walney Island.

HMHS *Newfoundland*, a passenger cargo ship, was built for Johnston Warren Lines, launched in January 1925, and converted to a hospital ship in 1940. She was bombed and sunk off Salerno on 13 September 1943, with the loss of thirty-eight lives. RMS *Nova Scotia*, a passenger cargo ship, was built for

Johnston Warren Lines, launched in 1926, and converted to a troopship in 1941. She was torpedoed and sunk in the Indian Ocean south-east of Natal Province on 28 November 1942 by *U-177*, while carrying Indian prisoners. Eight hundred and fifty-eight lives were lost.

RMS *Orama*, a passenger liner, was built for the Orient Steam Navigation Company, launched in 1924, and converted to a troopship in 1940. She was sunk off Harstad in Norway on 8 June 1940 by the German heavy cruiser *Admiral Hipper* during Operation Juno, a German naval offensive late in the Norwegian Campaign. Nineteen of *Orama's* crew were lost, including Chief Electrician Christopher Fagan, who is commemorated at Barrow cemetery, and 280 were taken prisoner. *Orama* had been used to transport children to Australia as part of the Kindertransport programme (November 1938 to September 1939), where Jewish children were helped to escape to safety, according to the US Holocaust Memorial Museum.

Cumbrian Clifford Wardropper (1903-1960), who married Gladys Innard (1912-1998) in Barrow in 1937, was on board *Orama* when she was sunk. He spent the next five years as a prisoner-of-war in Marlag und Milag Nord, according to Barrow Archive and Local Studies Centre. Marlag und Milag Nord was a Second World War German prisoner-of-war complex for men of the British Merchant Navy and Royal Navy, located around the village of Westertimke, about

This Wardropper diary was handed in to Barrow Library. (Tom Hughes)

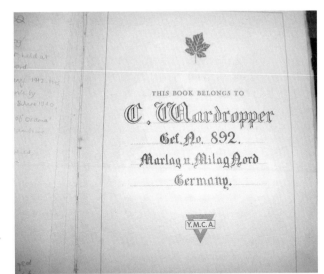

Right: An example
of Wardropper's
penmanship.
(Tom Hughes)

Below: Wardropper drew
this inside his diary.
(Tom Hughes)

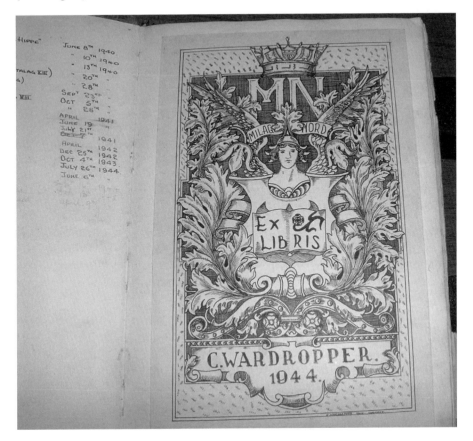

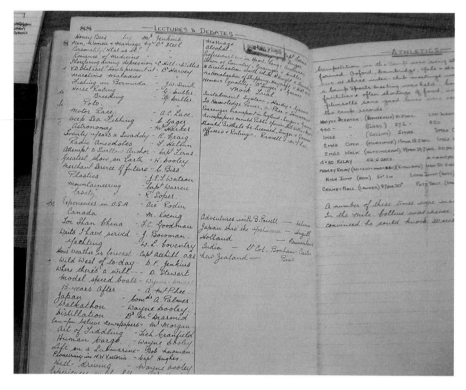

Wardropper's list of the lectures and debates that were given in a camp by the internees to the other prisoners-of-war. (Tom Hughes)

19 miles north-west of Bremen, Germany. However, in some sources the camp's location is given as Tarmstedt, a larger village about 2 ½ miles to the west

Wardropper, who died in Ulverston in 1960, kept a wartime diary. It was handed in to Barrow Library by persons unknown. The diary, dated 1942 to 1945, contains drawings, photographs and programmes that reflect the general routine of camp life as well as more special events including sports days and performances at the camp theatre. There was also a library with around 3,000 books.

RMS *Orion*, a passenger liner, was built for the Orient Steam Navigation Company, launched in 1934, and converted to a troopship in 1941. She was damaged in collision with HMS *Revenge*, but repaired. She was scrapped in Belgium in 1963. SS *Strathallan*, a passenger liner, was built for P&O Steam Navigation, launched in September 1937 and damaged by torpedo in the Mediterranean on 21 December 1942. A fire the following day capsized and sunk the ship. A listing of those aboard *Strathallan* when it was hit can be found on *uboat.net*.

Other Barrow-build vessels launched during the Second World War

Ficus/*Empire Grenadier*, an oil tanker, was built for Shell Tankers UK and launched in 1942. *Kennerleya*/*Empire Granite*, an oil tanker, was built for Shell UK and launched in 1941. *Empire Admiral*, a cargo ship built for Ministry of War Transport, was launched on 26 March 1945 and scrapped in Taiwan in 1969.

Empire Athelstan, a heavy lift ship, was built for Ministry of War Transport, launched on 15 January 1946, and scrapped in Yugoslavia in 1976.

Empire Charmian, a heavy lift ship, was built for Ministry of War Transport and launched on 25 November 1942. She was scrapped in India in 1962.

Italian cargo ship *Marco Foscarini* was bombed and damaged in the Mediterranean Sea off Tripoli, Libya, by British aircraft on 27 May 1941, and was beached on 30 May 1941. She was refloated and scrapped in Barrow from October 1948.

The most recent Barrow-built vessel to be lost during a military campaign occurred in 1982 during the Falklands War when HMS *Sheffield* was attacked and sunk by the Argentine Navy.

Operation Juno

There were heavy losses on the other allied ships also sunk on 8 June 1940 in Operation Juno: the aircraft carrier HMS *Glorious* with the loss of more than 1,200 lives, two destroyers HMS *Ardent* (152 died) and HMS *Acasta* (160 died), the trawler *Juniper*, and the oil tanker *Oil Pioneer*. Able Seaman Henry Adolphus Bunter (1920-1940) of Barrow, Able Seaman Charles Flynn of Dalton-in-Furness (d1940), Able Seaman Albert Ernest France (1919-1940) of Barrow, Able Seaman Stanley Hodgson (1917-1940) of Barrow, Ordinary Seaman Walter McMillan Kirkpatrick (d1940) of Carlisle, Stoker 2nd Class John Henry Long (1917-1940) of Barrow, Stoker 1st Class John Jackson Murray (1915-1940) of Longtown, Air Fitter Laurence Osler (1919-1940) of Stanwix, Carlisle, Able Seaman Thomas Edward Peters (1920-1940) of Barrow, Petty Officer Edward Arthur Stanford (1914-1940) of Barrow, and Ordnance Artificer 1st Class Montague James Foan Williams (1905-1940) of Barrow were on HMS *Glorious* and died.

Further research

William Noel Murray has written (2017 and 2018) about his twenty years as an electrician at Vickers. His text is available to read on *williamnoelmurray.*

wordpress.com. His grandfather, Pat, who lived on Walney Island and travelled to Barrow by the chain-driven ferry boat, was a riveter with Vickers in the late 1920s. Pat was going to retire when the war broke out in 1939. He carried on until the war was over in 1945. In 1939, William was accepted as a Vickers electrician, and started in the shipyard on HMS *Indomitable*. Shortly after, he was sent to Aircraft Carrier HMS *Illustrious* to do the flight deck lighting. Winter time came round, with its dark nights not helped by the blackout restrictions that had been imposed.

In 1940, William and Pat were given an Anderson shelter to erect in their back garden. William said: 'I was enrolled in the fire watchers, which at that time was a bit of a joke because nothing ever happened. It was only towards the end of the year that any bombs were dropped on Barrow, doing very little damage. One fell on a house at the top end of Prospect Road and damaged the gable end of the house slightly. That was quite close to where we lived in Clarence Road.'

William worked on various destroyers and frigates that came up for urgent repairs. A Canadian destroyer came into the Buccleuch Dock stern first under its own steam with most of its bows blown off, he said. The ship had been sent to the Clyde for repairs but, on entering the Clyde, hit a mine and was diverted to Barrow. An aerodrome had been built at the north end of Walney Island and it was used as an Air Gunners' Training School.

William was paralysed from the waist down following an accident on his bike in the blackout. He ran into a broken-down double decker bus. He regained the use of his legs. Once he arrived home, he had to see a doctor for a sick note for work. He was promptly told 'there's a war on', and signed off as fit for work.

Shortly after he completed his apprenticeship, he worked at the Vickers base at Cammell Lairds, Liverpool, to work on the guns. He wrote: 'Our main work was the Battle Class Destroyers being built in Lairds to which Vickers were fitting Twin Barrelled 4.5 inch High Angle/Low Angle Remote Power Controlled (RPC) Gun Mountings and Twin Barrelled 40mm RPC Bofor Mountings.' Once the sea trials were over, he returned to Barrow. A sea trial is the testing phase of a watercraft.

CHAPTER 32

Cumbria's Significance in the Cold War

The war was to have a lasting legacy in Cumbria as the county became part of the front line in the Cold War. Cumbria's comparative remoteness made it the ideal place to establish Calder Hall, a nuclear power station, and Windscale, a plutonium plant used to make nuclear weapons.

'W Cumberland Village May Be First Choice', read the headline in the *Lancashire Daily Post* of 19 May 1947. The Atomic Energy Council, with Cabinet approval, had planned a £7million scheme to produce electricity from uranium and pump it into the grid, and the necessary apparatus was to be established on the site of Drigg's Royal Ordnance Factory. There was, however, no confirmation of the story in west Cumbria. 'Only a few miles away, at Sellafield, a new Courtaulds factory was to be erected soon,' said the newspaper.

Work began in 1947 at the Sellafield site on two reactors – the Windscale Piles and a separation plant to extract plutonium needed for the atomic weapons programme. Recognising that atomic energy could be harnessed for commercial as well as military use, the United Kingdom Atomic Energy Authority (UKAEA) was formed and the site expanded with the commissioning of the world's first nuclear power plant, Calder Hall, in 1956 and the development of two generations

John Dalton (1766-1844), the discoverer of the atomic theory, is commemorated at his birthplace in a cottage in the village of Eaglesfield. (Photo © Graham Robson (cc-by-sa/2.0))

JOHN DALTON DCL LLD
THE DISCOVERER OF
THE ATOMIC THEORY
WAS BORN HERE SEPT 5 1766
DIED AT MANCHESTER JULY 27 1844

of plants for reprocessing commercial reactor Magnox and Oxide fuels. British Nuclear Fuels Ltd (BNFL) was formed in 1971 out of UKAEA as an organisation capable of preparing nuclear fuel, enriching and fabricating it, and equipped with the facilities for processing irradiated fuels. Under the direction of BNFL, Sellafield site's role in advancing economic use of nuclear energy was developed in parallel with the UK's energy requirements. Grandad Peter Weightman, a scientist, moved from Highbury Corner, London, to Springfield's, Salwick, Preston, in the 1940s, and then to Seascale for research work at Windscale. In 1946, Springfield's, a former wartime munitions factory, produced nuclear fuel for Calder Hall. In the 1950s, Seascale was known as 'the brainiest town in Britain', according to a report in the *Guardian* in October 2005.

Bassenthwaite Royal Observer Corps (ROC) underground post at Robin Hood, above Bassenthwaite, was a 'true' Cold War site, opening in 1948 and going underground in May 1961. There is now no trace of it. Dunmail Raise, Grasmere ROC post, was opened in December 1964 and closed in September 1991, now demolished. In 1951, the ROC worked to ROTORPLAN, a scheme to counter the threat posed by the huge increase in Soviet air-power. In April of that year, approval was given for 411 ROC posts to be re-sited from their Second World War locations, including the Threlked post.

In April 1948, a shepherd in the Scafell range found a crashed single-seater aircraft and the body of the pilot. The *Nottingham Evening Post* reported on 1 May 1948:

> Later, search parties led by the police and the RAF set out across the moors and the police carried the airman's body back to Eskdale over eight miles of difficult country. It is thought possible this may be the RAF Spitfire, piloted by Flight Lieutenant DJO Loudon and reported missing from Hawarden Aerodrome, North Wales, last November. Reports were then received that the plane was heard by a shepherd, flying in cloud over Scafell. The Spitfire was also on a flight to Edinburgh, and was also stated to have been seen over Seathwaite, which runs up into the heart of the Lake District from the Furness shore. An Air Ministry spokesman said today that the wreckage was that of a Spitfire lost on November 20th, 1947. The pilot has been identified as Flt.-Lt. Loudon.

Polaris submarine launched

HMS *Resolution*, the first of Britain's Polaris nuclear submarines, was built in Barrow and launched in Barrow on Thursday, 16 September 1966 by the Queen

Mother. It slid into the Walney Channel at noon as CND demonstrators paraded almost unnoticed with protest placards near the gates of the Vicker's yard. The Queen Mother, after the launching, paid tribute to the 'miracles of modern science' that had gone into the ship. About 10,000 spectators, most of them Barrow families with lives closely involved in the fortunes of Vickers, watched the launch. Commander Michael Charles Henry (1928-2008) and Commander Kenneth David Frewer (b1930) received the submarine on behalf of the RN.

Bibliography

Advocate, *From Normandy to the Baltic* (Pickle Partners Publishing, 2017)

Bates, Martha, *Snagging Turnips and Scaling Muck, The Women's Land Army in Westmorland* (Helm Press, 2001)

Battle, John D., *Underley Hall, A History of House and Occupants* (Unknown publisher, 1969)

Bertke, Donald A., Smith, Gordon & Kindell, Don, *World War Two Sea War* (Bertke, 2009)

Black, Brian, *The Solway Firth* (Regional Books, 1959)

Boniface, Patrick, *HMS Cumberland: a classic British cruiser in war and peace* (Periscope Publishing Limited, 2006)

Brassley, Paul, Segers, Yves & van Molle, Leen, *War, Agriculture, and Food: Rural Europe from the 1930s to the 1950s* (P Clavin, 2014)

Broad, Richard & Fleming, Suzie, *Nella Last's War: The Second World War Diaries of 'Housewife 49'* (Profile Books, 2006)

Brook, Henry, *True Stories of The Blitz* (Usborne, 2006)

Burt, Kendal & Leasor, James, *The One That Got Away* (Pen & Sword, 2006)

Chorlton, Martyn, *Cumbria Airfields in the Second World War, including the Isle of Man* (Countryside Books, 2006)

Crook, Paul, *Surrey Home Guard* (Middleton Press, 2000)

Crookenden, Spencer, *K Shoes – the first 150 years, 1842-1992* (K Shoes, 1992)

Dickon, Chris, *The Foreign Burial of American War Dead*, (McFarland & Company, 2011)

Driver, Leigh, *The Lost Villages of England* (Abe Books, 2009)

Earl, David W., *Hell on High Ground* (Airlife, 1999)

Edwards, Gloria, *Moota – Camp 103. The Story of a Cumbrian Prisoner of War Camp* (Little Bird Publications, 2005)

Fife, Malcolm, *British Airship Bases of the Twentieth Century* (Fonthill Media, 2015)

Foss, Brian, *War Paint: Art, War, State and Identity in Britain, 1939-1945* (Yale University Press, 2007)

Fraser, Maxwell, *Companion into Lakeland* (Methuen, 1936)

Greenhaugh, W., *Broughton-in-Furness and the Duddon Valley* (Broughton, 1989)

Harris, A., *Cumberland Iron, The Story of Hodbarrow Mine 1855-1968* (D. Bradford Barton Limited, Cornwall, 1970)

Harris, Robert & Paxman, Jeremy, *A Higher Form of Killing: The Secret Story of Chemical and Biological Warfare* (Random House, 2001)

Hay, Daniel, *Whitehaven: a Short History* (George Todd and Son, 1966)

Hughes, Peter, *Visiting the Fallen: Arras: North* (Pen & Sword, 2015)

Hurst, John, *Come Back to Eden: Lakeland's Northern Neighbour* (Sigma Leisure, 2000)

Leach, Nicholas, *Workington, Whitehaven, Maryport and Seascale Lifeboats: An Illustrated History* (Foxglove Publishing, 2017)

Lee, C.H., *The British Economy Since 1700: A Macroeconomic Perspective* (Cambridge University Press, 1986).

Massue, Melville Henry, *The Nobilities of Europe* (Elbion Classics, 2000)

McDonough, Frank, *Neville Chamberlain, Appeasement, and the British Road to War* (Manchester University Press, 1998)

Midlands Polish Community Association, *In War & Peace, Collected Memories of Birmingham's Poles* (Midlands Polish Community Association, 2011)

Munck, Ronaldo, *Reinventing the City?: Liverpool in Comparative Perspective* (Liverpool University Press, 2003)

Murfin, Lyn, *Popular Leisure in the Lake Counties* (Manchester University Press, 1990)

Newton, David, *Trademarked. A History of Well-Known Brands – from Aertex to Wright's Coal Tar* (Sutton Publishing, 2008)

Nicholson, Norman, *Portrait of the Lakes* (Hale 1963)

Nicholson, Norman, *Wednesday Early Closing* (Faber & Faber, 2008)

Nixon, John, *Wings over Sands* (Elanders, 2012)

Palmer, Mark, *Clarks, Made to Last* (Profile Books, 2013)

Patterson, John, *World War Two, An Airman Remembers* (General Store Publishing, Canada, 2000)

Pauling, Keith, *Discovering the Dales Way* (Keith Pauling, 2010)

Read, E.A., *Discovering Egremont*, (David Miles Books, 1992)

Rice, H.A.L., *Kirkby Lonsdale and its Neighbourhood* (The Westmorland Gazette, 1983)

Rollinson, Williamson, *Life and Tradition in the Lake District* (Littlehampton Book Services, 1974)

Shores, Christopher, *Aces High: A Further Tribute to the Most Notable Fighter Pilots in WWII* (Grub Street, 1999)

Thistlethwaite, June, *Cumbria The War Years, Lake District Life during the 1940s* (Kendal, 1997)

Trescatheric, Bryn, *Barrow-in-Furness Labour Party Records, 1914-1969* (Society for the Study of Labour History, 2000)

Trenowden, Ian, *The Hunting Submarine* (The Aspotogan Press, 2014)

Warner, Philip, *The D Day Landings* (Pen & Sword, 2004)

Woolnough, Guy, *Cumbria at War 1939-1945*, for use in secondary schools (Cumbria Archive Service, 2009)

Wotherspoon, Nick, Clark, Alan & Sheldon, Mark, *Aircraft Wrecks: The Walker's Guide* (Pen & Sword, 2008)

Websites

Alpinejournal.org.uk

Ancestry.co.uk

Britishnewspaperarchive.co.uk

Clydemaritime.co.uk

Eden.gov.uk

Halcyon-class.co.uk

Iwm.org.uk/memorials

Vistcumbria.com

Sellafieldsites.com

Fcafa.com

Forgottenairfields.com

Nicholaswinton.com

Peakdistrictaircrashes.co.uk

Royalnavyrsearcharchive.org.uk

skiptonww1camp.co.uk

Southlakes-uk.co.uk

Sports-reference.com

Thewi.org.uk

Torver.org

Ushmm.org

Wartimememoriesproject.com

Windermeresunderlandflyingboats

Index